The American
Revolution of 1800

The American Revolution of 1800

HOW JEFFERSON RESCUED DEMOCRACY FROM TYRANNY AND FACTION— AND WHAT THIS MEANS TODAY

FORTIETH ANNIVERSARY EDITION

Dan Sisson

with Thom Hartmann

BK

Berrett–Koehler Publishers, Inc.
San Francisco
a BK Currents book

Berrett-Koehler Publishers, Inc.
235 Montgomery Street, Suite 650, San Francisco, CA 94104-2916
Tel: (415) 288-0260   Fax: (415) 362-2512   www.bkconnection.com

Ordering Information

Quantity sales. Special discounts are available on quantity purchases by corporations, associations, and others. For details, contact the "Special Sales Department" at the Berrett-Koehler address above.

Individual sales. Berrett-Koehler publications are available through most bookstores. They can also be ordered directly from Berrett-Koehler:
Tel: (800) 929-2929; Fax: (802) 864-7626; www.bkconnection.com.
Orders for college textbook/course adoption use. Please contact Berrett-Koehler:
Tel: (800) 929-2929; Fax: (802) 864-7626.
Orders by U.S. trade bookstores and wholesalers. Please contact Ingram Publisher Services, Tel: (800) 509-4887; Fax: (800) 838-1149; E-mail: customer.service@ ingrampublisherservices.com; or visit www.ingrampublisherservices.com/Ordering for details about electronic ordering.

Berrett-Koehler and the BK logo are registered trademarks of Berrett-Koehler Publishers, Inc.

Printed in the United States of America

Berrett-Koehler books are printed on long-lasting acid-free paper. When it is available, we choose paper that has been manufactured by environmentally responsible processes. These may include using trees grown in sustainable forests, incorporating recycled paper, minimizing chlorine in bleaching, or recycling the energy produced at the paper mill.

Library of Congress Cataloging-in-Publication Data
Sisson, Dan, 1937–
    The American revolution of 1800 : how Jefferson rescued democracy from tyranny and faction and what this means today / Daniel Sisson with Thom Hartmann. — Fortieth anniversary edition.
        pages cm
    Original edition published in 1974.
    Includes bibliographical references and index.
    ISBN 978-1-60994-985-3 (hardcover)
1. United States—Politics and government—1789–1809. 2. Jefferson, Thomas, 1743–1826—Political and social views. 3. Presidents—United States—Election—1800. 4. Political science—United States—History. 5. Revolutions—United States—History. I. Hartmann, Thom, 1951– II. Title.
    E310.S57 2014
    973.4'6092—dc23

                                                                    2014016113

18   17   16   15   14   10   9   8   7   6   5   4   3   2   1

Cover design by Brad Foltz. Cover illustration by Eric Van Den Bruelle/Getty Images. Interior design and composition by Gary Palmatier, Ideas to Images. Elizabeth von Radics, copyeditor; Mike Mollett, proofreader; Rachel Rice, indexer.

To **BERNARD BAILYN**—
whose insights into our revolutionary heritage have defined my
perspective for nearly fifty years. I believe Bailyn's writings are so
original and imaginative no one will ever convince me he was not alive
and present at the founding—listening, questioning, taking notes,
even participating in the thousands of conversations about conspiracy,
imperialism, corruption, and, yes, revolution, from 1760 on—when
Otis, Adams, Jefferson, Paine, and Madison "began our world anew."
My intellectual debt to him is incalculable.

To **WILLIAM APPLEMAN WILLIAMS**—
a dear friend, whose ongoing assessment of how revolutionary
America transformed itself from a beacon of hope in the world
into an imperial state is unmatched in modern American scholarship.
We spent many days together, sitting on the beach near
Waldport on the Oregon coast, leaning against an uprooted
Douglas fir, sipping "clarity," and considering every angle
of Jefferson's and Madison's theories about how and
why and when and where and to what degree we were a nation
dedicated to liberty. In every instance Bill never lost sight of the
American idea, and at the end he always reaffirmed the Revolution
of 1800. Moreover he did so with elegance, a touch of irony,
and, above all, a marvelous sense of humor.

Contents

CHAPTER *5*

CHAPTER *6*

CHAPTER *7*

CHAPTER *8*

Introduction

*I*T IS RARE WHEN A BOOK ABOUT OUR EARLY REPUBLIC IS RELEVANT forty years after it was originally published. It is rarer still when that book provides insight into national problems we refuse to solve two centuries later.

You are therefore holding in your hands (or reading on your pad or computer) one of the most important books you will ever encounter. Here is why: Unlike other histories of this era, this book is written from a revolutionary perspective much like Jefferson's generation viewed the world.

The American Revolution of 1800 was not just about an election. It was about a life-and-death struggle for power between democratic-republican principles and oligarchic-plutocratic values based on corruption. In short, this book, by implication, is about the identical crisis America faces today.

The author's unique analysis is based on the idea of faction controlling party and how both undermine constitutional government. In an age where modern parties and the factions that control them have paralyzed our government, this book validates the politics of the Founders.

In still another contribution, the book demonstrates how preserving revolutionary ideas within our culture depends on understanding the classical tradition. The ability to recognize a demagogue is rooted deeply in the role Caesar played in destroying the republic of ancient Rome. That fear of a Caesar inspired Jefferson and others to organize citizens against the Federalists, thereby completely contradicting the political rules of their time.

The book, above all, presents a profoundly positive view of Jefferson and his creativity in the midst of crisis. It celebrates his gift—twenty-four years after he wrote the Declaration of Independence—and proves he never abandoned his principles or his revolutionary vision for America's future.

Ironically, it has become a cliché in political and economic circles that while we love Thomas Jefferson, we live in a country largely run by Alexander Hamilton's policies and John Adams's politics.

This may have been more true of the roughly two hundred years before the contemporary "free-trade" era, beginning in the 1970s under Richard Nixon and exploding in the mid-1990s, when Bill Clinton signed the North American Free Trade Agreement and the General Agreement on Tariffs and Trade. (Alexander Hamilton must be rolling over in his grave.) Nevertheless we have become a mercantilist nation dominated by banks and big industries, as Hamilton envisioned.

It is true that there were huge differences between Hamilton and Jefferson, particularly in their visions for the future of America and its economy, and those divisions tend to dominate interpretations of our political discussion when we reference the era of our first few presidents.

But a much larger and more dramatic battle of worldviews played out in the late 1790s between President John Adams and Vice President Thomas Jefferson, leading directly to what is arguably the most transformational presidential election in American history: the election of 1800.

In other books and places, both Dan Sisson and I have written at some length about the differences between these two men and their respective visions of America. Adams relished throwing newspaper editors in prison and demanded that when he and his wife visited a town the local militia come out to fire their cannons in salute of him and shout: "God save President Adams!"

Jefferson was so horrified by Adams's Alien and Sedition Acts that he left town the day they were signed into law, and, as president, often wore simple homespun garments. He was known to answer the front door of the White House in his bathrobe, and more than one visitor mistook him for a servant. As president, Jefferson literally acted out his egalitarian vision of America.

In my book *The Crash of 2016: The Plot to Destroy America—and What We Can Do to Stop It,* I described Jefferson's concern about aristocracy in American politics. On October 28, 1813, in a letter to his old rival John Adams, Jefferson commented on his distrust of America's growing wealthy elite—naming in particular the Senate, which was not democratically elected by the people.

Referring to the "cabal in the Senate of the United States," Jefferson wrote, "You [John Adams] think it best to put the Pseudo-aristoi into a separate chamber of legislation [the Senate], where they may be hindered from doing mischief by their coordinate branches, and where, also, they may be a protection to wealth against the agrarian and plundering enterprises of the majority of the people."[1]

Then Jefferson countered in the letter, writing, "I [do not] believe them [the Senate] necessary to protect the wealthy; because enough of these will find their way into every branch of the legislation, to protect themselves."

Instead, Jefferson, wrote, "I think the best remedy is exactly that provided by all our constitutions, to leave to the citizens the free election… In general they will elect the really good and wise. In some instances, wealth may corrupt, and birth blind them; but not in sufficient degree to endanger the society."

And in a final warning about the largely Federalist "cabal in the Senate," Jefferson wrote, "The artificial aristocracy is a mischievous ingredient in government, and provision should be made to prevent its ascendancy….I think that to give them power in order to prevent them from doing mischief, is arming them for it, and increasing instead of remedying the evil."

In a 1786 letter to George Washington, Jefferson gave his most explicit warning about this threat of a military allied with a plutocracy within and advocated for unwavering vigilance against it: "Tho' the day may be at some distance, beyond the reach of our lives perhaps, yet it will certainly come," he wrote, "when, a single fibre left of this institution, will produce an hereditary aristocracy which will change the form of our governments from the best to the worst in the world."[2]

He added, "I shall think little [of the] longevity [of our nation] unless this germ of destruction be taken out." It was not until 1913 that Americans became so disgusted by politicians dancing to the tune of state-level rich people essentially "buying" Senate appointments that the Seventeenth Amendment to the Constitution was passed to provide for the direct election of senators by the people themselves. More recently, the Supreme Court's *Citizens United v. Federal Election Commission* and *McCutcheon v. Federal Election Commission* decisions have reinstated the ability of wealthy and powerful people to buy members of Congress and, by implication, our government.

In broad strokes these are the ideas that should occupy most political histories published these days—and especially any discussions about the era around the election and the Revolution of 1800. Unfortunately, the two most popular biographies of Adams and Jefferson published in the past fourteen years do not mention Jefferson's Revolution of 1800—not even once! Thus after forty years, the story of the final completion of the American Revolution, and by Jefferson's own words one of his chief contributions to America and the world, remains a little-known story.

THE REAL CONCERNS OF THE FOUNDERS

While it is true that many modern historians mean well, all too many have missed or failed to focus on the most important differences and similarities between that time and now.

If Jefferson, or even Hamilton or Adams, were to witness the political gridlock extant in today's state and national capitols, they would be horrified. James Madison, perhaps, would be the most outraged, as he left us such an eloquent warning about the politics of faction in his Federalist No. 10. It opens with the following two sentences: "Among the numerous advantages promised by a well constructed Union, none deserves to be more accurately developed than its tendency to break and control the violence of faction. The friend of popular governments never finds himself so much alarmed for their character and fate, as when he contemplates their propensity to this dangerous vice."

But what is "faction"?

In our modern era, the word *faction* is often dismissed as an anachronism or simply interpreted to mean a "political party." But James

Madison, the Framer of our Constitution, and his contemporaries understood well the distinction between factions and political parties. And with that understanding, they would be shocked by how differently contemporary politics are interpreted today from similar events experienced by our Founders.

During that period the Framers saw faction *and* party paralyzing and then destroying governments—especially republics throughout history. As a consequence Jefferson suggested that "every generation" should have its own smaller form of revolution, reconfiguring the nation and its government to adapt to changing needs and changing times.

Jefferson wrote to his protégé, James Madison, the year the Constitution was ratified and our modern nation birthed: "The question, whether one generation of men has a right to bind another…is a question of such consequences as not only to merit decision, but place also among the fundamental principles of every government."[3]

No single generation, he wrote, has the right to saddle the next with a devastated commons [and/or environment], and it should be obvious "that no such obligation can be transmitted" from generation to generation.

Laying out his thinking on the issue, Jefferson continued: "I set out on this ground, which I suppose to be self evident, that the earth belongs in usufruct [common ownership] to the living; that the dead have neither powers nor rights over it. The portion occupied by any individual ceases to be his when himself ceases to be, and reverts to the society."

Jefferson's logic that no person or generation should be able to bind the next one was one of his core beliefs throughout his life. He added, "For if he could, he might during his own life, eat up the usufruct [commons] of the lands for several generations to come, and then the lands would belong to the dead, and not to the living, which is the reverse of our principle."

THEY WERE REVOLUTIONARIES!

But what was most revolutionary about Jefferson's thinking on this was the idea of *generational revolutions*—that the nation itself must fundamentally change roughly once every biological or epochal generation—and even that would not prevent larger periodic political transformations of the nation.

These were, he believed, not just ideals but a basic force of nature. He wrote,

> On similar ground it may be proved, that no society can make a perpetual constitution, or even a perpetual law. The earth belongs always to the living generation: they may manage it, then, and what proceeds from it, as they please, during their usufruct [shared ownership].
>
> They are masters, too, of their own persons, and consequently may govern them as they please. But persons and property make the sum of the objects of government. The constitution and the laws of their predecessors are extinguished then, in their natural course, with those whose will gave them being.

Jefferson believed that even the laws enshrined in our Constitution came with a time limit and that once the generation that wrote those laws passed on out of power, those laws must be rewritten by the new generation or at least every second generation: "Every constitution, then, and every law, naturally expires at the end of thirty-four years," Jefferson wrote. "If it be enforced longer, it is an act of force, and not of right. It may be said, that the succeeding generation exercising, in fact, the power of repeal, this leaves them as free as if the constitution or law had been expressly limited to thirty-four years only."

A revolution every twenty to thirty-four years? Could Jefferson have actually been proposing—or predicting—that?

In fact, yes.

And this is where Dan Sisson does such a brilliant job of showing how that old revolutionary, Thomas Jefferson—the guy who, as a young man in his thirties, had put pen to paper and triggered the American Revolution—fomented, as that much older and wiser man, a *second* American revolution a generation after the War of Independence.

This "second American revolution" was carried out in 1800, when Jefferson openly challenged the conservative, Federalist direction in which John Adams and his cronies had been leading America. Jefferson, then Adams's vice president, decided to fight Adams for the presidency. It was a brutal and hard-fought battle, but ultimately Jefferson won.

His victory fundamentally transformed America, and if we hope to maintain any fidelity to our founding principles, to American history, and to the ideals of a constitutionally limited democratic republic, it is essential that we understand what led up to the Revolution of 1800, how it played out, and how it left this country permanently changed.

Read on—and prepare to have your view of America altered forever.

Thom Hartmann
Washington, DC

The Idea of a
Non-party State

For it is the nature and intention of a constitution to prevent governing by party.

—Thomas Paine, 1795

So OFTEN IN THE PAST CENTURY, THE POLITICAL HISTORY OF America reveals a paralysis in the highest levels of our government. Legislation fails to pass, budgets are voted down, compromise seems impossible, and the problems of the nation are neither addressed nor solved. There have been brief periods, of course, when this was not the case: the New Deal is usually held up as an example of a time when American politicians came together to fundamentally transform the nature and the political landscape of our country. But in the generations since then, more often than not we have seen gridlock rather than collaboration.

"That's the way it should be!" says conventional wisdom. "The Founders of our country, the men who wrote the Constitution, wanted there to be a 'loyal opposition' to serve as a 'balance' against excessive power in the hands of any one political party or even a president."

Not only is this *not* true but this pervasive myth has done considerable harm to our nation—and continues to do so.

THE "LOYAL OPPOSITION"

The concept of a "loyal party opposition" has grown in the literature of the professional historians until it has assumed the stature of our most fundamental law. Not only historians but political scientists and everyone else who has sought to explain the stability of the American governmental system have looked to the origin of parties for the confirmation of our genius. The two-party system was the dominating idea in history and political science in the twentieth century. Historians and political scientists were so mesmerized by it that they, like English Whig historians, went back and reread all of American history (as well as British history) to demonstrate the continuity of the twentieth-century party system with the past. When they did so, the Revolution of 1800 dissolved. It had to.

This chapter is an attempt to redress that historical perspective and to deal with the political structure of the eighteenth century as a man of the times saw it. I am trying to make a case for using the contemporary lens of faction and of revolution as opposed to emphasizing the later emergence of political parties.

Moreover, by examining the period from a classical revolutionary perspective, it is possible to state several conditions not generally recognized.

- ૭ૐ First, the men in power from 1790 to 1801 did not even remotely conceive of a modern two-party system. In fact, the opposite is true. They wished to consolidate and perpetuate a one-party system of politics in America and were successful in their lifetime.

- ૭ૐ Second, their view of political administration was a classic political view, necessitating only one faction in power and abhorring the existence of an "opposition."

- ૭ૐ Third, because of this view it was necessary for those who were out of power to foment revolution, based on the classical political theory of "electoral Caesarism,"[1] simply to have access to or gain power. This last point will be discussed at length in the following chapters.

To develop these themes, it is necessary to realize that the eighteenth century had its own historical perspective. As one historian put it, "The most fruitful point of departure in studying their careers as statesmen is acceptance of the fact that all questions they asked and all the answers they found to them were eighteenth-century questions and answers that their intensive reading had already blocked out into a systematic pattern."[2]

These were not twenty-first-century concepts of political organization. Any attempt, therefore, to understand that "pattern," their political ideology, must examine the assumptions on which their political logic rested.

Nowhere is this truer than where the concepts *faction* and *party* are concerned. The former term belongs to the period generally up to Washington's Farewell Address, where the warnings against "factions" are often considered naïve. The latter term (*party*) is more confusing. It can be synonymous with faction, but it also is a term of opprobrium. It should not be confused with the establishment of political parties as we know them today.

Thus, for clarity's sake, and rather than discuss misconceptions of the terms *party* and *faction* by authors of secondary works in American history, it best suits our purpose to establish a working definition of the terms for an eighteenth-century politician.[3]

Common definitions before the nineteenth century treated the terms similarly, beginning in the sixteenth century. The *Oxford English Dictionary* gives a reference to *party* in 1535 as "inclined to form parties or to act for party purposes; seditious." *Faction* was described as "violent." *Sedition* held a connotation of insurrection and treason against the state, both revolutionary kinds of activity. Lord Bolingbroke (Henry St. John) referred to faction as that which "hath no regard to National Interest."[4]

One dictionary used by contemporaries, *An Universal Etymological English Dictionary,* explained that *party* and *faction* were synonymous.[5] Samuel Johnson in his dictionary suggested two meanings that essentially merged in the examples he cited. Giving similar descriptions of the two terms, he said *faction* was "a party in a state" and also "tumult, discord and dissension."[6]

Violence and dissension were common to both terms. It remained for Thomas Hobbes, however, to give the classic revolutionary description to *faction,* common from Aristotle's time to Charles Dickens's *A Tale of Two Cities.* He said *faction* "is as it were a city within a city."[7]

This was indeed recognition that potential revolutionary activity was associated with the term, for it raised the specter of the "two-city" theory of revolution.

These definitions perhaps sum up, better than any other, the eighteenth century's understanding of both terms. Seditious, revolutionary, "always with an opprobrious sense, conveying the imputation of selfish or mischievous ends or turbulent or unscrupulous methods."[8]

Distinctions between the words *party* and *faction* were slight, if made at all. Looking upon *party* as both a form of political organization and as an idea of violence, "most American writers seemed to have assimilated these two senses of the word to each other."[9]

Noah Webster throws an additional light on the term *party* if for no other reason than because he was an ardent foe of Jefferson. His original edition defined *faction* in a way that touched on all that we have discussed—including the importance of revolution.

Webster said *faction* is: "A party, in political society, combined or acting in union, in opposition to the prince, government or state; usually applied to a minority, but it may be applied to a majority. Sometimes a state is divided into factions nearly equal. Rome was always disturbed by factions. Republics are proverbial for factions, and factions in monarchies have often effected *revolutions*."[10]

SEPARATING OUT FACTION FROM PARTY

The terms *faction* and *party*, though appearing synonymous to the average eighteenth-century American, were nevertheless partially separable. Not only did they connote violence, turbulence, and a revolutionary threat against the state—its administration and national interest—they also implied a relationship to one another based on the complexity of human nature and its involvement with politics.

Perhaps it is best said by an author read by virtually every educated member of the revolutionary generation. Lord Bolingbroke wrote,

> It is far from being an easy matter to state to you, fairly and clearly, what the words party and faction really mean…
>
> A Party then is, as I take it, a set of men connected together, in virtue of their having, or, which in this case is the same thing, pretending to have the same *private* opinion with respect to *public* concerns; and while this is confined to sentiment or discourse, without interfering with the management of affairs, I think it wears properly that

denomination; but when it proceeds further, and influences men's conduct, in any considerable degree, it becomes *Faction*.

In all such cases there are revealed *reasons,* and a reserved *Motive.* By revealed reasons, I mean a set of plausible doctrines, which may be stiled the *creed* of the party; but the reserved motive belongs to *Faction* only, and is the Thirst of Power.

The creeds of parties vary like those of sects; but all Factions have the same motive, which never implies more or less than a *lust of dominion,* though they may be, and generally are, covered with the specious pretenses of *self-denial,* and that vehemence referred to *zeal* for the public, which flows in fact from Avarice, Self-Interest, Resentment and other *private views.*[11]

Bolingbroke, who had spent most of his political life opposing the administration of Robert Walpole, knew whereof he spoke. Acquainted with the motives of nearly all who objected to the Walpolean system, he could easily discern his colleagues' thirst for power no matter how they clothed it with patriotic disguises.

His distinction between *party* and *faction* looms important in the politics of the early republic if merely for the reason that most American statesmen complained about party and faction on the same grounds.

Two other observations by Bolingbroke about "motives" common to both terms deserve comment.

First, members of parties or factions, despite their "revealed" motives, were men obsessed with power and a "lust for dominion." It follows then that these same men, given and perhaps even creating the opportunity, are capable of reaching for power through seditious means. This would be especially true if the administration in power considered their opposition illegal.

Second, if parties *become* factions when their behavior affects the public realm, it is important to keep this distinction in mind. For one characteristic of eighteenth-century statesmen, little understood by twenty-first-century writers, is the absolute vehemence with which they denounced party and faction.

The reasons lay in their extreme fear and anxiety of what occurred once parties became factions and began to influence public opinion.

The results were almost guaranteed: disruption of the public realm. This distinction is important because it means that historians have misunderstood the terms *party* and *faction* by imputing public action only to the former. Nineteenth-, twentieth-, and twenty-first-century historians have brushed this distinction aside; and, in fact, they have *reversed* the distinction between party and faction.

David Hume's *The History of England*, widely read in the colonies before, but even more after, the American Revolution, described the idea of faction in this manner: "Factions subvert government, render laws impotent, and beget the fiercest animosities among men of the same nation, who ought to give mutual assistance to each other."

"Founders of...factions," he wrote, should be "detested and hated."[12]

Edmund Burke, who enjoyed immense popularity among Americans, spoke of party in 1770. His "Thoughts on the cause of the Present Discontents" laid the source of England's troubles at the door of party and its relationship to the court. Burke went beyond theory to include the actual consequences of party practice:

> The [party] machinery of this system is perplexed in its movements, and false in its principle. It is formed on a supposition that the King is something external to his government; and that he may be honoured and aggrandized, even by its debility and disgrace. The [court as well as party] plan proceeds expressly on the idea of enfeebling the regular executory power. It proceeds on the idea of weakening the State in order to strengthen the Court. The scheme depending entirely on distrust, on disconnection, on mutability by principle, on systematic weakness in every particular member; it is impossible that the total result should be substantial strength of any kind.[13]

In yet another famous remark, this time on the nature of a representative, Burke indicated a total unwillingness to sacrifice his views to those of any party. Here Burke presents the theory behind his observations on practical instruction from either his district or his party: "His [the representative's] unbiased opinion, his mature judgment, his enlightened conscience, he ought not sacrifice to you, to any man, or any set of men living....But government and legislation are matters of reason and judgment, and not of inclination; and what sort of reason is that, in which determination precedes the discussion; in which one set of men deliberate, and another decide; and where those who form the conclusions are perhaps three hundred miles from those who hear the arguments?"[14]

A more devastating intellectual critique of the function of party could hardly be made. Refusing to become the creature of party, stating that the very rationale of party—with its willingness to dispense with deliberation and dialectical reason—contradicted the basic reason for government, Burke had made his decision on party.

The terms *party* and *faction* had such a long history that they were widely assumed by American statesmen to be part of human nature. This at least was the approach taken by the two men most responsible for establishing the theoretical guidelines of the early republic. James Madison and Alexander Hamilton attempted to analyze the terms in light of their influence on the political system. Their *Federalist* essays presented an analysis of party and faction that is more than consistent with the history of the terms we have reviewed.

Madison referred to "the violence of faction" as a "dangerous vice" characteristic of free governments.

"By a faction," he says, "I understand a number of citizens, whether amounting to a majority or a minority of the whole, who are united and actuated by some common impulse of passion, or of interest, *adverse* to the rights of other citizens, or to the permanent and aggregate interests of the community."

He continued, "The latent causes of faction are thus sown in the nature of man; and we see them everywhere."

Thus party, as Madison understood it, was not something of recent origin. Parties have been around since the beginning of man. And, he noted, "the *most numerous party, or in other words, the most powerful faction* must be expected to prevail."

He ends his analysis on this note: "To secure the public good and provide rights against the danger of such a faction…is then the great object to which our inquiries are directed."[15]

Thus Madison captured the essence of the terms as they were understood by his contemporaries: that faction and party were inescapably rooted in human nature and produced violence, zeal, animosity, oppression, and danger—all *adverse* to the interests of the community.

He added: "Men of factious tempers, of local prejudices, or of sinister designs may, by intrigue, by corruption, or by other means, first obtain the suffrages, and then betray the interests, of the people."[16]

His conclusion is that factions must be broken and controlled. They are, at all costs, not to be legitimately recognized or encouraged.

Madison was not alone in his aversion to party and faction.

HAMILTON AGREES WITH MADISON: PARTIES ARE EVIL

Alexander Hamilton too warns the reader: "Ambition, avarice, personal animosity, party opposition, and many other motives not more laudable than these" were typical of that "intolerant spirit which has, at all times, characterized political parties."[17]

Registering his disgust for faction, Hamilton continued, "It is impossible to read the history of the petty republics of Greece and Italy without feeling sensations of horror and disgust at the…rapid succession of revolutions by which they were kept in a state of perpetual vibration between the extremes of tyranny and anarchy."[18]

Hamilton, we might note, connects ancient history with modern America. "The tempestuous situation," he writes, "from which Massachusetts has scarcely emerged [Shays's Rebellion], evinces that dangers of this kind are *not merely speculative*. Who can determine what might have been the issue of her late convulsions, if the malcontents had been headed by a Caesar or a Cromwell?"[19]

In Federalist No. 77, he describes the influence of faction and party intrigue, connections, and "personal influence" in government in a way that was characteristic of the terms from classical times through the age of Robert Walpole: "Every mere council of appointment, however constituted, will be a conclave, in which cabal and intrigue will have their full scope.…And as each member will have his friends and connections to provide for, the desire of mutual gratification will beget a scandalous bartering of votes and bargaining for places."[20]

What is worth noting here is not only Hamilton's description of the influence of party and faction upon an administration but his general description of politics. He is describing the politics of England for the past century and a half.

Moreover he understood that encouraging party and faction, at the theoretical as well as the practical level, guaranteed that the emergent system of American politics would be propelled into the futile violence and dissension that had plagued every republic in history.

Throughout the remainder of his political career, Hamilton reserved a special contempt for parties. At various times he caricatured them as "the petulance of party," "the rage of party spirit," "sedition and party rage," the "unaccommodating spirit of party," the "delirium of party," the "baneful spirit of party," and the "heats of party." One of Hamilton's biographers notes that "To the end of his life he refused to believe that the party he led was a party at all. It was, rather, a kind of *ad hoc* committee of correspondence of men with a large view of America's destiny."[21]

THEY WERE ALL AGAINST PARTIES

Contrary to some historians' opinions, the consistency with which these statesmen held their views against faction and party in every phase of their political careers is indicative of a lifelong attachment to the antiparty cause. Moreover they were willing to write down their biases in theoretical terms, explaining in extreme detail the consequences of party activity.[22]

Indeed it is striking the quality of the men who expressed their opinions against party. They were the brightest, most reflective, often the wittiest, and easily the most philosophical men of their time. James Madison, Alexander Hamilton, George Washington, Sam Adams, John Adams, Thomas Jefferson, James Monroe, Patrick Henry, Albert Gallatin, John Jay, Thomas Paine, John Taylor of Caroline, John Quincy Adams, Benjamin Rush, Fisher Ames—the list could go on, reading like a Who's Who of the 1790s.

Fisher Ames wrote,

> *Faction* is an adherence to interests foreign to the interests of the
> state; there is such a faction among us devoted to France....There
> is some hope of reclaiming a very few of them; but if they travel far
> on the party road, or associate long with the desperados in the van,
> who explore the thorny and crooked by-ways, they will not remain
> honest. They will be corrupted, and so deeply, that, in every approach

towards civil war and revolution, the dupes, who sincerely believe
the whole creed of their *party,* will be found to go the farthest.[23]

Ames, writing in 1800, accepted the same definitions of the terms as
his contemporaries. And like them he makes a connection among faction,
party, and the idea of revolution. Ames also dealt with the origins and
causes of party and faction exactly as did Madison and Hamilton. He asks,
"Is it in the nature of free governments to exist without parties? Such a
thing has never yet been and probably will never be. Is it in the nature of
party to exist without passion? Or of passion to acquiesce, when it meets
with opposers and obstacles? No....Party moderation is children's talk.
Who has ever seen faction *calmly* in a rage? Who will expect to see that
carnivorous monster quietly submit to eat grass?"[24]

Ames's prose may seem lurid to us now, but to his contemporaries
it was commonplace. The consequences of unbridled faction and party
activity meant revolution, civil war, violence, and perhaps the most feared
development of all: a change in the form of government.

John Jay, writing to Jefferson in 1786, observed, "If faction should
long bear down law and government, tyranny may raise its head, or the
more sober part of the people may even think of a King."[25] It was a remark
that left an indelible impression on his correspondent and was to become
the most crucial issue of the next fifteen years.

PARTIES DESTROY LIBERTY

Tom Paine was another writer who considered party an evil that must be
kept within traditional bounds.

Writing in 1795, he states, "For it is the *nature and intention of a
constitution to prevent governing* by *party,* by establishing a common
principle that shall limit and control the power and the impulse of party,
and that says to all parties, *thus far shalt thou go and no further.* But in
the absence of a constitution, men look entirely to party; and instead of
principle governing party, party governs principle."[26]

Paine placed the constitution as a barrier between the violence of
party and the principles of republican government. He also noted in the
absence of an effective constitution, even when rulers adhered to the

letter and the spirit of the constitution, the spirit of party will destroy those principles. This is an important observation, as it demonstrates the reasoning that Paine, as well as most of his colleagues, agreed on: party, if allowed to develop, would inevitably destroy the constitution, the principles of republican government, and the form of the republic itself.

This theme is important because it constitutes the main thrust of Jefferson's intriguing statement: "The Revolution of 1800…was as real a revolution in the principles of our government as that of 1776 was in its form."[27] The reader will do well to keep Paine's construction in mind as he ponders the ideas of faction and revolution.

THE ONE-PARTY STATE

James Monroe, one of Jefferson's closest confidants, urged Jefferson in 1801 to formally create a one-party state. He wrote, "This public expects some tone to be given your Administration immediately. There is a conflict of principle, and either democracy or royalty must prevail. The opposing parties can never be united…because their views are as opposite as light and darkness."[28] Monroe, who took an unusually hard line, believed the opposition could not be reconciled; therefore it must be controlled.

Another revolutionary figure, a Virginian, but one who could scarcely be considered a confidant of Jefferson's, also shared a horror of faction and party. Writing to Jefferson in 1799, anticipating the crisis of the approaching revolution of 1800, Patrick Henry declared, "United we stand, divided we fall. Let us not split into factions which must destroy that union upon which our existence hangs…not exhaust it in civil commotion and intestine wars."[29]

The clearest statement on the theory of the one- or non-party state comes from a man whom everyone admired—George Washington. Father figure, warrior, model of virtue, a monument in terms of his symbolic value to the country, he was also considered a repository of wisdom and common sense. Therefore his specific warnings against party and faction in his Farewell Address merit special attention. Not only are they consistent with the definitions stated thus far, they were written in the context of a dissertation on the principles of constitutionalism and free government.

Washington notes,

The basis of our political system is the right of the people to make
and to alter their constitutions of government. But the constitution
which at any time exists till changed by an explicit and authentic act
of the whole people is sacredly obligatory upon all. The very idea
of the power and the right of the people to establish government
presupposes the duty of every individual to obey the established
government.

All obstructions to the execution of the laws, all combinations and
associations, under whatever plausible character, with the real design
to direct, control, counteract, or awe the regular deliberation and
action of the constituted authorities, are destructive of this fundamental principle and of fatal tendency. They serve to organize *faction;*
to give it an artificial and extraordinary force; to put in the place of
the delegated will of the nation the will of a *party,* often a small but
artful and enterprising minority of the community, and, according
to the alternate triumphs of different *parties,* to make the public
administration the mirror of the ill-concerted and incongruous
projects of *faction...*

[Faction and party] are likely in the course of time and things to
become potent engines by which cunning, ambitious, and unprincipled men will be enabled to subvert the power of the people, and to
usurp for themselves the reins of government, destroying afterwards
the very engines which have lifted them to unjust dominion.[30]

Washington's exposition needs little commentary. Suffice it to say he
sees parties as natural to society, realizes they cannot be destroyed, and
urges his countrymen to control them. In all of this, he is in complete
agreement with the best minds of his time.

While we have examined in detail the thoughts on party and faction
expressed by leading statesmen of the period, we have reserved for the
end of our review the comments of two thinkers and actors during the
1790s: John Adams and Thomas Jefferson.

Adams, throughout his long career, had written and spoken out
against the influence of faction and party. As early as 1780, he wrote two
truly prophetic sentences, as strong an indictment of party as anyone

could possibly write: "There is nothing which I dread so much as a division of the republic into two great parties, each arranged under its leader, and concerting measures in opposition to each other. This in my humble apprehension is to be dreaded as the greatest political evil under our constitution."[31]

Once Adams had reached the pinnacle of his own power, he raised the issue in his Inaugural Address, saying we must "preserv[e] our Constitution from its natural enemies, the spirit of sophistry, the spirit of party...[and] the profligacy of corruption."[32]

In another prophetic line, his address dealt with the relation between party and elections. He said, "We should be unfaithful to ourselves if we should ever lose sight of the danger to our liberties if anything partial or extraneous should infect the purity of our free, fair, virtuous, and independent elections. If an election is to be determined by a majority of a single vote, and that can be procured by a party through artifice or corruption, the Government may be the choice of a party for its own ends, not of the nation for the national good."

In correspondence with Jefferson, Adams said, "Every one of these Parties [monarchical, aristocratical, and democratical], when possessed of power, or when they have been Undermost, and Struggling to get Uppermost, has been equally prone to every Species of Fraud and Violence and Usurpation."[33]

While Jefferson agreed with every line of his friend's complaints, he probably would not have expressed himself so pungently. But beginning in 1789, he left a trail of evidence against party and faction that, over the years, adds up to the most severe indictment by anyone against the role they played. Jefferson characteristically began his onslaught by casting his opposition in philosophical and moral terms. Writing to a friend who attempted to sound him out as to whether he was a party member, Jefferson advised him: "I am not a Federalist, because I never submitted the whole system of my opinions to the creed of any party of men whatever, in religion, in philosophy, in politics, or in anything else, where I was capable of thinking for myself. Such an addiction is the last degradation of a free and moral agent. If I could not go to heaven but with a party, I would not go there at all."[34]

In 1798 Jefferson wrote John Taylor of Caroline an analysis of party:

> Be this as it may, in every free and deliberating society, there must, from the nature of man, be opposite parties, and violent dissensions and discords; and one of these, for the most part, must prevail over the other for a longer or shorter time. Perhaps this party division is necessary to induce each to watch and relate to the people the proceedings of the other. But if on a temporary superiority of the one party, the other is to resort to a scission of the Union, no federal government can exist.[35]

Here is no categorical statement of an endorsement of party. For Jefferson being involved in politics was a matter of principle, above both party and faction.

JEFFERSON AND THE ONE PARTY STATE

This concern about principles, strangely enough, is never connected with Jefferson's first Inaugural Address. And it is that address, conspicuous by its absence in the works of those who claim Jefferson was establishing the first modern political party, that brings together his philosophy of government without party rule. On the eve of his triumph, Jefferson could afford, indeed he needed, to be conciliatory by making a plea for harmony and unity in his new administration. Those who remain in "opposition," he says, will stand as "monuments," but their opposition, it is important to notice, is equated with civil war, violence, and changing the form of government:

> Let us then, fellow-citizens, unite with one heart and one mind. Let us restore to social intercourse that harmony and affection without which liberty and even life itself are but dreary things....During the throes and convulsions of the ancient world, during the agonizing spasms of infuriated man, seeking through blood and slaughter his long-lost liberty, it was not wonderful that the agitation of the billows should reach even this distant and peaceful shore; that this should be more felt and feared by some and less by others, and should divide opinions as to measures of safety. But every difference of opinion is not a difference of principle. We have called by different names brethren of the same principle. We are all Republicans, we are all Federalists. If there be any among us who wish to dissolve this Union

or to change the republican form, let them stand undisturbed as monuments."[36]

Jefferson's comment "We are all Republicans, we are all Federalists" is an appeal to every citizen to forsake party and return to the original principles of the American Revolution, the Constitution, and the republic—principles which, as Jefferson viewed them, rise above party and are the common property of everyone. Years later Jefferson would recollect the "sad realities" of the years before his successful drive for the presidency and remark, "I fondly hope we may now truly say, 'we are all republicans, all federalists,' and that the motto of the standard to which our country will forever rally, will be, 'federal union, and republican government.'"[37]

This then appears to be the true meaning of Jefferson's oft-quoted statement. What he expected was not the continuation of the Federalist party in opposition but the recognition by those Federalists that they had a dual responsibility to the government: to uphold the principles of federalism (the division of the Union's power into state and national jurisdictions) and the principles of republicanism (guaranteeing the people's right to self-government through the representative system). This was a central theme of his revolution: the renewal of a decentralizing process that had begun with the American Revolution. Nearing the end of his address, Jefferson makes an explicit connection between the principles of the American Revolution and those of his republican victory. In Jefferson's mind there was no difference:

> These principles form the bright constellation which has gone before us and guided our steps through an age of revolution and reformation. The wisdom of our sages and blood of our heroes have been devoted to their attainment. They should be the creed of our political faith, the text of civic instruction, the touchstone by which to try the services of those we trust; and should we wander from them in moments of error or of alarm, let us hasten to retrace our steps and to regain the road which alone leads to peace, liberty and safety.[38]

After Jefferson came into power in 1801, he wrote to a friend, confirming his long-held antiparty bias: "I learn from all quarters that my inaugural Address is considered as holding out a ground for conciliation and union....I was always satisfied that the great body of those called Federalists were real Republicans as well as federalists."[39]

A dozen years later, Jefferson placed his views in a philosophical and historical perspective:

> To me then it appears that there have been differences of opinion, and party differences, from the first establishment of governments, to the present day; and on the same question which now divides our country; that these will continue thro' all future time: that everyone takes his side in favor of the many, or of the few, according to his constitution, and the circumstances in which he is placed: that opinions, which are equally honest on both sides, should not affect personal esteem, or social intercourse: that as we judge between the Claudii and the Gracchi...of past ages, so, of those among us... the next generations will judge, favorably or unfavorably.[40]

Jefferson's letter might have been written for posterity, as it places considerable confidence in the judgment of future generations. He believes, of course, that history will vindicate the stand he and Adams took on party. We might also note the historical perspective that Jefferson reveals. The Gracchi brothers, who, two thousand years before, had dealt with party agitations of a similar nature, had, according to their constitutions, taken the side of the people. Jefferson, it seems, identified with them and not with Appius Claudius Caecus, one of the despotic emperors in Roman history. This identification was "natural," as the Gracchi had provided the model for Jefferson's democratic Revolution of 1800.

Jefferson's final and complete statement on party was made to the Marquis de La Fayette in 1817. Relating the facts of the aftermath of the War of 1812, Jefferson told his friend that the "the best effect has been *the complete suppression of party.*"

The election of James Monroe was the final triumph against party: "Four and twenty years, which he will accomplish, of administration in *republican forms and principles,* will so consecrate them in the eyes of the people as to secure them against the danger of change."[41]

Indeed, when Tom Paine wrote, "It is the nature and intention of a constitution to prevent governing by party," he summarized the theory of an age.

The final observation is one that links the concern over party violence with the most important argument of all. As Jefferson framed the issue, it came down to a choice between "kingly government" or the principles of the American Revolution. It was a centuries-old battle in which everyone made their natural choice. Indeed he saw his and his contemporaries' efforts to construct a non-party state contained within a single ancient framework: the struggle of liberty against despotism.

And that, after all, is the story of revolution throughout history.

2 The Idea of Revolution

But what do we mean by the American Revolution? Do we mean the American war? The Revolution was effected before the war commenced. The Revolution was in the minds and hearts of the people...This radical change in the principles, opinions, sentiments, and affections of the people, was the real American Revolution.

> —John Adams to Hezekiah Niles
> February 13, 1813

The revolution of 1800...was as real a revolution in the principles of our government as that of 1776 was in its form.

> —Thomas Jefferson to Spencer Roane
> September 6, 1819

WHILE IT IS THE PURPOSE OF THIS CHAPTER TO DEMONSTRATE the continuity of revolutionary ideas from the 1760s through the 1790s, I intend to analyze the idea of revolution during the period after the Constitutional Convention and refer to the period before 1787 only when necessary. Anyone who has read Bernard Bailyn's *The Ideological Origins of the American Revolution* will realize that to begin my narration in the 1760s would be mere repetition. Indeed those who are revolutionary "quick-witted" will have already noted, by their perusal of the table of contents, my indebtedness to Bailyn's masterful work.

I intend to establish an ideological framework for revolution as it developed during the decade after the Constitution. From that perspective this chapter will deal with revolution as a complicated idea, what its components were, and how it remained, at least in a definitional sense, a constant force in the minds of the revolutionary generation.

The most logical starting point, one used by Bailyn, is John Adams's oft-quoted remark on the American Revolution written fifty-five years after he believed it had begun. I begin with Adams's query because it throws into sharp relief, perhaps more succinctly than any other in eighteenth-century America, the most important elements regarding the nature of revolution.

It was characteristic of Adams to raise important questions like this—and fortunate for us that he did so with Thomas Jefferson—because it provoked a lengthy as well as an intriguing discussion between the two on the idea of revolution. They had both been pondering the American Revolution for years, writing back and forth, assessing the importance of that great event in their own lives and observing the success and the failure of all the revolutions that had taken place since then.[1]

REVOLUTION IS IN THE MIND

Adams always worried that his ideas were "peculiar, perhaps even singular." And often, as befits an irascible individual, they were. But when Adams asked Jefferson, "What do we mean by the [American] Revolution?" he was not being stubborn or peculiar. He was seeking clarification of the most significant event of their lives and the most complex political phenomenon known to man. Adams, aware that limitations had already been placed on understanding that revolution, that the secrecy of the major decisions had made it impossible to discern the truth, that adequate histories were not being written, even in his own lifetime,[2] must have had posterity in mind when he addressed Jefferson:

> What do we mean by the Revolution? The War? That was no part of the Revolution. It was only an Effect and Consequence of it. The Revolution was in the Minds of the People, and this was effected, from 1760 to 1775, in the course of fifteen Years before a drop of blood was drawn at Lexington. The Records of thirteen Legislatures, the Pamp[h]lets, Newspapers in all the Colonies, ought [to] be consulted, during the Period, to ascertain the Steps by which the public Opinion was enlightened and informed concerning the

authority of Parliament over the Colonies. The Congress of 1774, resembled in some respects, tho' I hope not in many, the Counsell of Nice in Ecclesiastical History. It assembled the Priests from the East and the West, the North and the South, who compared Notes, engaged in discussion and debates and formed Results by one Vote and by two Votes, which went out to the world as unanimous.[3]

Adams stated explicitly that revolution was separate from war. Moreover, he believed that revolution had occurred over a long span of time and that not one drop of blood had been shed.

Revolution, then, had everything to do with ideas and opinions and less to do with battlefield confrontations. In his view the changing of ideas and opinions through the then-known media—newspapers, pamphlets, and legal records—was the real revolution. What Adams was also describing was a complete change of people's minds regarding the principles of their constitution (i.e., between their rights and the authority of Parliament).

Indeed, if one were to use the eighteenth-century definition of the term *revolution* and compare it with Adams's description, the meanings would be identical. In the Enlightenment all revolutions, whether political or mechanical in nature, were referred to in terms of the earth revolving around the sun, the full circle, and completion of a cycle.

And this was precisely what the American Revolution had been: the cyclical turning back to an original British constitution at the time of the Glorious Revolution.

Adams, far from being "singular," was supported by many of his generation in a general understanding of the term. For most of them, *revolution* also referred to the action of turning over an idea in the mind: reflection and consideration. Nathan Bailey described *revolution* as "the turning round, or motion of any body, till it returns to the same place that it was before," "a rolling back or change in government."[4]

Noah Webster gave several meanings to *revolution* that had a common theme: all dealt with changes in the principles of a constitution. Webster viewed revolution thusly: "In politics, a material change or entire change in the constitution of government. Thus the revolution in England, in 1688 produced…the restoration of the constitution to its primitive state." Webster also referred to *revolutionized* as "changing the form and principles of a constitution."[5]

REVOLUTION IS SEPARATE FROM WAR

John Quincy Adams noted how the change in people's minds related to revolution in this way: "For if the people once discover (and you cannot conceal it from them long) that you maintain the war for the army, while you tell them you maintain the army for the war, you lose their attachment forever, and their good sense will immediately side against you.... You will have effected in *substance if not in forms a total revolution* in the government...and the chaos of civil war will ensue."[6]

The younger Adams's observation is worthy of notice because it points to more than simply a change in ideas; it calls attention to what he says is the "substance" of revolution. In Adams's mind it was not necessary to change the form of government to have a revolution. Like his father, John Quincy Adams also made a distinct separation between revolution and war.

Implicit in Adams's remarks is another distinction: the intellectual separation of violence from revolutionary change. This refers to physical violence, of course, unless one wishes to include psychological anguish, a form of violence that tears one's affections from family, friends, and the institutions we have been taught to revere.

If one ponders Adams's query for still another moment, it is possible to detect perhaps the most important and enduring fact of all revolutions throughout history: the democratic nature of the revolutionary process as it occurred from 1760 to 1775.

The appeal to the people through written and verbal forms, the election of representatives to a congress, and the rational discussion and debate that defined the course of revolution—all were calculated to extend revolutionary ideas to as many people as possible.

This last point—the influence of reason in discussion—also implied that revolution, at least as it was understood by the revolutionary generation, was not an irrational phenomenon. The ability to reason in the midst of political crisis was indeed one of their proudest achievements and seems lost to most twenty-first-century anatomists of revolution.

While the Adams quotation succinctly raises many important questions regarding the fundamental nature of revolution, his colleague, Thomas Jefferson, in rambling fashion and over a longer period of time, provides us with a more extensive treatment of the subject in both theory and practice.

Like Adams, Jefferson reveals a lifelong fascination with the idea. Yet Jefferson's letters go beyond Adams's and his attempts to understand the subject philosophically. Throughout his correspondence Jefferson revealed a passionate commitment to and an involvement with revolution that not only surpassed any other American statesman's but spanned his entire adult life.

Whatever differences there were between them stemmed from their basic attitudes toward governmental authority, despite the fact that they had had similar, almost identical, political careers. It was Adams who nearly suffered a nervous breakdown making the psychological commitment to revolution in the 1760s.

By contrast, Jefferson, as a young lawyer, never gave the slightest evidence that he suffered in his decision to undermine British authority. Jefferson had a belief, as we shall see later, that authority, especially constitutional authority, was limited in duration and ought to be renewed periodically—that governments should adapt to change like a man refuses to wear the coat of a boy. His was a "generational" idea of change.

Adams, on the other hand, saw government and even administration as the repository of authority and, certainly in a new nation, even of tradition. No one admired tradition, especially the tradition of the British constitution, more ardently than John Adams.

Adams also had a longer view of constitutional government than Jefferson did. He believed that continuity, over time, provided stability without which any government would fail. Consequently, Adams's view of government was one that spanned many generations. His faith in human nature, more pessimistic than Jefferson's, failed to believe that man could change rationally or reasonably in a short time.

For Adams, men were creatures of habit. Writing to Jefferson in 1794, he remarked, "The Social compact and the laws must be reduced to writing. Obedience to them becomes a national habit and they cannot be changed but by Revolutions which are costly things. Men will be too economical of their blood and property to have recourse to them very frequently."[7]

This view expressed by Adams may be the source of their disagreement, for Jefferson firmly believed that rebellions and revolutions, like "a storm in the atmosphere," should be as frequent as necessary. Adams saw stable governments resisting or putting to rest all fears and threats of revolution. Contrarily, Jefferson, committed to his belief that any government could not enjoy stability for long, was certain that there could be no post-revolutionary society.

This meant Jefferson, more than Adams, feared that the social compact and the laws would have only limited success in checking the power of government. Revolution would then become a necessity to maintain liberty against the encroachments of tyranny.

At the same time, Jefferson realized that the state had been the enemy of revolution throughout history, and this was why revolutions had been so bloody and costly. He knew that if a people once lost their liberty, there was one recourse that the state would oppose over all others: revolution. For revolution was always directed against the existing political order, and those currently in power would resist being overthrown with all the resources at their command. Despotic rulers would, almost by instinct, develop engines of repression that in turn would make revolution inevitable.

To Jefferson this dynamic struggle had seemed to be the entire history of Western civilization.

REVOLUTION INVOLVES SYSTEMIC CHANGE

There was another dimension to this reasoning that placed Jefferson in sharp opposition to Adams. As we have seen, Jefferson was deeply committed to principles and to substantive change. This might be described more accurately, especially in reference to revolutionary theory, as "systemic change."

Jefferson's constant references to despotic regimes indicate that he viewed them as a system with an internal logic of their own. That logic had, as its prime motivation, the aggrandizement of wealth and power for a privileged few at the expense of the many. "History has informed us," said Jefferson, "that bodies of men, as well as individuals, are susceptible to the spirit of tyranny."[8]

As his statements about the character of parties and the men who choose sides according to the "few or the many" show, tyranny manifested a character and a condition that could be broken only by a complete constitutional (read systemic) revolution. This tension, this necessity to break apart an old system and replace it with a new one, was the primary reason why Jefferson believed revolutions would continue throughout history.

REVOLUTION IS A PERMANENT FORCE IN THE WORLD

Despite their basic disagreements, however, there were many areas where their opinions overlapped. Here is Jefferson anticipating Adams's separation of war and revolution almost thirty years before the latter's famous query:

> There is always war in one place, revolution in another, pestilence in
> a third, interspersed with spots of quiet. These chequers shift places
> but they do not vanish, so that to an eye which extends itself over
> the whole earth there is always uniformity of prospect.[9]

Jefferson is recording here a profound observation on the nature of revolution: It is a permanent force in the world we inhabit. It does not vanish; it merely breaks out in another place. Jefferson's recognition of this permanence of revolutionary activity was in the classical political tradition. It meant that he saw revolution as others saw wars—a recognizable, permanent phenomenon in history that could be studied, analyzed, and perhaps made predictable. But this was an old story.

Polybius, one of the few who grasped the significance of revolution in ancient times, saw that all societies were subject to the dynamics of revolution and could look forward to one immediately or in some future time. This was a cyclical view of history, believed by most educated men in eighteenth-century America.

Like Polybius, what Jefferson was pointing to was a historical dialectic of revolution. Because the cycle of governments revealed a state of constant change, in principle as well as in form, it meant that changes, no matter what they might be (monarchy, aristocracy, democracy, polity, tyranny, or oligarchy), would be constantly challenged by revolutionary forces and ideas.

From time immemorial revolution had been in opposition to the state. Indeed that was the very meaning of the word—against the regime in power. It was therefore the antithesis of "the system," hated, feared, and detested by rulers throughout history. By viewing itself as a negating force, revolution would be successful; otherwise it could be coopted, mere reform; or, worse, it would signify a return to greater repression. These conditions, recognized by Jefferson, fulfilled the requirements of a true dialectic in history and made his theories revolutionary.

In Jefferson's mind the Revolution of 1776 had taken on this dialectical, negating quality that over the years influenced the checkered pattern of war and revolution around the globe.

In fact, at the end of his life Jefferson saw the Revolution of 1776 as a permanent revolutionary force in the world. Included in this idea was the implication that the forces unleashed in a particular revolution, if universalized, might be the catalyst for revolutions elsewhere. That is, if a revolutionary "engine" could be developed capable of destroying the "engines" of despotism, systemic change could be accomplished on a world scale.

This was the dream of a true revolutionary: the creation of a theory of revolution that could be applied to any and every condition of man.

The evidence that Jefferson believed he had formulated a revolutionary ideology can be seen at varying intervals throughout his career. His family motto, *Rebellion to tyrants is obedience to God,* nearly summed up his entire political philosophy. Jefferson's original Declaration of Independence firmly established the "right to revolution" among all mankind and introduced a notion of equality that, he believed, would democratize the idea of revolution. It was in this context of speaking for all men, in all future ages, "the memory of the American revolution will be immortal,"[10] that one can see Jefferson's identification with a world revolutionary perspective.

During the period of the French Revolution, Jefferson endorsed Tom Paine's universal application of the Rights of Man. All his life he subscribed to the revolutionary ideology of republicanism, which at the time no one knew how to translate successfully into a functional government. Republicanism was revolutionary simply because no one, for at least two thousand years, had seen a republic. Yet reminiscing on the origins of the nation's commitment to republicanism, Jefferson revealed that at the first idea of independence the revolutionaries were determined to try it: "From the moment that to preserve our rights a change of government became necessary, no doubt could be entertained that a republican form was most consonant with reason [and] with right."[11]

Jefferson thus made it a principle to urge it upon others whenever possible.

Jefferson wrote to Joseph Priestley in 1802, "We feel that we are acting under obligations not confined to the limits of our own society. It is impossible not to be sensible that we are acting for all mankind."[12]

Seven years later Jefferson would carry the torch of revolution even further and define the United States as a revolutionary nation: "The station which we occupy among the nations of the earth is honorable, but awful. Trusted with the destinies of this *solitary republic of the world*, the only monument of human rights, and the sole depository of the sacred fire of freedom and self-government, from hence it is to be lighted up in other regions of the earth."[13]

Twelve years later Jefferson wrote Adams a letter that showed his consistent faith in the power of the revolutionary ideas he had helped formulate:"I will not believe our labors are lost. I shall not die without a hope that light and liberty are on steady advance...in short, the flames kindled on the 4th of July 1776 have spread over too much of the globe to be extinguished by the feeble engines of despotism. On the contrary they will consume those engines, and all who work them."[14]

Thus Jefferson observed the struggle that has throughout history characterized the nature of revolution; that is, the struggle of men to become free of despotism.

We might also note ironically that Jefferson firmly believed that the Spirit of 1776, crystallized in the election of 1800, would make it impossible that this nation would ever ally itself with the despotic forces in the world but would work to destroy them.

REVOLUTIONS TAKE TIME TO ACCOMPLISH

Jefferson's optimism, within realistic bounds, had always comprehended a time span that reflected his understanding of the historical forces at work in any century, including his own. Writing to Adams again, he concurred with him on the difficulty that revolutions experience in their transition from despotism to freedom. In the letter Jefferson supplies us with his notion of revolution in history:

> The generation which commences a revolution can rarely compleat it. Habituated from their infancy to passive submission of body and mind to their kings and priests, they are not qualified, when called on, to think and provide for themselves and their inexperience, their ignorance and bigotry make them instruments often, in the hands of the Bonapartes and Iturbides to defeat their own rights and purposes. This is the present situation of Europe and Spanish America. But it is not desperate. The light which has been shed on mankind by the art of printing has eminently changed the condition of the world. As yet that light has dawned on the midling classes only of the men of Europe. The kings and the rabble of equal ignorance, have not yet received its rays; but it continues to spread. And, while printing is preserved, it can no more recede than the sun return on his course. A first attempt to recover the right of self-government may fail; so may a 2d. a 3d etc., but as a younger, and more instructed race comes on, the sentiment becomes more and more intuitive, and a 4th. a 5th. or some subsequent one of the ever renewed attempts will ultimately succeed.[15]

Jefferson's observation that the bourgeoisie, or "midling class," was emerging as a revolutionary class is worth noting here because it reveals Jefferson's dependence on it to advance the idea of revolution.

REVOLUTIONS ALWAYS POSSESS A DUAL CHARACTER

Pervading this statement is a doctrine of inevitability, as if the forces of revolution represented in the dialectic of history are so powerful they cannot be denied. In fact, what Jefferson was hinting at is a theory that reflects not just an emerging revolutionary dialectic but the logic of faction and the non-party state mentioned in chapter 1. Jefferson's description of revolution deals with a similar idea. Taking this view, one can read his letter as an analysis of the basic components of the idea of revolution.

The first component, Jefferson's description of an "eminently changed" condition in parts of the world, reflects his recognition of the potential for revolutionary societies in Europe and Latin America, something no statesman had ever referred to before.

Here Jefferson is painting a picture of the dual character of societies in which two cities exist, each opposing the other. This opposition, according to Jefferson, has taken on among the younger generation an ingrained "instinct," which in time produces "two competing cultural systems warring against each other in the same society."[16]

Next, Jefferson described the "institutional" and "ideological" components in this emerging two-city thesis. The institutions were monarchy and its trappings—religious superstition and ignorance—versus the more enlightened institutions of "self-government." The ideological components were the divine-right theories of the state versus the emerging republican ideology. The monarchical types represent "the establishment"; the successive generations represent the competing classes or counterculture.

Jefferson's notion of "intuitive" sentiments is merely another way of expressing the strengthening of the second city—the faction in society that challenges the establishment.

In the third component, represented by the historical view that Jefferson held, the revolutionary dialectic would increase in intensity until a crisis situation was reached. The influence of science and the printing press would spread among the younger generation, almost invisibly; yet it would be denied by the kings and the priests who refused to understand the changes around them. That was, and is, the characteristic behavior of an establishment that fails to respond to or solve its crises.

It also signaled to Jefferson that the second city would grow in strength and resolve. It might be ten, forty, or sixty years in the future, but when the crisis occurred—when traditional, institutional, ideological, and cultural reforms failed—the revolution would inevitably succeed.

REVOLUTIONS ALWAYS
EXPERIENCE CRISES

Jefferson's realistic sense of what must be accomplished over generations was not limited to time. Included in his assessment was the toll that permanent revolution would exact in violence. He completed his letter to Adams by warning that the price would not be cheap: "To attain all this however rivers of blood must yet flow, and years of desolation pass over. Yet the object is worth rivers of blood...for what inheritance so valuable can man leave to his posterity?"[17]

This notion of leaving a legacy of revolution and violence to posterity was not the idle speculation of a philosopher in old age. Jefferson had, as a young man of thirty-one, been immersed in the political violence of the Revolutionary War. He had also seen firsthand limited violence at the beginning of the French Revolution and knew of the purges that followed his departure. Thus a recognition of potential violence had been a consistent part of Jefferson's experience from the beginning.

REVOLUTION MUST BE DISTINGUISHED
FROM REVOLT AND REBELLION

This recognition expressed itself in the references Jefferson made to rebellion and revolution. Strangely, he seemed to have merged the two. At least he was not careful about making distinctions between them. But from past experience, Jefferson felt that revolt or rebellion was directed against individual rulers or specific abuses and not against states. He also felt that rebellion was spontaneous, often a reaction to specific grievances that had nothing to do with the society as a whole. Yet *Rebellion to tyrants is obedience to God* was Jefferson's credo, and the inference is that he saw rebellion on a continuum with revolution. Had he lived in the seventeenth century, he might have founded a divine-right theory of revolution; as it was, the Declaration nearly amounted to the same thing.

While Jefferson might have acknowledged that rebellions rarely threaten the state, they had the potential to, and that made them important. Rebellions also had the potential to enlarge—at least in a ruler's mind—and therefore their utility lay in keeping rulers honest.

There was also another characteristic of rebellion that appealed to Jefferson's principles—that their actions were often directed against a consolidating and distant power. This consolidation of power was something that Jefferson feared. Moreover, if rebellions could prevent the gradual growth of power in the state, he wished to encourage them. If they occurred regularly, they would have the effect of maintaining society on a course consistent with its principles of government.

Thus Jefferson, in what amounted to a convergence theory of revolt and revolution, might be regarded as a rebel who was profoundly revolutionary. Incapable of tolerating injustice in any form, Jefferson seemed unwilling, like many nineteenth- and twentieth-century revolutionaries, to play a counterrevolutionary role. Rather than wait for the opportune moment in history, when the "objective conditions" were favorable, Jefferson simply wished to see injustice eradicated. Because injustice would always exist in an imperfect world, a theory of permanent rebellion emerged along with his idea of revolution through history.

Violence could not be divorced from either rebellion or revolution. Referring to the "rivers of blood" that would flow in the future revolutions of Europe and Latin America, Jefferson believed in the classical sense that liberty could grow and flourish only through bloodshed. Indeed it was as if violence against tyrants was liberty's "natural manure." Referring to Shays's Rebellion at the time of the Constitutional Convention, Jefferson stated explicitly his notion of rebellion and its relation to violence. No American statesman before or since has so completely embraced the idea of violence as a means to realize the end of state. He wrote,

> Can history produce an instance of a rebellion so honourably conducted? I say nothing of its motives. They were founded in ignorance, not wickedness. God forbid we should ever be 20 years without such a rebellion. The people cannot be all, and always well informed. The part which is wrong will be discontented in proportion to the importance of the facts they misconceive. If they remain quiet under such misconceptions it is a lethargy, the forerunner of death to the public liberty....What country before ever existed a century and a half without a rebellion? And what country can preserve its liberties if their rulers are not warned from time to time that their people preserve the spirit of resistance? *Let them take arms.* The remedy is to set them right as to facts, pardon and pacify them. What signify a few lives lost in a century or two? The tree of liberty

must be refreshed from time to time with the blood of patriots and tyrants. It is its natural manure.[18]

Because Jefferson linked his idea of revolution to a constitution, he must have been considering total and systemic change. Revolution, then, must have a plan; it must be systemic in its approach. Rebellion, on the other hand, labors under misconception and ignorance. Therefore it could not be systemic in the changes it wrought unless, of course, it became something else.

In that same year, 1787, Jefferson again expressed his strong commitment to the idea of rebellion. Writing to James Madison in January of that year, he said with a warning: "I hold it that a little rebellion now and then is a good thing, and as necessary in the political world as storms in the physical. Unsuccessful rebellions indeed generally establish encroachments on the rights of the people which have produced them. An observation of this truth should render honest republican governors so mild in their punishment of rebellions, as not to discourage them too much. It is a medicine necessary for the sound health of government."[19]

THE SPIRIT OF REBELLION
MUST ALWAYS BE KEPT ALIVE

Shays's Rebellion was one of those thunderstorms that Jefferson felt was necessary. Comparing the political events of Europe with those of America, he had determined that the furor over Shays's Rebellion was highly exaggerated. In strong language to his friend Madison, Jefferson warmed to his favorite theme, the topic of rebellions:

> No country should be long without one. Nor will any degree of power in the hands of government prevent insurrections. France, with all its despotism, and two or three hundred thousand men always in arms, has had three insurrections in the three years I have been here every one of which greater numbers were engaged than in Massachusetts and a great deal more blood was spilt. In Turkey, which Montesquieu supposes more despotic, insurrections are the events of every day. In England, where the hand of power is lighter than here [France], but heavier than with us they happen every half dozen years. Compare again the ferocious depredations of their insurgents with the order, the moderation and the almost self extinguishment of ours.[20]

What seems different about this letter is the comparison Jefferson is making between despotism and free governments and their relationship to rebellion. Normally, one assumes that a free society is the most tumultuous. Jefferson, however, seems to be saying the opposite: in those states where absolutism prevails, the citizens tend toward greater extremes of violence.

While his reference to "insurrection" is unclear in the sense that he is drawing a sharp distinction between it and revolution, the implication of his first sentence is crystal clear: no "degree of power" held by the state will prevent either rebellion or revolution from occurring. Both are natural phenomena.

As Jefferson went about his duties in France, the Constitutional Convention was meeting to decide the future of the American states. This event loomed significantly in Jefferson's mind, for, as we shall see later, it held the connotations of a "second" American revolution.

While Jefferson argued that we ought to have a revolution every century and a half, he was also pointing to the *object* of the revolution, namely despotism or governments "of force." In his mind those governments were synonymous with monarchies and aristocracies, the kind of regimes whose power to abuse was rarely limited. This is important because it registers the eighteenth century's great concern for the forms of government and the influence that form had on the conduct of administration.

On this last point, Jefferson seems to be sliding over distinctions between insurrection and revolution. The comparison between American and European governments keeps the distinction; but his hope is that a revolutionary change—in principle and systemic in nature—will emerge from insurrection: the proof that men can govern themselves without kings. This would indicate that the relationship between the two is almost indistinguishable for Jefferson in 1787.

A REVOLUTION MUST AVOID PROVOKING THE MILITARY

The role that violence would play in any revolution, measured against the nature of the regime, was crucial to the success the revolution would enjoy. Jefferson had agreed with Adams that revolution was separate from war. He had even observed to a friend that war "is not the most favorable moment for divesting the monarchy of power. On the contrary, it is the moment when the energy of a single hand shews itself in the most seducing form."[21]

Although Jefferson was, in this instance, observing the emerging revolution in France, his statement is in the form of a principle and can be generalized. His idea of revolution, which always seemed to be opposed to monarchy or aristocracy, was becoming practical.

Jefferson was developing an idea of peaceful revolution.

He was already aware of the connection between the idea of revolution and his own fame. His authorship of the Declaration of Independence had established his reputation as a hero to the most "ardent spirits" in Europe and especially to those in France. Wherever revolutionary activity was potential, contemplated, or in the process of taking place, Jefferson was a man to be consulted. His colleagues at home, many of whom did not understand, often caricatured him as a "man of some acquirements…but [having] opinions upon Government…the result of fine spun theoretic systems, drawn from the ingenious writings of Locke, Sydney and others of their cast which can never be realized."[22]

While this was true of those he would later accuse of courting the principles of "kingly government,"[23] his admirers in France and elsewhere appreciated his talents with deeper understanding. Even at the risk of violating his diplomatic neutrality, Jefferson was willing to engage in revolutionary intrigue.

Once, after presiding over a revolutionary dialogue in his own home "truly worthy of being placed in parallel with the finest dialogues of antiquity," Jefferson felt moved to explain his behavior to the French minister, Armand Marc, Count de Montmorin. Montmorin's guarded reply furnishes a good insight into Jefferson's ability to influence, in a practical way, the developing idea of revolution. "He [Jefferson] told me… he earnestly wished I would habitually assist at such conferences, being sure I should be useful in moderating the warmer spirits, and promoting a wholesome and practicable reformation only."[24]

But in truth Jefferson did not need encouragement or flattery. By May 1787 he was already writing long letters to his friends in America, keeping them abreast of the progress of the idea of revolution throughout the world. Referring to Brazil he wrote,

> The men of letters are those most desirous of a revolution. The people are not much under the influence of their priests, most of them read and write, possess arms, and are in the habit of using them for hunting. The slaves will take the side of their masters. In short, as to the question of revolution, there is but one mind in that Country. But there appears to be no person capable of conducting a revolution, or willing to venture himself at its head, without the aid of some powerful nation.... There is no printing press in Brazil. They consider the North American revolution as a precedent for theirs.... [And] in case of a successful revolution, a republican government in a single body would probably be established.[25]

Here Jefferson is making a distinction between those who may be expected to participate in revolution and those who will languish in despotism. Jefferson's assessment seems to be made on the basis of the population's *literary* skills and how receptive they are to *written* appeals. Noting the absence of a printing press, he seems to believe that this device, used to disseminate revolutionary ideas, is crucial—in practical terms—to a burgeoning revolution.

He also recognizes, in a limited way, that certain objective conditions must exist in the society before revolution is possible. For revolution to occur, there must be someone who has the will to lead it, someone who can assimilate a view of a future society and act on his vision. Jefferson would have argued that men must have some awareness of their place in history. They must know or realize from past examples in history that they can actually complete a revolution.

At the same time, he implied the people themselves must be conscious of their role in a revolution. Like their leaders, they must understand the idea of liberty sufficiently to expand it. If they are either ignorant or illiterate, with no understanding of the potential of a constitutional system, they merely endanger their lives and the few rights they enjoy.

A REVOLUTION MUST BE
CONNECTED TO IDEOLOGY

We ought to note, too, that Jefferson *assumes* a "probable" connection of the revolutionary ideology of his time—"republicanism"—to the successful outcome of revolution. This would imply that Jefferson, like revolutionaries in all ages, linked the prevailing ideology to any successful revolution, whether probable, potential, or actual.

Jefferson was aware that you could not simply say you were going to start a revolution and then have one. His concern for "enlightening and emancipating the minds" of the people was uppermost in his notion of what was important in an emerging revolution. It was, he felt, the very first consideration one had to make in assessing the possibility of revolution.

To show his consistency on this position, Jefferson was still concerned about educating the people of Latin America thirty years later. He seemed to believe it was better to have revolution piecemeal than to endure a violent confrontation that would set back the cause of liberty, perhaps for generations. Answering a query from John Adams on the revolutionary potential in South America, he wrote,

> I enter into all your doubts as to the event of the revolution of South America. They will succeed against Spain. But the dangerous enemy is within their own breasts. Ignorance and superstition will chain their minds and bodies under religious and military despotism. I do believe it would be better for them to obtain freedom by degrees only; because that would by degrees bring on light and information, and qualify them to take charge of themselves understandingly; with more certainty…as may keep them at peace with one another.[26]

Thus Jefferson, serving in the capacity of a revolutionary adviser, was always tailoring his advice to the conditions he found locally or nationally. No blanket theorist, he found himself making distinctions regarding the potential for revolutions in a way that many critics, and even a few revolutionaries in the twenty-first century, have lost sight of. Jefferson was always speaking of an "appeal to the nation…and yet not so much as to endanger an appeal to arms."[27]

A REVOLUTION MUST NOT INITIATE ARMED STRUGGLE

Jefferson's greatest fear was that revolutionaries would act prematurely, before the "public mind was ripened by time and discussion and was one opinion on the principal points."[28] He seemed to believe that without an understanding of what the forces of power were, what the delicate balance of the constitution was, even what was worth fighting for, any revolution would be strangled in its cradle.

At the same time, Jefferson also kept in mind that unity or agreement among the people was essential if only to demonstrate that a sufficient force of public opinion existed in the state. That was the first objective of any revolution. Means must be found to communicate that force to those in power, who, hopefully, would then change their policies or realize that resistance was futile. Jefferson never abandoned his hope that revolution could be successful without a resort to arms.

Thus Jefferson writes to Washington, informing him what the issue of revolution has been so far: "The nation [France] is pressing on fast to a fixed constitution. Such a revolution in the public opinion has taken place that the crown already feels its powers bounded, and is obliged by its measures to acknowledge limits."[29]

It is obvious that Jefferson is studying the emerging constitutional developments, hoping the French Revolution would continue its nonviolent course during this early period of consolidation.

One critical factor in furthering any revolution was to "cleverly" prevent any violent turn from taking place. It was the responsibility of the leaders to nurture a rational policy that would not provoke those in power to "draw the sword." Indeed Jefferson's reflections on the future of France, placed in the context of the favorable issue of the second American revolution, raised the question of whether other nations could imitate America.

As Jefferson had seen just two months earlier, the forces of despotism in France were so powerful that a peaceful solution was by no means guaranteed. Another critical factor he sees as a problem for any revolution is the question of the army. Writing to a friend, he notes rather sharply the tragic role that party and the armed forces play in producing counterrevolution:

> We can surely boast of having set the world a beautiful example of a government reformed by reason alone without bloodshed. But the world is too far oppressed to profit of the example. On this side of the Atlantic [France] the blood of the people is become an inheritance, and those who fatten on it, will not relinquish it easily. The struggle in this country is as yet of doubtful issue. It is in fact between the monarchy, and the parliaments. The nation is no otherwise concerned but as both parties may be induced to let go some of its abuses to court the public favor. The danger is that the people, deceived by a false cry of liberty may be led to take side with one party, and thus give the other a pretext for crushing them still more. If they can avoid an appeal to arms, the nation will be sure to gain much by this controversy. But if that appeal is made it will depend entirely on the dispositions of the army whether it issue in liberty or despotism.[30]

By the middle of 1788, as the first sentence would imply, Jefferson has the model of the second American revolution firmly in mind. Moreover, he is now preparing that model on a global scale, explicitly stating that other nations would do well to imitate America's example.

His is a recommendation for revolution without violence and bloodshed. Yet nothing is lost in the sense that he and Adams defined the term almost three decades earlier. Pondering the potential violence of the emerging French Revolution, Jefferson made a distinction between the ongoing revolution and civil war.

POLITICAL CONDITIONS REQUIRED FOR REVOLUTION

By March 1789 Jefferson was still optimistic that France would avoid bloodshed. One reason was a belief that the idea of revolution must be accepted by the people. And from his vantage point in Paris, he daily saw the public becoming deeply involved. Jefferson traced this involvement in a letter that outlined the essential politics of a developing revolution. The conditions included the following:

- The nation's intellectual potential to become aware of a political crisis

&❧ The role of the press in shaping public opinion

&❧ An economic crisis, especially one related to taxes

&❧ The rate of nonviolent change

&❧ The differences between the newly emerging and the past forms of government

&❧ The people's understanding of their relation to the constitutional powers present in the government of the day and even of the hour

&❧ The degree of liberty expressed in a declaration of rights toward which the revolution aims

Each of these points must be seen in relation to the others as they occur. Considered collectively, they compose a near complete idea of revolution. Judged singly, they simply represent another problem in government or administration that can be adjusted to or solved.

In this letter to his friend David Humphreys, Jefferson is conveying the picture of a "complete revolution":

> The change in this country, since you left it, is such as you can form no idea of....The king stands engaged to pretend no more to the power of laying, continuing or appropriating taxes, to call the States general periodically, to submit *letters de cachet* to legal restriction, to consent to freedom of the press, and that all this shall be fixed by a fundamental constitution which shall bind his successors. He has not offered a participation in the legislature, but it will surely be insisted on. The public mind is so ripened on all these subjects, that there seems to be now but one opinion....In fine I believe this nation will in the course of the present year have as full a portion of liberty dealt out to them as the nation can bear at present, considering how uninformed the mass of their people is.[31]

At the same time, Jefferson's optimism regarding the avoidance of bloodshed in a revolution was not without qualification. He even seems to be saying that despite all precautions, some merging of the two is inevitable. In what was to be a prophetic warning to his friend Gilbert du Motier, the Marquis de La Fayette, Jefferson revealed his pessimism

regarding the future progress of the French Revolution. On the eve of
his departure, he wrote,

> So far it seemed that your revolution had got along with a steady
> pace; meeting indeed occasional difficulties and dangers, but we are
> not to expect to be translated from despotism to liberty, in a feather-
> bed. I have never feared for the ultimate result, tho' I have feared
> for you personally...Take care of yourself, my dear friend. For tho'
> I think your nation would in any event work out her salvation, I am
> persuaded were she to lose you, it would cost her oceans of blood,
> and years of confusion and anarchy.[32]

As Jefferson contemplated the idea of revolution during the year
before he left France, he could not help but believe that the most important concern of any revolutionary movement must be the constitutional
process.

ROLE OF ELECTIONS
IN AN EMERGING REVOLUTION

From his own experience in the 1770s, Jefferson realized that only when
the ideals of a revolution were written into law was it possible for the
people to realize them. If ideals remained pure rhetoric, they would
continue to divide the people and lead to confusion and anarchy.

One major part of this concern was the process of electing officials to
represent the people. Elections had played a major role in Jefferson's rise
to power during the American Revolution. Being a delegate to the Continental Congress had thrust him suddenly onto the national stage. But
more significant was the fact that elections had made the revolution
appear legitimate in the eyes of the people.

Like the "men of influence" in the midst of revolution in America,
Jefferson had resigned his seat in Congress and taken his "place in the
legislature of Virginia." There he introduced bills in 1776 that had as their
goal the complete destruction of the British administration. Among
them were the "establishment of courts of justice" and "trial by jury"; a
"bill declaring tenants in tail to hold their lands in fee simple"; a "bill to
prevent...the...further importation" of slaves, abolish primogeniture,
abolish the tyranny of the Church of England, "establishing religious

freedom"; and finally an attempt to revise the "whole code" of laws and adopt them to "our republican form of government."[33]

These were the revolutionary aims Jefferson had in mind in 1789, and he hoped that the French might also. Certainly, he believed they were capable of promoting those aims.

In sum, Jefferson's experience of constitution making had become an integral part of his notion of how a revolution was to proceed.

CRITICAL ROLE IN CALLING A CONSTITUTIONAL CONVENTION IN THE MIDST OF REVOLUTION

A reflection of his American experience, a revolution emphasized principles, organization, and functions of every governmental entity. Indeed this emphasis was, in Jefferson's eyes, virtually an axiom for all the other revolutions he saw occurring in the world.

He never tired of believing that America could set an example that would ultimately provide a way to avoid civil wars. Thus in 1787, before he could know its results, he remarked upon hearing of the Constitutional Convention, "Happy for us, that when we find our constitutions defective and insufficient to secure the happiness of our people, we can assemble with all the coolness of philosophers and set it to rights, while every other nation on earth must have recourse to arms to restore their constitutions."[34]

Contrast Jefferson's axiom regarding initiating armed struggle with the military to avoid violence. Virtually all modern revolutions throughout the twentieth and twenty-first centuries—those led by Lenin, Mao, Castro, and Ho Chi Minh and even those surrounding the "Arab Spring"—have uniformly resulted in not decentralizing the power of the state or maximizing the liberty of the individual. They have produced states dominated by military regimes, unending civil wars, and the denial of human rights, civil liberties, the Rights of Man, and the rule of law—in short, everything Jefferson believed a revolution should avoid. This axiom alone, of avoiding the initiation of violence, should enable the reader to appreciate the sophistication of Jefferson's idea of revolution.

His sense of optimism overflowing, Jefferson wrote to David Humphreys, "The operations which have taken place in America lately, fill me with pleasure. In the first place they realize the confidence I had that whenever our affairs get obviously wrong, the good sense of the people will interpose and set them to rights. The example of changing a constitution by assembling the wise men of the state, instead of assembling armies, will be worth as much to the world as the former examples we have given them."[35]

The transfer of constitutional power from one form of government to another, peaceably, with the will of the majority presiding, was for Jefferson the only successful idea of revolution.

This was systemic change—the true characteristic of revolution—achieved peacefully. Any other transfer of power that failed to produce an expansion of liberty, that remained attached to principles of monarchy or aristocracy, both forms of despotism, was not revolution at all. It was counterrevolution.

Because of this continuous possibility, the principles of government became just as important for revolution as the form. The fact was, as Jefferson had recognized earlier, those successive generations that "instinctively" demanded greater freedom were the core of the second city. As they continued to expand their idea of freedom, gradually and through written constitutional guarantees, the growth of the revolution, based on the principles of a new value system, was assured.

THE RIGHTS OF MAN
IN THE CONSTITUTION

Jefferson saw that it did nothing for mankind to advocate revolution and then discover that the reasons for turning to revolution had been lost in the struggle. This is why he expressed concern over the failure of the "wise men" in Philadelphia to incorporate the Rights of Man into the Constitution itself. Declaring his willingness to accept the majority view, he nevertheless stated those rights which, if abused collectively in the minds of the people, formed the right to revolution.

Commenting on the new constitution, he wrote,

> I am one of those who think it a defect that the important rights, not placed in security by the frame of the constitution itself, were not explicitly secured by a supplementary declaration. There are rights which it is useless to surrender to the government, and which yet, governments have always been fond to invade. These are the rights

of thinking, and publishing our thoughts by speaking or writing: the right of free commerce: the right of personal freedom. There are instruments for administering the government, so peculiarly trust-worthy, that we should never leave the legislature at liberty to change them. The new constitution has secured these in the executive and legislative departments; but not in the judiciary. It should have established trials by the people themselves, that is to say by jury. There are instruments so dangerous to the rights of the nation, and which place them so totally at the mercy of their governors, that those governors, whether legislative or executive, should be restrained from keeping such instruments on foot but in well defined cases. Such an instrument is a standing army. We are now allowed to say such a declaration of rights, as a supplement to the constitution where that is silent, is wanting to secure us in these points.[36]

While Jefferson's optimism regarding the successful conclusion of the American Revolution remained strong, his imagination ranged over the possibilities of using reason and the "coolness of philosophers" to ensure that revolution in a single society would be permanent as well as bloodless.

By now he was not content to simply see the "chequers" shifted on the board. Recognizing that tensions in society that cause revolutions often result from oppressive regimes that over time have lost all touch with current problems or the needs of a new generation, Jefferson sought to provide a rationale that would prevent those tensions from accumulating.

If we recall his reference to the Constitutional Convention as the second American revolution, we may gain an insight into his changing idea of revolution. Perhaps, he believed, a society dedicated to rational principles could *institutionalize* revolution in a constitutional form.

In a little-known and even less understood essay titled *The Earth Belongs to the Living,* Jefferson was apparently sounding out his most trusted colleague, James Madison, to this possibility. Written at the height of his involvement with the emerging French Revolution, it answers the problems he saw developing there and elsewhere in the world:

No society can make a perpetual constitution, or even a perpetual law. The earth belongs always to the living generation. They may manage it then, and what proceeds from it, as they please, during their usufruct. They are masters too of their own persons, and consequently may govern them as they please. But persons and property make the sum of the objects of government. The constitution and the laws of their predecessors extinguished then, in their natural course, with those whose will gave them being. This could preserve that being till it ceased to be itself, and no longer. Every constitution, then, and every law, naturally expires at the end of 19 years. If it be enforced longer, it is an act of force and not of right.

It may be said that the succeeding generation exercising in fact the power of repeal, this leaves them as free as if the constitution or law had been expressly limited to 19 years only. In the first place, this objection admits the right, in proposing an equivalent. But the power of repeal is not an equivalent. It might be indeed if every form of government were so perfectly contrived that the will of the majority could always be obtained fairly and without impediment. But this is true of no form. The people cannot assemble themselves; their representation is unequal and vicious. Various checks are opposed to every legislative proposition. Factions get possession of the public councils. Bribery corrupts them. Personal interests lead them astray from the general interests of their constituents; and other impediments arise so as to prove to every practical man that a law of limited duration is much more manageable than one which needs a repeal.

This principle that the earth belongs to the living and not to the dead is of very extensive application and consequences in every country, and most especially in France. It enters into the resolution of the questions Whether the nation may change the descent of lands holden in tail? Whether they may change the appropriation of lands given antiently to the church, to hospitals, colleges, order of chivalry, and otherwise in perpetuity? Whether they may abolish the charges and privileges attached on lands, including the whole catalogue ecclesiastical and feudal? It goes to hereditary offices, authorities and jurisdictions; to perpetual monopolies in commerce, the arts or sciences; with a long train of et ceteras.[37]

The essay turned out, in Jefferson's own words, to be the "dream of a theorist," for he never attempted to have it written into law. In truth, Jefferson's essay was too revolutionary even for his most intimate colleagues—all members of the power structure. Reading it over, they most likely realized that nothing in the society would remain untouched or unchanged; no one's base of power would or could remain secure.

Jefferson's departure from the one-dimensional vision of change that characterized nearly all of his eighteenth-century contemporaries was too powerful.

HOW TO RECOGNIZE A PREREVOLUTIONARY SOCIETY

Yet the idea had profound revolutionary implications. As Jefferson realized, its principle had very "extensive application" and would serve as an obstacle to despotism around the globe.

The essay went to the heart of every important power relationship in the commonwealth, specifically those that Jefferson, in his own revolutionary experience, had drafted legislation to remedy. But most significant, within Jefferson's essay were leveling principles, institutionalized, that would democratize the idea of revolution.

What Jefferson saw himself doing was anticipating the normal development of a prerevolutionary situation. Those conditions he enumerated at the end of his letter had been present in all despotisms throughout history and were particularly characteristic of the ancient regimes yet in power. Further, they could be summarized as those conditions that existed in America from 1760 to 1775: attempts by the government in power to maintain its authority were gradually undermined; laws became arbitrary; "obligations," once bearable, "became impositions"; traditional loyalties faded and new forms of attachment (outside the existing circle of government) became noticeable—the second city; the idea of community— defined by the establishment—no longer held people's attention to the interests of the nation; factions arose that exploited the frustrated classes in society; representatives no longer were representative but spoke for a privileged few; accepted forms of wealth and income suddenly appeared corrupt; existing concepts of prestige changed; those in positions of power were viewed with hostility and suspicion; and, finally, those with talent, normally integrated into society, began to feel "left out."

This is the picture of an emerging two-city theory of revolution: a "dialectic of two competing cultural systems warring against each other in the same society."[38] This was a condition that, if allowed to develop over a long period of time, would inevitably produce a "crisis of community," "political, economic, psychological, sociological, personal, and moral at the same time."[39] The conflict of values could plunge the nation into civil war.

Revolution need not be the culmination of these conflicts, but the loss of liberty and harmony most certainly would be. What was needed at a time like this—and Jefferson had seen this condition in America and in France—was the intelligent search for a new sense of community, a new set of principles or a return to older ones, and a way to reestablish conditions that would become acceptable to those who were disillusioned and felt "left out."

A new constitution for every generation was one way to establish this new sense of community. It was an exercise guaranteed to keep the government responsive to the people while inhibiting the growth of factions that established oligarchies and corrupted the laws. It would, Jefferson pointed out, make government and constitutions respect the rights of the individual and not become the instruments of force. If every generation had to decide what to throw away, as well as what to keep, in a constitution, it would be an educational process that would force it to understand, as well as to protect, its rights. This was consistent with Jefferson's belief that the Rights of Man were at the heart of every revolutionary struggle.

Jacques Ellul has observed that in the eighteenth century the idea of "revolution was a juridical concept that met the demands of reason."[40]

Jefferson's revolutionary essay was an expression of this eighteenth-century Age of Reason belief in reason as the supreme arbiter in society. It was also a recognition of the political nature of revolution. Only reason could avoid the fanaticism, the excesses, and the bloodshed that ultimately defeated the cause of liberty. Accordingly, Jefferson's essay was this juridical concept carried to its logical conclusion: a system of abstract laws designed to ensure that each generation would be able to construct its own system of political relationships. Jefferson's system was not likely, as other revolutions would prove, to perpetuate and increase the power of the state at the expense of the individual.

His theory was designed to do the opposite: to signal a radical departure from the theme of centralization that has characterized all revolutions before or since. His theory would enable each generation to use established laws and institutions to decentralize anew the power of the state every twenty years.

INSTITUTIONALIZING PERMANENT, PEACEFUL, CONSTITUTIONAL REVOLUTION

Further, Jefferson, in his long essay, guaranteed that every twenty years there would be a certain amount of chaos in the transition to the new government. This meant that, instead of increasing its power by placing succeeding generations in awe of its immortal sovereignty and majesty, the state would become a means to an end and not the end in itself. The essence of Jefferson's revolution every twenty years was to humanize the prospects of remodeling society.

It meant that and more: Jefferson's essay was the philosophical expression of a device that, assuming the worst situation developed, any trend toward tyranny would be abolished or altered every second decade; that those who accumulated wealth at the expense of their fellow citizens would see it redistributed; that class rivalry would be eliminated or started anew; and that mobility would be ensured.

Finally, the hope was that liberty and justice would be renewed with each generation. Because of its thoroughness, its near-complete alteration of the relations of established society, it was a system that would channel all of society's discontents and integrate them in a radical yet nonviolent solution.

Jefferson's logic culminated in what would be the greatest benefit of all. Because each generation would have complete control over its own life span, plus the ability to enact laws regulating its own behavior, it would have no need to resort to violence or civil war to change the government's form or principles.

Liberty and the Rights of Man embedded in the constitution would therefore never be endangered. In sum, *The Earth Belongs to the Living* was intended by Jefferson to be a theoretical statement of the possibility of institutionalizing permanent, peaceful, and constitutional revolution.

What we have been describing thus far is an idea of revolution propounded by a few eighteenth-century men. But not every part of that description has been limited to the pure idea of revolution. The dominance of politics, in an architectonic sense, has asserted itself in every phase of revolution we have discussed.

CLASSICAL POLITICS AND REVOLUTION

The nature of revolution in eighteenth-century America was, above all, political. Neither Jefferson nor Adams nor anyone else who discussed the topic ever divorced it from its classical political framework. Constitutions, ideologies, wars, committees, factions, and congresses are political ideas and forms that were known before Aristotle. They were in Adams's and Jefferson's time viewed as part of one's natural political constitution. This framework, then, was rooted in human nature and was as old as man himself.

While many of these concepts relate to forms as well as ideas, they have a dialectical relationship that makes it impossible to discuss one meaningfully without the others. It is important then, in rounding out the idea of revolution, to consider these forms in some detail and establish their connection with the politics that will be reviewed in the remaining chapters.

We have seen both Adams and Jefferson associate their revolutionary experience in the 1770s with revolutions that occurred for the rest of their lives. Their concern for opinion, elections, constitutional forms, declarations of rights, the power of the press, and so forth—all were carryovers from their experience. As they well knew, these specific forms of organization had given form and energy to the American Revolution.

Jefferson, in his search for a new mode of revolution, was attempting to maintain a similar energy level that he had experienced in 1776 but not so much that it would commit revolution to violence.

THE CYCLE OF REVOLUTIONS

This distinction is important because it reveals Jefferson's imagination at work, spinning out a theory that would enable him to realize his goal of permanent world revolution.

He knew already that governments are not free once and then for all time. He realized, perhaps more fully than anyone in his century, that the nature of man made it inevitable that a government would sooner or later founder in corruption. When this occurred, the two-city thesis of revolution asserted itself. Principles needed to be reestablished, constitutions reaffirmed, and liberty renewed in an ongoing natural process. It was this transition in the cycle of revolutions, the division of society into two warring camps, that fascinated Jefferson and spurred him on in pursuit of a nonviolent theory of revolution.

The cycle of revolution had occurred at least three times within Jefferson's lifetime. The Revolution of 1800 was, in more ways than not, a repetition of the Revolution of 1776, and, by Jefferson's own description, another was the Constitutional Convention of 1787.

The one major difference was a shift from form to principle almost exclusively; another lay in the peaceful transition made by the Revolution of 1800. Yet this peaceful transition did not occur by accident.

THE FORMS AND PRINCIPLES OF REVOLUTION

We have seen how Jefferson always placed the framework of revolution in a struggle between the principles of despotism and those of freedom—between monarchy or aristocracy and the democratizing efforts of the people. This formulation of principles had looked back to Jefferson's original revolutionary experience (the classic example of an imperial power opposed to granting freedom to a colonial people). As the concern for principle arose, Jefferson again looked to his own experience and realized that he must rely on the trusted "old-fashioned" or classical forms of organization.

Of the organizational principles used to combat despotism all over the world, quite a number had been invented in America and had become, after the 1770s, the bag and baggage of revolutionaries everywhere.

The formation of conspiratorial caucuses "to concentrate leadership abilities," the organization of clubs, committees of correspondence, the post, circular letters, newspapers, pamphlets, broadsides, speeches, elections, legislative resolves, and constitutional resolutions—all were used to advance the cause of revolution.

The culmination of these political forms *after* the election of congresses was the establishment of courts of law and provisional governments.

These organizational forms and principles all took place within, but were opposed to, the existing system of government. They were literally "the state within the state," "the city within a city," the result of a group of organized factions cooperating to achieve similar revolutionary ends. Together they created a democratic ideology and a fashioned unity. They won the minds and the hearts of the people and laid the foundations for a new government.

It is in this framework that we must view Jefferson's approach to politics and revolution in the coming decade. Knowing his deep concern for republican principles and the revolutionary Spirit of 1776, plus his absence of nearly six years, we might place his idea of revolution into a perspective that has not been made explicit before.

That perspective, moreover, is consistent with the classical definition of revolution: a cyclical return to the time when the rights and the liberties of the people were untainted by corruption, when the ideals and the principles of the American Revolution were accepted by all, and when the American Revolution was—in a word—glorious.

In 1789 Jefferson, enthused with the optimism of the emerging French Revolution, contemplated his return to America. He wrote to a friend, "I hope to receive permission to visit America this summer, and to possess myself anew, by conversation with my countrymen, of *their spirit and their ideas.* I know only the Americans of the year 1784. They tell me this is to be much a stranger to those of 1789. This renewal of acquaintance is no indifferent matter to one acting at such a distance."[41]

As he would soon find out, the distance between ideas was great, if not greater than the width of the ocean he would cross. And it would take time, almost a decade in fact, before he could report that the Spirit of 1776 was "not dead. It...[had] only been slumbering."[42]

3

The Idea of Revolution: Conspiracy and Counterrevolution

Every republic at all times has it[s] Catalines and its Caesars.

— Alexander Hamilton, 1792

HE ROLE OF CONSPIRACY AS THE BREEDING GROUND FOR RESIS-tance and revolution is known to every student of early American history. For conspiracy, as a latent behavioral trait and characteristic of the American mind, was a part of the birthing of the new nation. But the literature of American history dealing with conspiracy antedates even that founding act.

The 1770s, for example, were filled with constant charges by English and American pamphleteers of the British ministry "having formed a conspiracy against the liberties of their country."[1]

The wide belief in the idea of conspiracy, which gained easy acceptance in America, and the relationship it has to revolution can be translated as follows: the fundamental rights of all citizens under the Constitution, and indeed the Constitution itself, are endangered; and tyranny, in the guise of a few unscrupulous men seeking power, threatens.

A fear then arises that the principles by which the laws operate are under assault. The additional fear that the laws are being corrupted, whether they are or not, nevertheless appears real and serves to trigger a right to revolution in the minds of the people.

From the 1770s on, knowledge that the principles of free government had been under assault by politicians considered sinister in the British Parliament, by cabinet officials in the administration, and even by the king himself was transferred across the Atlantic and held in reserve for their administrative counterparts in America.

Edmund Burke's comment that Americans could "snuff tyranny in the breeze" was as much a description of their education, character, and disposition as it was of their reaction to the designs of the British ministry.

EVERY LEADER FEARED A CAESAR

Founders of a republican form of government, the first since classical times, the revolutionary generation reacted against the intrigues of elitist aristocracies. Bred to the classics, they were especially familiar with the conspiracy of Julius Caesar, the man who overturned the liberties of the Roman republic.

A unique and sinister connotation was attached to Caesar's name. It was linked with every revolutionary plot, cabal, or conspiracy that arose. Indeed "Caesarism" had become a symbol synonymous with demagoguery because Caesar had established a dictatorship enforced by his army. Caesarism thus became a stigma associated with any and every attempt to enervate the principles of the republic. An example of this can be seen in one of Thomas Jefferson and John Adams's discussions on the merits of aristocracy. The latter could have been speaking of conspiracy in the broadest sense:

> When Aristocracies, are established by human Laws…honor Wealth and Power are made hereditary by municipal Laws and political Institutions…but this never commences, till Corruption in Elections becomes dominant and uncontroulable. But this artificial Aristocracy can never last. The everlasting Envys, Jealousies, Rivalries and quarrells among them, their cruel rapacities upon the poor ignorant People their followers, compel these to *sett up a Caesar,* a Demagogue to be a Monarch and Master…Here you have the origin of all artificial Aristocracy, which is the origin of all Monarchy.[2]

Adams's quote captured the essence of a conspiracy to return monarchy to America.

Factional rivalries and jealousies, corruption in elections, undue regard for wealth and honors—all of these would characterize the politics of the 1790s. And to perceptive observers like Jefferson, Madison, Hamilton, Henry, and others, all that was necessary was a man to play the role of Caesar.

The idea of conspiracy was, moreover, entwined with the meaning of revolution in more than a superficial sense. Revolutions that failed to live up to the expectations of those who began them were called rebellions, and so were conspiracies.

A successful rebellion always had a few key conspirators; likewise successful conspiracies were normally considered, at least by those in the establishment, as counterrevolutions. Conspirators themselves were generally regarded as men whose political characters were identified with a lust for power or dominion. Always energetic, proud, even arrogant, they were men with forceful personalities and political aspirations that knew no bounds. They often appealed to the pride and the vanity of a birthright, their own fallen status, or the continuance of one to which they had recently become wedded.

They were often men whose experience was of a military nature, which enabled them to develop a constituency independent of the civilian society. Because of this support, suspicion attended their involvement in the open politics of society.

If they suffered the disappointment of a lost electoral candidacy, the fear always arose that they would attempt to recoup their losses through armed force or corruption. It was characteristic of political conspirators to instigate legislation that appealed to class interests, the sole intent of which was to increase their own personal power. These character traits culminated in the suspicion that the conspirator would stop at nothing short of total power, that he would not be deterred by principles or tradition, and that, ultimately, he would change the form of the constitution to perpetuate his own power.

This, briefly, was the common understanding of the meaning of conspiracy linked with "Caesarism," "Cromwell[ism]," and "Bonapartism" among the revolutionary generation. These three were constantly linked with revolution, monarchy, and the loss of liberty.

In 1792 Alexander Hamilton set down a description of conspiracy in the new republic that could have been directed only at Jefferson and the republican faction. But what is so remarkable about his description is that it revealed so much about its author: "There is yet another class of men, who in all the stages of our republican system, either from desperate circumstances, or irregular ambition, or a mixture of both, will labour incessantly to keep the government in a troubled and unsettled state, to sow disquietudes in the minds of the people and to promote confusion and change. Every republic at all times has it[s] Catalines and its Caesars."[3]

We have often assumed that the struggle between monarchy and the republican form, complete with democratic principles, was ended once and for all with the Declaration of Independence. But to many, especially the Federalists, this apparently was not the case.

A RETURN TO MONARCHY WAS SEEN AS A CONSPIRACY

The fact was there were many citizens who believed that monarchy was the only way in which a stable government could be achieved. Indeed a case can be made that the revolution, instead of deciding the issue, simply polarized the sentiment between the advocates of monarchy and republicanism.

William Maclay, a senator from New York, expressed his fears in a journal:

> Yet…[we] were not wanting a party whose motives were different [i.e., monarchists]. They wished for loaves and fishes of government, and cared for nothing else but a translation of the diadem and scepter from London to Boston, New York or Philadelphia; or, in other words, the creation of a new monarchy in America, and to form niches for themselves in the temple of royalty.

> This spirit manifested itself strongly among the officers at the close of the war, and…developed in the Order of Cincinnati.[4]

Writing to Washington about the Order of the Cincinnati, Jefferson expressed himself in strong terms, knowing full well that the former commander in chief had it within his power to stamp out the "germ" of aristocracy:

[The aristocracy is] the germ whose development is one day to destroy the fabric we have reared....Tho' the day may be at some distance, beyond the reach of our lives perhaps, *yet it will certainly come,* when, a single fibre left of this institution, will produce an hereditary aristocracy which will change the form of our governments from the best to the worst in the world....I shall think little also of...[our government's] longevity unless this germ of destruction be taken out.[5]

Jefferson was not optimistic regarding the extinguishing of the monarchical sentiment in America; in fact, he predicted its inevitable triumph. The connection between monarchy, aristocracy, titles, and the pomp and ceremony of military life—all opposed to the simple egalitarianism inherent in a republic—was as obvious to Jefferson the philosopher as to Jefferson the politician.

It was all the more striking to Jefferson because he had known of a discussion among the military council of war at the close of the American Revolution. As he described the discussion in *The Anas,* the issue came to a head "whether all [the states] should be consolidated into a single government...and whether that national government should be a monarchy or a republic....Some officers of the army, as it has always been said and believed (and Steuben and Knox have ever been named as the leading agents), trained to monarchy by military habits, are understood to have proposed to General Washington to decide this great question by the army before its disbandment, and to assume himself the crown on the assurance of their support."[6]

Jefferson praised Washington for his answer and consequent rejection of their advice. He then went on to describe the "Cincinnati's" attempts to "ingraft" onto "the future frame of government" a "hereditary order"[7] during the time of the army's disbandment. Jefferson, it seems, always feared the latent monarchical tendencies in America as political conspiracies.

Yet, as Jefferson would acknowledge more than twenty-five years later, "a short review of the facts will show, that the contests of the day were contests of principle, between the advocates of republican, and those of kingly government."[8]

This attitude did not develop overnight. It had its origins in the aftermath of the peace settlement in Great Britain. As early as 1785, Jefferson had begun to express his antipathy toward the defeated enemy: "In spite of treaties, England is still our enemy. Her hatred is deep-rooted and cordial, and nothing is wanting with her but the power, to wipe us and the land we live on out of existence."[9]

A year later, antipathy had been joined with fear, as Jefferson wrote to John Page, "That nation hates us, their ministers hate us, and their King, more than all other men."[10] To Charles W. F. Dumas, he even raised the specter of the final solution: "I shall not wonder to see the scenes of ancient Rome and Carthage renewed in our day."[11]

Jefferson was ready to believe that such a conspiracy in fact already existed. His logic reached the point of illogic. Referring to the inevitability of war with England, he prophesied that America would be coerced into abandoning her neutrality: "I fear, the English, or rather their stupid King, will force us out of it. For thus I reason. By forcing us into the war against them, they will be engaged in an expensive land war, as well as a sea war. Common sense dictates, therefore, that they should remain neuter: ergo, they will not let us remain neuter. I never yet found any other general rule for foretelling what they will do, but that of examining what they ought not to do."[12]

WEALTH PRODUCES CONSPIRACY AND COUNTERREVOLUTION IN REPUBLICS

John Adams, drawing on his "experience" and forswearing pessimism, nevertheless gave a dour forecast for the future of the republic:

> In short, my dear Friend you and I have been indefatigable Labourers through our whole Lives for a Cause which will be thrown away in the next generation, upon the Vanity and Foppery of Persons of whom we do not now know the Names perhaps. The War that is now breaking out will render our Country, whether she is forced into it, or not, rich, great and powerful in comparison of what she now is, and Riches and Grandeur and Power will have the same effect upon American as it has upon European minds. We have seen enough already to be sure of this.[13]

After Adams had expressed his sentiments, the news came from America that a Constitutional Convention had been called and would address itself to the defects of the Confederation. At first the news buoyed Jefferson's spirits, but David Ramsay, a historian and longtime correspondent of Jefferson's, raised the specter again: "Our eyes now are all fixed on the continental convention to be held in Philada. in May next. Unless they make an efficient federal government I fear that the end of the matter will be an American monarch or rather three or more confederacies.[14]

Within a few months, Jefferson would write to Benjamin Hawkins that while "I look up with...[you] to the Federal convention for an amendment of our federal affairs...above all things I am astonished at some people's considering a kingly government as a refuge."[15]

Sensing the battles for ratification that would follow the Constitutional Convention, Jefferson poured out his frustrations to the one man he felt most likely would become president. His remarks link the role of the future president to his fears of monarchy and aristocracy: "The perpetual re-eligibility of the President. This I fear will make that an office for life first, and then hereditary. I was much an enemy to monarchy before I came to Europe. I am ten thousand times more so since I have seen what they are. There is scarcely an evil known in these countries which may not be traced to their king as its source, nor a good which is not derived from the small fibres of republicanism existing among them."[16]

It is difficult, if not impossible, to ascertain whether Jefferson believed that a conspiracy against liberty and the republic was imminent. But, at a later date, he said so in *The Anas*. Describing the motives of those who attended the Annapolis Convention of 1786, he describes what can only be interpreted as a fear of men changing the form of government:

> Friends of...[monarchy] confined themselves to a course of obstruction only, and delay, to everything proposed; they hoped, that nothing being done, and all things going from bad to worse, a kingly government might be usurped, and submitted to by the people, as better than anarchy...The effect of their manoeuvers...resulted in the measure of calling a more general convention, to be held at Philadelphia. At this, the same party exhibited the same practices,

and with the same views of preventing a government of concord, which they foresaw would be republican, and of forcing through anarchy their way to monarchy.[17]

Thus, from the Annapolis Convention through the Philadelphia Convention, Jefferson must have feared a conspiracy or even a counter-revolution. A trusted friend had apprised him that "an extraordinary revolution in the sentiments of men, respecting political affairs," had occurred in America.[18]

He could not help pondering conditions in America and the mind and the spirit of its citizens. A steady stream of correspondence continued to inform him of Britain's refusal to give up the frontier posts, of British threats to American commerce, and of attempts to sabotage its neutrality and impress its seamen.

These British "designs," coupled with, as Monroe put it, the potential political designs of Washington's advisers, reinforced a fear that has been part of every successful revolutionary's psychology since the first revolution: the fear of counterrevolution. If such a revolution were to take place in America, it definitely meant a return to monarchy. Moreover, because Jefferson believed that the majority of people were firmly republican, it also meant that any attempt to restore monarchy would be led by a minority faction.

Monarchy could only come about through a conspiracy. And, indeed, when Jefferson returned to America, the first impressions he received unfortunately caused his mind to reel in shock and wonder. As we read his statement in *The Anas,* and recollect the mood of those who wined and dined the great revolutionary figure on his return from France, one can easily imagine Jefferson, sitting at a table amidst the sounds of clinking wineglasses, listening to the buzzing yet audible voices of elitist conversation, and forming the question ever so silently in his mind: *Is it possible that a return to monarchy is imminent?*

> I returned from [France]…and proceeded to New York in March, 1790, to enter on the office of Secretary of State.…The courtesies of dinner parties given me, as a stranger newly arrived among them, placed me at once in their familiar society. But I cannot describe the wonder and mortification with which the table conversations

filled me. Politics were the chief topic, and a preference of kingly over republican government was evidently the favorite sentiment. An apostate I could not be, nor yet a hypocrite; and I found myself, for the most part, the only advocate on the republican side of the question.[19]

As Jefferson assumed his duties in Washington's cabinet, he quickly became aware that the principles of republicanism were under assault.

Before he had even arrived on the scene, "Hamilton's financial system had been passed." And its "first object," Jefferson noted later, was to "exclude popular understanding and inquiry."[20] That system, Jefferson would claim, "destroyed" any hopes that the republic could have been launched on its true principles.[21]

In Hamilton's first report, January 14, 1790, on the public credit, he set into operation a fiscal design incorporating the nation's foreign debt, its domestic debt, and the government's assumption of state debts. The debates over the implementation of these fiscal policies were to divide the republic on the fundamental nature of the government.[22]

Hamilton's subsequent report on a national bank was clearly intended to "consolidate" the power of the national government at the expense of the states. Indeed, Hamilton's vision of a wealthy, capitalist society and a government supported mainly by a wealthy class was a direct challenge to Jefferson's idea of the limitations imposed by the Constitution and his preference for states' rights and an agricultural society.

HAMILTON VERSUS JEFFERSON: CONSPIRACY TAKES FORM

The first inkling of this challenge was to take place within three months of Jefferson's arrival. It involved a moral as well as a financial question: Who would receive payment of the "arrearages in soldier's pay"? Would it be the soldiers who had fought in the War of Independence and were now, many of them, penniless? Or, as speculators triumph, those men who had bought up the securities issued by the Continental Congress for a fraction of their worth? As Julian P. Boyd has remarked, the dispute over soldiers' pay "brought about the first open, direct, and uncompromising collision between the secretary of the treasury and the secretary of state.... This, therefore, was a case symbolic of all that was to follow."[23]

In their separate opinions on the subject, both men revealed different approaches to the application of power. Jefferson, as he would note later, knew that "immense sums were thus filched from the poor and ignorant, and fortunes accumulated"[24] by those with inside information. These latter men—speculators—were allegedly friends of Hamilton's. Jefferson, then, in urging Washington to veto the bill, argued that a "fraud" had occurred in the administration.[25]

Hamilton ignored Jefferson's evidence of fraud and allowed that the passage of his economic policies was critical, that time was of the essence. Alluding to "Caesar's wife," Hamilton implied that he was above suspicion. Washington, confronted with the choice of remaining silent or getting to the bottom of Jefferson's allegation, chose to allow the dilemma to remain unresolved. When the bill passed, it became apparent to Jefferson that his rival was well on his way to realizing the second objective of his economic system: "a machine for the corruption of the legislature."[26]

It would seem, then, that Jefferson should have been on his guard when Hamilton approached him regarding the passage of the assumption bill. This was a bill that would allow the federal government to assume the separate state debts built up during the Revolutionary War. But because some states had paid portions of their debt and many had not, disagreements arose in Congress as to who would receive the federal monies. The ensuing debate "seemed to unchain all those fierce passions" that overly ambitious men were capable of.[27]

CORRUPTION VIOLATES REPUBLICAN PRINCIPLES

Assumption was passed, and Hamilton gained a tighter hold on his ultimate objective: It made the Treasury's "Chief the master of every vote in the legislature which might give to the government the direction suited to his political views."[28] The "real history of the assumption," Jefferson would later protest:

> was unjust, in itself oppressive to the states, and was acquiesced in merely from a fear of disunion, while our government was still in its most infant state. It enabled Hamilton so to strengthen himself by corrupt services to many that he could afterwards carry his bank scheme and every measure he proposed in defiance of all

opposition; in fact it was a principal ground whereon was reared up that Speculating phalanx, in and out of Congress which has since been able to give laws and to change the political complexion of the government of the U.S.[29]

Within a period of six months then, Jefferson believed he had seen the government—an independent republic with principles and separate but equal branches—transformed into a system dependent on corruption and the will of one man. And what was perhaps worse, he, the worldly, urbane secretary of state, had been an unwitting tool in his rival's accomplishment.[30]

The "bank scheme," as Jefferson called it, would make the future look especially bleak. What was at stake here, and Jefferson fully realized it, was the chief principle of the Constitution: the separation of powers. Realizing that Hamilton must "contrive" an "engine of influence more permanent" than the funding and assumption plans, Jefferson, Madison, and their cohorts all watched with grim understanding the scenes playing round them.

CORRUPTION OF THE SEPARATION OF POWERS DOCTRINE

Jefferson stated much later that even at that early date, December 1790, Congress had divided into two groups "styled republican and federal. The latter being *monarchists* in principle, adhered to Hamilton…as their leader in that principle, and this mercenary phalanx added…ensured him always a majority in both Houses: so that the whole action of the legislature was now under the direction of the Treasury."[31]

In the long debate over the bank bill, begun in December 1790, the important issue soon became not the bank itself but the principles of the Constitution. Madison rose up to remind the House of Representatives that the Constitutional Convention had denied the government the powers of incorporation. He then proceeded to argue for a strict construction of the Constitution. Jefferson, echoing Madison in the cabinet, warned that "a single step beyond the boundaries thus specially drawn around the powers of Congress is to take possession of a boundless field of power, no longer susceptible of any definition."[32]

Jefferson's logic had penetrated the ultimate danger to the Constitution. Madison too, perhaps even the interpreter in this instance, had begun to alter his broad nationalist construction of the Constitution made only two years earlier. For both the danger in principle was the absolute and unlimited consolidation of power by the central government. When they saw this possibility, in conjunction with Hamilton's domination of the Legislature, the future of republican principles became ominous.

HAMILTON'S "SYSTEM" CREATES MONOPOLIES FOR THE RICH CORPORATIONS

Knowing Jefferson's hatred of the British system, we can begin to understand what suspicions must have been going through his mind, even at this early date, when he contemplated the direction of the government. Gouverneur Morris, an old friend of Hamilton's, would sum up, perhaps better than Jefferson could himself, what lay at the source of his conflict with the secretary of the treasury: Hamilton "apprehended a corrupt understanding between the Executive and a dominating party in the Legislature which would destroy the President's responsibility, and he was not to be taught (what everyone knows) that where responsibility ends, fraud, injustice, tyranny, and treachery begin."[33]

Indeed this was what Jefferson feared. He stated, "Hamilton was not only a monarchist, but for a monarchy bottomed on corruption." The proof for this assertion was, for Jefferson, an anecdote that told the full story. In April 1791 Jefferson, Adams, Hamilton, and Henry Knox had a dinner in which the subject of the British constitution came up for discussion.

SPECIAL INTERESTS AND LOBBYISTS EQUAL CORRUPTION

Hamilton, in the course of disagreeing with Adams on whether the British constitution needed reforming, said, "Purge it of its corruption…and it would become an *impracticable* government: as it stands at present, with all its supposed defects, it is the most perfect government which ever existed." Jefferson's conclusion was that Hamilton was for "an hereditary King, with a House of Lords and Commons corrupted to his will, and standing between him and the people." Jefferson further concluded that Hamilton had been "so bewitched and perverted to the British example, as to be under thorough conviction that corruption was essential to the government of a nation."[34]

Jefferson had already tasted the fruits of Hamilton's managerial corruption.[35] The funding and assumption plans, augmented by the bank bill, had given Hamilton immense leverage in the new government. Already Hamilton had interfered in foreign policy by consulting with the British representative, Major George Beckwith.[36] Within a year Jefferson would complain to Washington that over the past twelve months "the Secretary of the Treasury, by his cabals with members of the Legislature…has forced down his own system, which was exactly the reverse" of Jefferson's.[37]

The fact was, Hamilton had been emulating the late prime minister of England, Sir Robert Walpole. In the latter's role as prime minister, he used, at different intervals, George II and George III as his "Aegis very essential," established the Bank of England and a national debt, brought the moneyed interests into the administration, manipulated the various factions by intrigues, distributed patronage, kept a tight rein on legislation and the timing of bills, involved himself in foreign policy, and created a chain of influence around the king—all in a decidedly nonpartisan fashion.

Hamilton could only have been mirroring the politics of management created by Walpole in the 1720s, 1730s, and 1740s. This style of politics relied on the maintenance of faction, personal connections, special interests, lobbyists, friendship, and all the undercurrent practices "bottomed on corruption" that supported the British constitution Hamilton so admired.[38]

If we attempt to ask whether Hamilton had an exact blueprint, or whether Jefferson believed he did, we are missing the point of historical analysis. Hamilton obviously had little regard for the separation of powers; and if we take Jefferson, Madison, and Henry seriously, he had even less regard for the limitations on the powers of government.

By August 1791 it appeared to Jefferson that Hamilton was the leader of a conspiracy to transform the government from a republic to an aristocratic form. In a conversation between them, Hamilton startled Jefferson by saying "that the present government is not that which will answer the ends of society by giving stability and protection to its rights, and that it will probably be found expedient *to go into the British form.*"[39] To a man of absolute principle, this reliance on expediency was heresy in a republican government. It was at this point that Jefferson saw that it would be necessary to redouble his efforts to crush Hamilton, or republican principles would be compromised out of existence.

A DEFINITION OF CORRUPTION: GOVERNMENT OFFICIALS BECOMING RICH

Jefferson's idea of being in government was to serve the public, not cheat it; nor would he deceive anyone or particularly aim to make himself rich.

The idea that a government would grow strong in proportion to the fraud, corruption, and manipulation that occurred among its leaders, or that secrecy and deception were the means by which policy was advanced, was anathema to Jefferson. As Gouverneur Morris had suggested, and what "everybody else knew," those devices produced "fraud, injustice, tyranny, and treachery."

These principles of administration were fundamentally at stake in the years of Jefferson's struggle with Hamilton and would be resolved only by the Revolution of 1800. But in 1792 Jefferson had no idea that they would be resolved in any way other than the immediate course the government seemed to be taking.

By March, Jefferson's suspicions of Hamilton's involvement with the British minister George Hammond had grown so great that he stated, "I believe he [Hamilton] communicated to Hammond all our views, and knew from him, in return, the views of the British court."[40]

Jefferson claimed a small victory in October, as Washington allowed the State Department to assume control of the mint rather "than to multiply the duties of the other [the Treasury]."[41] But this was to be his last success. His attempt to reduce Hamilton's control of the Treasury by splitting it into two sections, customs and internal taxes, met with failure in the Senate.[42]

Meanwhile, Hamilton had gone on the offensive. In Fenno's *Gazette of the United States,* he published an attack against Jefferson which revealed that Jefferson had "embarrassed [Hamilton's] plans…but continued in opposition to them, after they had been considered and enacted by the legislature…and had been approved by the chief magistrate." Hamilton ended by calling for Jefferson to resign.[43] Finally, he asserted that Jefferson "aims with ardent desire at the Presidential chair." Jefferson's "influence, therefore,…becomes a thing, on ambitious and personal grounds, to be resisted and destroyed."[44]

By October, Washington was again attempting to reconcile his two advisers. When the president told Jefferson "he did not believe there were ten men in the United States" who wished to transform "this Government into a monarchy," Jefferson replied that "there were many more than he [Washington] imagined."[45] And he added that "the Secretary of the Treasury was one of these."

Jefferson then told the president that Hamilton had called the Constitution a "shilly shally thing, of mere milk and water which could not last long and was only good as a step to something better." Jefferson reminded Washington that at the Constitutional Convention of 1787 Hamilton had attempted "to make an English constitution of it" and ended by describing the "regular system" of the Treasury as responsible for collapsing the separation of powers. As the most powerful man in the executive, he [Hamilton] "had swallowed up the legislative houses."[46]

In February 1793 once again Washington asked Jefferson if he and Hamilton might "coalesce" in the interest of giving confidence to the government. This was a revelation to Jefferson, for it meant that Washington still had not grasped what was at stake, what he had been trying to tell him for almost two long years.

Jefferson's answer is also illuminating because he based his objections on principle: "That as to a coalition with Mr. Hamilton, if by that was meant that either was to sacrifice his general system to the other, it was impossible. We had both…principles conscientiously adopted, [which]…could not be given up on either side."[47]

Hamilton would have agreed and, in fact, had stated so as much as nine months earlier in his letter to Edward Carrington. Complaining about Jefferson's opposition to the funding system, Hamilton said, "I do not mean that he advocates directly the undoing of what has been done, but he censures the whole, on principles which, if they should become general, would not but end in the subversion of the system."[48]

FACTION AND CONSPIRACY
ARE INSEPARABLE

Thus Hamilton, nursing his own conspiratorial mentality, was accusing Jefferson, and by implication Madison, of acting in a manner that would bring about a change in not only the administration but also the system of government. Placing his fears into perspective, he told Carrington, "On the whole, the only enemy which Republicanism has to fear in this country is in the spirit of faction and anarchy."[49] Of course, Hamilton saw Jefferson acting in the spirit of one and producing the other. That Hamilton believed that Jefferson was the leader of a faction cannot be doubted. Jefferson, he stated, was leading a "uniform opposition" involving a campaign of "whispers and insinuations."

The opposite view was held by Jefferson. Not only had everyone in the chief councils of the government become suspect but the circles of the conspiracy seemed to be growing wider. Jefferson had drawn the line from the cabinet to the society at large and encompassed the affluent and aristocratic portions: "The line is now drawn so clearly as to show on one side. 1. The fashionable circles of Philadelphia, New York, Boston and Charleston, (natural aristocrats.) 2. Merchants trading on British capital. 3. Paper men, (all the old tories are found in some one of the three descriptions.) On the other side are, 1. Merchants trading on their own capital. 2. Irish merchants. 3. Tradesmen, mechanics, farmers, and every other description of our citizens."[50]

Jefferson had begun to see the emergence of a class division: rich against poor, the old and familiar division of a republican society verging toward revolution and a change in the form of government. When Jefferson refused to accommodate his principles to Hamilton's, it was because he was steeped in the history of republican governments.[51]

Unfortunately, there is little evidence that Washington understood what was at stake. Himself beyond suspicion, at least in terms of motives, he wished only to reduce the friction that he saw dividing his councils. And when Jefferson refused to compromise, Washington, while not openly siding with the secretary of the treasury, at least inclined his way.

Hamilton's influence, by this time pervasive, would continue to grow, even through Adams's entire administration.[52] But it was the influence that Hamilton had had on Washington that was truly dangerous.

For, according to Jefferson, Washington had become incompetent, if not senile. "From the moment...of my retiring from the administration," he wrote, "the federalists got unchecked hold of General Washington. His memory was already sensibly impaired by age, the firm tone of mind for which he had been remarkable, was beginning to relax...a listlessness of labor, a desire for tranquility had crept on him, and a willingness to let others act, and even think for him." (Hamilton, in Jefferson's eyes, had already been doing too much of that.) Finally, Jefferson concluded by observing that Washington "had become alienated from myself personally, as from the republican body generally of his fellow-citizens."[53]

Thus Jefferson, isolated from the one man who earlier had asked him to be a "check" on his administration,[54] saw that he could do nothing but return to Monticello. There he kept up a rapid but distant correspondence with Madison on the main issues confronting Congress. By March 1794 Jefferson saw Hamilton's hand in a Senate speech by William Smith opposing Madison's bill regulating commerce. Writing to Madison, Jefferson noted, "I am at no loss to ascribe Smith's speech to its true father. Every title of it is Hamilton's except the introduction."[55]

This was a sign that Hamilton's influence, like that of an English prime minister's, was reaching farther and deeper into the Legislature. The question now was, How far could Hamilton go in assuming control of the government? Jefferson saw no obstacle to Hamilton's having his way.

HAMILTON AT THE HEAD OF THIRTEEN THOUSAND MEN: A POTENTIAL CAESAR?

But the worst was yet to come. Before Jefferson retired to Monticello, a movement had been under way that bore all the signs of a revolutionary conspiracy. Beginning in July 1791, in the "western country" of Pennsylvania, a number of farmers had held meetings and complained against land speculation, trials in remote federal courts, lack of concern for their defense and navigation rights on the Mississippi, and the imposition of an excise tax on whiskey.[56] The culmination of the meetings came on August 1, 1794, when roughly eight thousand men marched through the town of Pittsburgh.[57]

Henry Knox, secretary of war, ordered a total of 12,950 men to be requisitioned to put down the insurrectionists.[58] By August 7, assuming the rebels intended to continue their resistance and that their behavior "amounted to treason," Washington decided on force.[59] The word of Washington's determination spread quickly as an army of approximately thirteen thousand men had assembled at Carlisle and was ready to march. Another development, however, had taken place, with potentially sinister overtones.

When Washington left Philadelphia, he had at his side General and Secretary of the Treasury Alexander Hamilton.[60] Madison believed that the consequences of Hamilton's role would be the creation of a standing army and passed on the gossip of the day: "It is said the militia will return with that doctrine in their mouths."[61]

Hamilton, left in command by Washington, had suddenly assumed the role of a potential Caesar. His antidemocratic sentiments leaped out of one of his first communications to Washington: "It is long since I have learned to hold popular opinion of no value."[62]

The very thought of Hamilton's leading an army of thirteen thousand men was almost too much for Jefferson to bear. But Washington's next act, the denunciation of the democratic societies, was, in Jefferson's words, "one of the extraordinary acts of boldness of which we have seen so many from the *fraction of monocrats.*"[63]

WASHINGTON'S ASSAULT ON THE FIRST AMENDMENT: THE CONSPIRACY GROWS

Jefferson believed that Washington had acted in direct consequence of the rebellion. If this was the policy of the government, he had no doubt that it constituted an "attack on the freedom of discussion, the freedom of writing, printing and publishing." Hamilton, it appeared, was using Washington and the rebellion as an excuse to assault the First Amendment to the Constitution. It was indeed the part of the Constitution that Jefferson held sacred.

As he contemplated Hamilton's role as a general officer, he also pondered the relationship that his adversary had with "the society of the Cincinnati, a *self-created one, carving out for itself hereditary distinctions, lowering over our Constitution eternally, meeting together in all parts of* the Union, periodically, with closed doors, accumulating a capital in their separate treasury, corresponding secretly & regularly, &…denouncing the democrats." "Their sight," he added, "must be perfectly dazzled by the glittering of crowns & coronets."[64]

Jefferson still believed that the Order of the Cincinnati had not been extinguished, that they had not given up their designs to obtain a glittering coronet, even a "crown." He stated that he fully "expected to have seen some justification of arming one part of the society against another; of declaring a civil war *the moment before* the meeting of that body which has the sole right of declaring war."[65]

Jefferson was describing here nothing less than a conspiracy aimed at the overthrow of the Constitution, the general freedom of the people, and the republic itself. The striking image of Hamilton's assuming command of the largest military force assembled since the days of the American Revolution would not leave Jefferson's mind.

To Jefferson and Madison, those thirteen thousand men were the frightening reality. They knew that Hamilton, poised at the head of an army, potentially a standing army, was capable of declaring a "civil war" despite the authority of Congress.

Both Madison and Jefferson knew that Hamilton had little regard for the separation of powers. Jefferson suspected his ties with Hammond and the British interests. He believed in Hamilton's loyalty to the "eternal enemy" and his institutions. Madison suspected him of attempting to create a standing army.[66] They both knew he had a thirst for power, that on occasion he used Washington, that he had a military background and no small constituency of his own, that he was sympathetic to the Cincinnati, and that he believed men could be governed only by force and corruption.

They also thought Hamilton believed that the current republican system would not work and that he looked upon it only as a steppingstone to something else. It was not surprising, then, that they both regarded him as a modern-day Caesar, a man whose perverse genius could overturn the republic.

HAMILTON'S HERO:
A SYMBOL OF CONSPIRACY

That genius was now at the height of his power. The chief councils of the government were close to being entirely in his hands. Poised on the banks of the Rubicon, Hamilton would be the one to decide when to cross, when to declare civil war, when to ask for aid from Britain, when to risk changing the form of government from a republic to a monarchy, and, finally, when to activate the counterrevolution.

And if there were any doubt, all that Jefferson had to do was remind Madison of an anecdote that had occurred in his home in April 1791. A chilling recollection, it would, Jefferson observed, always serve to "delineate Mr. Hamilton's political *principles*." After a special cabinet meeting held in Washington's absence, Hamilton, Adams, and Jefferson gathered in the latter's living room to converse. Jefferson speaks: "The room being hung around with a collection of the portraits of remarkable men, among them were those of Bacon, Newton and Locke, Hamilton asked me who they were. I told him they were my trinity of the three greatest men the world had ever produced, naming them. He [Hamilton] paused for some time: "*the greatest man*," said he, "*that ever lived, was Julius Caesar!*"[67]

4

The Principles of the American and French Revolutions

That the principles of [the] American [Revolution] opened the Bastille is not to be doubted.

— Thomas Paine to George Washington
May 1, 1790

ONE OF THE MOST INFLUENTIAL POLITICAL EVENTS IN AMERICA during the decade of the 1790s was undoubtedly the French Revolution. It was so influential that, in Jefferson's words, "the form our own government was to take depended much more on the events of France than anybody had before imagined."[1]

None other than John Marshall agreed with Jefferson in his assessment of the importance of the French Revolution in America. It was a cataclysmic event, "the admiration, the wonder, and the terror of the civilized world," and it made such an impression on Americans and how they viewed the idea of revolution that it is impossible to comprehend the Revolution of 1800 without considering its influence.

We tend to forget, viewing that event from a distance of more than two hundred years, that the upheaval in France was seen as a direct outgrowth of the American Revolution. And because its results were so radically different in its violence and social consequences from all prior revolutions, we forget too that it had its origins in the *principles* of the American Revolution.

In addition to the drama, the changing nature of the French Revolution, from one extreme to another, provided an ongoing model to *compare and evaluate the idea of revolution* as it was understood by its American spectators. This is why the French Revolution, when considered in the context of Jefferson's phrase "the Revolution of 1800 was…a revolution in principles," assumed such importance in American politics for the next decade.

But to begin our search for the principles of the French and American Revolutions we must conduct our investigation in reverse and note the expectations that Americans had of the new developments in France. Thomas Paine, an American in spirit, noted, "The Independence of America, considered merely as a separation from England, would have been a matter but of little importance, had it not been accompanied by a revolution in the principles and practice of Governments. She made a stand, not for herself only, but for the world, and looked beyond the advantages herself could receive."[2]

The American Revolution, it was widely believed, would have repercussions far beyond its borders. This was a belief shared by a few of the crowned heads of Europe as well as by Americans. John Paul Jones, for example, reported that the empress of Russia was "persuaded that the American revolution cannot fail to bring about others, and to influence every other government."[3]

George Washington regarded the extension of American revolutionary ideas abroad as the dawn of a new epoch: "Indeed the rights of Mankind, the privileges of the people, and the true principles of liberty, seem to have been more generally…understood throughout Europe since the American revolution than they were at any former period."[4]

We have seen how Jefferson personally attempted to influence the progress of the French Revolution. As early as 1788, Jefferson was claiming that France "had been *awakened by our revolution,* they feel their strength, they are enlightened, their lights are spreading and they will not retrograde."[5]

Peter Porcupine, consistently the harshest critic of France in America, recognized the widespread support occasioned by the revolution:

When the French Revolution commenced there were very few republican Americans, perhaps *not one,* but felt a most cordial interest in the event, and anxiously wished it complete success. It was a revolution of principles, and bid fair to give freedom and happiness to a great nation. Every account which announced its progress was read with pleasure; and aspirations of gratitude to the Supreme Disposer of human affairs, for so signal a triumph of liberty over despotism, issued from every truly American heart.[6]

The reasoning behind this favorable sentiment lay in the extraordinary parallels of principle, strategy, and tactics that were seen initially (and we must note what stage of the French Revolution we refer to) by participants in both revolutions. It is this concern for principles in the midst of revolution that we must comprehend.

HOW PRINCIPLES CHANGE REVOLUTION

What were the principles that Paine and Jefferson saw as responsible for the progress of both revolutions? And how did these principles differ from past revolutions? Paine's answer, in language that reflected the Declaration of Independence, was this:

What were formerly called Revolutions, were little more than a change of persons, or an alteration of local circumstances. They rose and fell like things of course, and had nothing in their existence or their fate that could influence beyond the spot that produced them. But what we now see in the world, from the Revolutions of America and France, is a renovation of the natural order of things, a *system of principles* as universal as truth and the existence of man, and combining moral with political happiness and national prosperity.

I. *Men are born, and always continue free and equal in respect of their rights. Civil distinctions, therefore, can be founded only on public utility.*

II. *The end of all political associations is the preservation of the natural and imprescriptible rights of man; and these rights are liberty, property, security, and resistance of oppression.*

III. *The Nation is essentially the source of all Sovereignty; nor can any individual, or any body of men, be entitled to any authority which is not expressly derived from it.*

In these principles...monarchical sovereignty, the enemy of mankind, and the source of misery, is abolished; and Sovereignty itself is restored to its natural and original place, the Nation.[7]

Paine also recognized a moral dimension to his revolutionary principles when he addressed himself to the "disease that afflicts all mankind": war. Paine recognized the universal concern for peace and morality in a world of power politics. The power to make war was to reside in the people, not in a king or his corrupt ministers.

RIGHTS, DIGNITY, AND RULE OF LAW VERSUS WEALTH

For Paine, the principles of the revolutions in France and America were bound up in the republican ideology he and Jefferson espoused. "In the instance of France," Paine wrote, "we see a revolution generated in the rational contemplation of the rights of man, and distinguished from the beginning between persons and principles."[8]

There were to be no distinctions between one class of men and another; no artificial divisions based on wealth; no titles of nobility; no tinseled aristocracy. Indeed this was the principle upon which all governments must be founded: a distinction between arbitrary rule and the rule of law.

What Paine was saying here was in complete agreement with what Jefferson would write in his last letter: "The mass of mankind has not been born with saddles on their backs, nor a favored few booted and spurred, ready to ride them legitimately, by the grace of God."[9] Paine's principles, like those in Jefferson's essay *The Earth Belongs to the Living,* went to the heart of the state's legal machinery and those mechanisms that had enabled the few to oppress the many for centuries.

Paine's idea of the original government compact was not between an individual and his sovereign or his government but between individuals (government came after the people, not before). The principles in *The*

Rights of Man recognized the basic political nature of man, more so than any other document in the eighteenth century.

These sentiments were both radical and revolutionary: radical because they attempted to get to what Paine called the "root problem," and revolutionary because Paine believed, once universalized, they were capable of transforming or changing the minds of the entire world.[10] For Paine the idea of revolution in France was consistent with his idea of revolution in America. He defined the revolution as "no more than the consequence of a *mental* revolution previously existing in France. The mind of the nation had changed beforehand, and the new order of things has naturally followed the new order of thoughts."[11]

Revolution then was, as Adams had stated, "in the minds of the people."[12] Moreover, the change of opinion had become the basis for substantive change in France, even before the *ancien régime* was abolished.

OPPOSITION TO REVOLUTION BASED ON POWER, NOT RIGHT

Opposition to the revolution in France was led by Edmund Burke, who argued that the people or their representatives had no right to overthrow a monarch or establish a government. Paine's answer to Burke was that "it is power and not principles that Mr. Burke venerates."[13] In a perfect echo of Jefferson's essay *The Earth Belongs to the Living,* Paine took Burke to task: "There never did, there never will, and there never can exist a parliament, or any description of men, or any generation of men, in any country, possessed of the right or the power of binding and controlling posterity to the 'end of time,' or of commanding forever how the world shall be governed."

Paine summarized his argument: "I am contending for the rights of the living, and against their being willed away, and controlled and contracted for, by the manuscript assumed authority of the dead; and Mr. Burke is contending for the authority of the dead over the rights and freedom of the living."[14]

Paine's criticism of Burke was an assertion of a new idea of freedom and equality, based on principles that both he and Jefferson hoped would enable mankind to destroy despotism. These principles could be expressed symbolically in one of the first acts of the French Revolution: "The fall of the Bastille," said Paine, "included the idea of the downfall of despotism."[15]

Many who had fought in the American Revolution and wished to support the French struggle began to feel uneasy about the increasing violence. Paine attempted to make a clear separation between the causes of violence and revolutionary principles. Becoming impatient with what he considered irrelevant criticism, Paine asked his critics to account for the influence of human nature in a revolutionary situation:

> While the characters of men are forming, as is always the case in revolutions, there is a reciprocal suspicion, and a disposition to misinterpret each other, and even parties directly opposite in principle, will sometimes concur in pushing forward the same movement with different views [motives], and with the hope of its producing very different circumstances.[16]

What Paine was implying here is a convergence theory of revolution. He is saying that it is necessary to subordinate ideological disputes to the basic character of the revolution. It is also necessary to submerge factional dispositions in the interest of revolution. And the way one can do this is to ally oneself with a political organization that transcends the difference between factions.

There was another view of revolution shared by almost all Americans, not only enthusiastically but as a simple matter of principle. This was the definition of revolution stated by François Barbé-Marbois, and it summed up eloquently the prevailing American sentiment: "I define revolution as the advent of law, the resurrection of human rights and the revival of justice."[17]

Americans sympathetic with the republican ideology expressed approval of the extension of what they considered their revolution to France and, indeed, the world. And Jefferson was certainly one, if not the leader, of those who understood and foresaw that revolutions would continue. This was for many the real meaning of the American Revolution: the beginning of a new age of revolutions.

At first Americans generally saw the French Revolution taking the same course and exhibiting the same forms as the American Revolution before it. Jefferson had written to Madison about La Fayette's declaration of rights, which, he thought, contained "the essential principles of *ours* accommodated as much as could be to the actual state of things here."[18] That declaration, which essentially stated the principles of the American Revolution, was presented to the king on September 3, 1791.

The chief concern of the revolutionaries during these first years of the revolution was to guarantee liberty through a constitution. They were determined to proceed, step by step, in forming a government whose constitutional authority would be presented as a fait accompli to a monarch, totally changing the political nature of a regime. Article 16 stated, "A society in which the guarantee of rights is not assured, nor the separation of powers, has no constitution."[19]

"The basis of the present struggle," wrote Jefferson, is "the establishment of a constitution which shall assure to them a good degree of liberty. They flatter themselves they shall form a better constitution than the English."[20]

Jefferson gave an indication of how he believed the French could benefit from England's example, especially upon principle. It was Jefferson's hope that France would establish "a real constitution, which cannot be changed by the ordinary legislature; whereas England has no constitution at all: that is to say there is not one principle of their government which the parliament does not alter at pleasure. The omnipotence of parliament is an established principle with them."[21]

Jefferson, approving the actions of the French revolutionaries, wished to see the Rights of Man so embedded in a "fixed constitution" that there would be no turning back, no counterrevolution.

Only in this slow, cautious yet deliberate manner could the fundamental alterations of power be achieved without massive violence.

The constitution that was being debated and adopted by the French Assembly was, so far as Jefferson was concerned, revolutionizing the country in the manner that the original republican constitutions had in America.

The objects the assembly sought to guarantee in Virginia were "a free press," "a habeas corpus law," the rights to "periodical convocation of the States," "their exclusive right to raise and appropriate money," a "participation in legislation," a "right to propose amendments," "infallibly end[ing] in a right of origination."[22] The only principles lacking, according to Jefferson, were "trial by jury" and the abolishment of "a standing army."

This was a definition of the politics of revolution in principle: the coordination of ideology and institutions adapted to the changing needs of a revolutionary society. It meant involving a wide spectrum of people in novel political organizations that enabled them to become educated and prepared for political action.

Ultimately, it involved dealing with those forces and institutions directly responsible for implementing a constitution. A modern way of describing Jefferson's analysis would be to say that the politics of revolution finds its peculiar mode of organization and then "inevitably channels itself into institutions and constitutions."[23]

As Paine himself related by late 1789, "Societies were formed in Paris, and committees of correspondence and communication established throughout the nation, for the purposes of enlightening the people, and explaining to them the principles of civil government; and so orderly was the election [of the first National Assembly] conducted, that it did not give rise even to the rumor of tumult."[24]

Indeed these forms had been seen by the Americans, and they knew what they meant. Jefferson would refer to them collectively as signs of the Spirit of '76. Obviously, these same forms of organization gave rise to enormous amounts of energy in France. As Paine indicated, they made it possible to coordinate the activities of men in committees and clubs with elections that decided national questions.

AVOIDING VIOLENCE

The "favorable issue" of revolution depended on the mode of organization plus the strength of a fixed constitution. The mode was, theoretically, nonviolent. The basic distinction made between potential violence and the progress of a "constitutional revolution" was how both related to great national questions. According to Jefferson and most of his associates, instances of violence based on local needs not affecting the entire citizenry only disrupted the revolution and distracted the people. Jefferson firmly believed that a revolution could be advanced by the "wheedling and intimidation" of leaders in a parliamentary body, as in the case of the National Assembly.

But the intimidation would be calculated to always fall short of force.[25]

If any rough spots occurred in the transition of power from an aristocracy to the representatives of the people, especially within an assembly, France should follow the example of the "second American revolution." "You must have observed, when in America," Jefferson had earlier written to Francis dal Verme, "that time and trial had discovered defects in our federal constitution." A new essay, made in the midst of the flames could not be perfect."[26]

This concern for the reasoned, steady growth of a constitution was Jefferson's way of suggesting a remedy to a constitutional defect. And it was why he felt it necessary to grasp the principles of the politics of revolution. Indeed a "political revolution," Jefferson's protégé in France echoed, "may be considered as effected so far as it relates to the transfer of all power into the hands of the representatives of the people."[27]

If a revolution resulted in despotism or uncontrollable violence, Jefferson considered it a disaster.

THOUGHTS ON THE VIOLENCE IN FRANCE

Jefferson could not singlehandedly prevent anti-French sentiment. Edmund Genet had soured many Americans, while the depredations of French privateers against American commerce alienated even more. But the real culprit was violence. Americans were treated to the spectacle of violence on a scale never before dreamed of. Leaders fell almost daily. Those who attempted to act moderately were as likely to be victims as those who demanded excessive and ruthless policies.

To Americans, unused to prolonged terror and bloodshed, the carnage seemed unreasonable. Although they had seen terror, bloodshed, and guerrilla warfare in the southern colonies and between Loyalists and

Rebels in New England, they had witnessed nothing like the wholesale bloodletting that characterized the revolution in France.

The real fear of those opposed to the French Revolution was the influence that it would have in America. Porcupine had noted shrilly that "the elections that have lately taken place [1796] have proved that the *French faction is increasing.* There are to be found, in every beer-house, scores of fellows, who will not only justify the French in all they have done, but will tell you flat and plain, that they would *join them,* if they were to land in the country!"[28]

Even such a calm observer of the political scene as Alexander Hamilton could see events from Porcupine's perspective:

> Symptoms of the too great prevalence of this system [the French revolutionary system] in the United States are alarmingly visible. It was by its influence that efforts were made to embark this country in a common cause with France...to induce our government to sanction and promote her odious principles....It is by its influence that every succeeding revolution has been approved or excused; all the horrors that have been committed justified...even the last usurpation, which contradicts all the ostensible principles of the Revolution, has been regarded with complacency, and the despotic constitution engendered by it slyly held up as a model not unworthy of our imitation.[29]

That the French played politics in America cannot be doubted. By 1795 the attitude of many Americans in the spirit of the French Revolution had become rebellious. The aftermath of the Whiskey Rebellion prompted many to raise questions about the number of revolutionaries returning to America from France.

William Cobbett produced an insight of which even he did not grasp the full meaning: "I do not say that they had any immediate hand in the western affair: but when rebels, from all quarters of the world are received with open arms, as persecuted patriots, it is no wonder that rebellion should be looked upon as Patriotism."[30] Indeed rebellion, equated with patriotism, was fast becoming a national mood.

Meanwhile the continuing French Revolution caused consternation and bitterness among factions in America. Those who were cynical, who could see nothing of value in the changing nature of the revolution, who, perhaps, never truly understood what the revolution was about, even from an American viewpoint, were wont to reduce that struggle to a domestic one.

Federalists, notably Fisher Ames, would excoriate the revolutionary process in language typical of an American: "The French Revolution has been made the instrument of faction; it has multiplied popular errours,... and, on every inviting occasion for mischief and the oppression of a minority [the democratic leaders], make it...*appear to be the abandonment of its principles and cause.*"[31]

FACTION DESTROYS CONCERN FOR PRINCIPLE

Ames, like Paine, was pointing out the role of faction in destroying a concern for principle. The French partisans were incapable of restraint and gave themselves over entirely to their factional interests. In the process, it appeared, they had abandoned the republican principles so carefully inculcated by Jefferson and Paine.

Minority factions split the republican majority in the French National Assembly until that majority consumed itself in terror, brought on the despotism of Napoleon, and eventually a counterrevolution and the restored monarchy.

Other Americans had also begun to perceive the tragedy in France. As early as 1796, Patrick Henry wrote his friends in Virginia: "I should not be surprised if the very man, at whose victories you now rejoice, should, *Caesar-like, subvert the liberties of his country.*"[32]

Expressions such as these signaled a complete abandonment of principle, without which a revolution would slide backward.

Because the French had failed to unite the nation and have their gains perpetuated by degrees in the constitution, the revolution *had* failed. Paradoxes abounded: the greater the violence, the less self-discipline was imposed; no sooner was one aspect of despotism destroyed than, suddenly, the threat of total despotism seemed even greater; the more the French did to establish the Rights of Man, the less secure they became; and the more that was done to destroy the centralized power of the monarchy, the greater became the irreversible and consolidated power of the revolution.

The climax of these contradictions, as seen by Jefferson and his friends, was that an entirely new set of problems had arisen. Revolution suddenly had the opposite effect from that which was intended.

TOO MUCH TOO SOON IS DANGEROUS IN A REVOLUTION

The primacy of the state was enhanced at the expense of the individual. If revolution proceeded too fast and too soon, it destroyed whatever opportunities it had to guarantee liberty and conserve principles.

Jefferson had noted in 1790 that "the ground of liberty is to be gained by inches...we must be contented to secure what we can get, from time to time, and eternally press forward for what is yet to get. It takes time to persuade men to do even what is for their own good."[33]

PRINCIPLES INFLUENCE FORM

Destroying the oppressive feudal aristocracy of the *ancien régime,* the new constitution ushered in a new system of relationships, transforming completely the French citizen's notion of himself and his society.

"In contemplating the French constitution," wrote Paine in 1790,

> we see in it a rational order of things. The principles harmonize with the forms, and both with their origin. It may perhaps be said as an excuse for bad forms, that they are nothing more than forms; but this is a mistake. Forms grow out of principles, and operate to continue the principles they grow from. It is impossible to practise a bad form on anything but a bad principle. It cannot be ingrafted on a good one; and whenever the forms in any government are bad, it is a certain indication that the principles are bad also.[34]

The emphasis was placed equally on both principle and form. The two were interconnected in a way that Jefferson, as well as Paine, understood was essential for liberty. A revolution that began on republican principles must assume a republican form in its constitution and its governing administration.

If not, the two would lack harmony and one or the other, and ultimately both, would become corrupt. This was as true for America as it had been for France. And for Americans, the Consulate was a vivid example. As the years passed by, and the revolution in France went through its successive changes, Paine saw the implications for liberty in dark and disillusioned terms.

Three years later, Paine would write to Jefferson, underscoring the concern for principles that occupied their attention: "Had this revolution been conducted consistently with its principles there was once a good prospect of extending liberty through the greatest part of Europe, but I now relinquish that hope."[35]

AN OVEREMPHASIS ON UNITY AND PARTY DESTROYS A REVOLUTION

Jefferson himself made a connection between the form and the principle of revolution in America and how they differed from the issue of the French Revolution. In a letter to Destutt de Tracy in 1811, he stated, "The republican government of France was lost *without a struggle* because the party of 'un et indivisible' had prevailed; no provincial organizations existed to which the people might rally under authority of the laws, the seats of the Directory were virtually vacant, and a small force sufficed to turn the legislature out of their chamber, and to salute its leader chief of the nation."[36]

Because the revolutionary party had become so powerful, its very slogan—*un et indivisible,* used to achieve power—denied that there might be a division of power. Indeed there was no possibility of a reversal of power to the people. The principle of liberty for "the people" had been usurped by the central government.

As Jefferson implied, no institutions existed in which an alternative locus of power remained. All political power and authority had been concentrated in the Directory and, later, consolidated in the Consulate.

DECENTRALIZED STATES: THE SINE QUA NON OF REVOLUTION

By comparison, the American revolutionaries had been wiser. Jefferson remarked in 1811,

> the true barriers of our liberty in this country are the State govern-
> ments; and the wisest conservative power ever contrived by man,

is that of which our Revolution and present government found us possessed. Seventeen distinct States, amalgamated,...regularly organized...[by] the choice of the people, and enlightened by a free press, can never be so fascinated by the arts of one man, as to submit voluntarily to his usurpation. Nor can they be constrained to it by any force he can possess. While that may paralyze the single State in which it happens to be encamped, sixteen others...rise up on every side, ready organized for deliberation by a constitutional legislature, and for action by their governor, constitutionally the commander of the militia of the State.[37]

This was a "constitutional prescription" for revolution if the need arose, or if a usurper attempted to overthrow the liberties of the people. Jefferson's description of the French Assembly, "virtually vacant," and of the French provinces, without legal organizations that had reserved powers under the law, is juxtaposed to the state legislatures in America with their powers to unite under the legal auspices in rebellion against the national government.

Jefferson's greatest fear was that, like France, the federal government of the United States would "consolidate" all power unto itself.[38]

This principle—a decentralized organization of states opposing a consolidation of power by a central government—was so important to Jefferson and his colleagues that they were willing to tolerate its contradictions: "To wit, that certain States...might attempt to secede from the Union," Jefferson noted. "This is certainly possible; and would be befriended by this regular organization. But...if ever they should reach the majority [of states], they would then become the regular government."[39]

This was the principle of dual sovereignty that many saw could potentially lead to a confrontation like the American Civil War.

But this was also the one principle that could continue to legitimate a dynamic, changing society.

It was a principle consistent with Jefferson's notion of a permanent, constitutional revolution. When the governing elite became unrepresentative, the states individually, and then reaching a majority, would validate the revolution. The implication of this theory, applied to the states, could also be applied to the individual. Through the constitutional process, the individual could make a conscious, legitimate choice for or against revolution.

Moreover, as we view the consolidation argument posed by Jefferson as a threat to American liberty, and we see his argument for the necessity of constitutionally reserved powers to enable states to resist national encroachments, we may better understand his concern for the purity of both principle and form.

We may also clearly understand the idea of revolution that Jefferson propounded. Jefferson saw the necessity of maintaining a form that would allow and facilitate resistance but, at the same time, be consistent with the principle of revolution. This was essential for one basic purpose: to prevent counterrevolution.

Learning his lesson from that "abortive" experiment abroad, Jefferson was determined that France's loss of liberty would not be duplicated in America. As Paine's letter signaled the death of liberty in Europe, Jefferson's commitment to the idea of revolution deepened. If, as noted, Jefferson believed that the cause of world liberty rested with the revolution in France, he must have believed by 1797 that the future of liberty in the world rested with America. And he was determined more than ever that America would not lose its "without a struggle."

5

The Politics of Faction

Faction is to party what the superlative is to the positive: Party is a political evil, and faction is the worst of all parties.

> —Henry St. John, Lord Bolingbroke
> *The Idea of a Patriot King*

The violence of faction is the mortal disease under which popular governments have everywhere perished.

> —James Madison, Federalist No. 10

THUS FAR WE HAVE EXPLORED THE PRINCIPLES OF THE ONE-PARTY state and of revolution and have examined the ideas, as well as the fears, of conspiracy and counterrevolution. We have seen that leading politicians believed they were observing the development of administrative, political, and revolutionary models that were similar, if not identical, to those in England and the revolutionary period of the colonies. These statements would imply that the American political system as it developed from 1787 to 1801 was not, at least in the minds of the actors, materially different from what they had known.

The political system, in the context of its basic ideological conflicts, remained largely unchanged from the early 1770s to 1800. And this hypothesis, if true, contradicts the conclusion of every American historian to the present.

Before we dismiss or reject it as being out of step with contemporary scholarship, we need to examine the assumption upon which this assertion rests. Opposition to government in the eighteenth century was regarded as a political evil of the greatest magnitude. There was only one government, one administration; and everyone was bound (at least in theory) to support it.

Those who failed to give their allegiance did so at their own peril. For the most part, political opposition was considered illegal, subversive, and always dangerous.

OBSTRUCTING THE GOVERNMENT EQUATED WITH TREASON

Indeed, as we have seen, those who were members of an extreme opposition faction were regarded as members of a city within a city, a state within a state, potentially violent revolutionaries. No matter what area of politics one might choose to become active in—administration, the newspaper media, pamphleteering—it was impossible to be ignorant of the fact that the purpose of the government in power was to suppress faction before it could promote civil war and tear apart the state.[1]

In a typical passage of the times, Peter Porcupine was quoted in the *New York Gazette:* "It is an axiom in republican politics that the majority must rule. This power is exercised by proxy; and whoever erects, or is accessary in erecting a systematic opposition to this proxy, or government established by the people, is a bad citizen and merits the resentment of the people. If a party be formed under the auspices of any foreign state to clog the wheels of government, it is treasonably engaged in resisting the will of the people, and of course deserves *capital* punishment."[2]

This was the theory of the one- or non-party state. Yet clearly, more than one party or faction existed in America, just as it had in every other republic in history. The ideal contemporary political theory, then, recognized that society was divided into different factions, but that for the benefit of the commonwealth they were not to raise their voice in the community. And since political parties were not allowed, they *had* to be parties of a "foreign state."

FEAR OF CONSPIRATORIAL FACTIONS

This was also characteristic of politics during the revolutionary era in America. Bernard Bailyn writes of Massachusetts Governor Sir Francis

Bernard, "Bernard's fear of a conspiratorial faction is the main theme that runs through his extensive correspondence of the 1760s."[3]

This fear of a conspiratorial faction also ran through the entire decade following the American Revolution. It was characteristic of the period under the Articles of Confederation and the era immediately following the Constitution. And this style of politics, dominated by faction, continued through the remainder of the 1790s.

The purpose of this chapter is to point out how the politics of faction grew into the politics of revolution, ultimately climaxing in Thomas Jefferson's accession to power in 1801.

One of the principal theories of government in the eighteenth century, designed to counter the influence of faction, was harmony. Richard Hofstadter has written that "they [the Founding Fathers] were far from clear as to how opposition should make itself felt, for they valued social unity or harmony and they had not arrived at the point that opposition, manifested in organized political parties, could sustain freedom without shattering such harmony."[4]

This historical judgment accurately reflected George Washington's attempts to "coalesce" Jefferson's and Alexander Hamilton's differing views for the sake of unity in his administration. It was also Hamilton's point in initially achieving Jefferson's agreement on the assumption plan.

While Jefferson would later regret the bargain with Hamilton as his greatest political error,[5] he had compromised on the basis that harmony in the administration was essential. To an old friend he had written: "In general I think it is necessary to give as well as take in a government like ours."[6] This would seem to reflect the theory of the Constitution as well as a belief that disagreement in the formation of policy was allowed up to a certain point. Then, majority rule would assert itself upon the vote taken for any particular bill, and the opposition, in whatever branch, would acquiesce in its binding provisions.

This opposition, necessary as well as natural for wise deliberation, was restricted in its most virulent form to the legislative chambers. But it too was limited.

Thus, in the earliest days of the new government, the fear of faction threatening the fragile harmony of the administration spread among those concerned with public affairs. Arguing over the residence bill in 1790, one political observer wrote that if the seat of government was moved, "there will be one party endeavoring to carry the bill into effect, and another... that will exert themselves to oppose it....The influence of these factions will go into every measure of government."[7]

Other newspapers sounded the tocsin: "If a faction can violate the Constitution; this sacred charter of government, which they are sworn to support, may be considered as blank paper."[8]

OPPOSITION FACTIONS EQUATED
WITH "POLITICAL SUICIDE"

The administrative council too expected that a certain amount of disagreement would assert itself in the making of policy; but it was not accustomed, or prepared, to see the opposition continue unabated. Washington certainly reflected this view when he stated that bringing someone to the highest councils "whose tenets are adverse to the measures which the general government advocates...would be a sort of political suicide."[9]

From an administrative point of view, the same fear motivated Hamilton as he contemplated Virginia's protest against the assumption bill: "A spirited remonstrance to Congress is talked of. This is the first symptom of a spirit which must either be killed or will kill the constitution of the United States."[10] Obviously, Hamilton believed such opposition reflected the spirit of a faction opposed to his policies. And a faction the size of Virginia, phrasing its disagreement in such terms as "subversive" and "dangerous," could lead to serious consequences: the threat of revolution against the national government.[11]

In the spirit of the times, Hamilton also believed, to use his own word, that that kind of opposition must be "killed." He had good theoretical grounds for expressing his fear in such extreme language. If a faction did not expire, it would grow until it had overwhelmed the state. Thus, starting from two different poles of reason, both Hamilton and Jefferson appeared to believe that the Constitution was threatened by the politics of faction. The latter intoned to John Harvie, "If it [the assumption plan] is obdurately rejected, something much worse will happen" than his "aversion" to assumption.[12] That allusion was double: it referred to the potential failure of compromise and the death of the new government.

The point we might keep in mind, however, is that a state, passing resolutions against the policies of the national government, was considered a threat to the Constitution.

From the generally accepted theory of faction, it would appear that the causes, if understood, proceeded from permanent divisions in the nature of man. The only temporary consideration was whether the government had or did not have the power to suppress violent factions. Hamilton registered his deep-seated fears and was quick to reach an affirmative conclusion:

> It was not till the last session that I became unequivocally convinced of the following truth: *that Mr. Madison, co-operating with Mr. Jefferson, is at the head of a faction decidedly hostile to me and my administration; and actuated by views, in my judgment, subversive of the principles of good government and dangerous to the Union, peace, and happiness of the country.*
>
> These are strong expressions…I have not lightly resolved to hazard them. They are the result of a *serious alarm* in my mind.[13]

Hamilton, it seemed, had articulated a conspiracy theory of his own: Jefferson and Madison at the head of a faction were determined to subvert the government. In addition, Hamilton revealed what Jefferson had suspected all along: he saw himself acting as the prime minister, the head of Washington's cabinet, even labeling it "my administration."

Most importantly, he labeled Jefferson's and Madison's actions as "subversive," implying that "principles of good government" would not tolerate an opposition, especially from a *faction*.

FACTIONS DO NOT COMPROMISE BUT SEEK TO DESTROY ONE ANOTHER

Jefferson's reaction, once he heard that the terms had been applied to him personally, was one of anger. He told Madison, "You will discover Hamilton's pen…daring to call the republican party *a faction*."[14] The term infuriated Jefferson and for good reason. Yet the charge was more generally applied than even he knew. Because of the strife, Washington had thought of retiring and had asked Madison to author a valedictory address for him. The request included a wish by the president to say something that would dampen the spirit of party. But the president, postponing his retirement for four more years, failed to use the speech until 1796. Nevertheless it indicates the concern over faction had become grave.

At nearly the same time, Hamilton was gloomily reporting his worst fears: "The spirit of party has grown to maturity sooner in this country than perhaps was to have been counted upon."[15] Hamilton not only saw his system threatened but began to fear that the implications of Virginia's solid resistance might portend the end of the Union.

Hamilton's recognition that party spirit had "matured" was tantamount to saying it constituted a threat to the government. This was particularly true where the Democratic societies were concerned. As we have already noted, Jefferson defended these societies and opposed Washington's condemnation of them. The reason they were so viciously attacked was a reflection of the nature of their activity. They were viewed as potentially revolutionary.

SELF-CREATED SOCIETIES SEEN
AS PREPARING FOR REVOLUTION

Washington himself reflected the fears of many when he wrote to Jay, "That the *self-created societies* which have spread themselves over this country have been laboring incessantly to sow the seeds of distrust, jealously, and of course discontent, thereby hoping to effect some *revolution* in the government, is not unknown to you."[16]

Indeed the meetings, the passing of resolutions, the distribution of circular letters, the vociferous statements of opposition to the administration, the correspondence exchanged, the identification with the revolutionary fervor in France, and the Whiskey Rebellion—all had added up, as Jefferson suggested, to a "rekindling" of the old Spirit of 1776."[17]

Madison, the leader of the opposition in Congress, thus saw the attempt to crush the Democratic societies as a threat to American liberty. Indeed, Madison felt the crisis so great that he spelled out the threat to his friend James Monroe in even more precise terms. In the process he revealed his idea of the use of power in dealing with counterrevolution. And, interestingly, he placed his reflections on power in the context of the republican ideology. Reporting on the Whiskey Rebellion, he began,

The event was in several respects a critical one for the cause of liberty, and the real authors of it…were…doing the business of Despotism. *You well know the general tendency of insurrections to increase the momentum of power*….I have no doubt that a formidable attempt would have been made to establish the principle that a standing army was necessary for *enforcing the laws*….The game was, to connect the democratic Societies with the odium of the insurrection—to connect the Republicans in Congress with those Societies—to put the President ostensibly at the head of the other party, in opposition to both, and by these means prolong the illusions in the North, and try a new experiment on the South.[18]

That experiment, Madison believed, was an attempt to coerce the South.

FEAR OF A STANDING ARMY

If Hamilton, at the head of an army, could maintain the illusion of republican resistance to the administration's policies, perhaps the force of a standing army could overawe the South.

Earlier in the year, Madison had seen the threat coming. Referring to the lower House, he wrote to Jefferson, "The attempt of this Branch to give the President power to raise an army of 10,000, if he should please, was strangled more easily in the House of Representatives than I had expected. This is the third or fourth effort made in the course of the Session to get a powerful military establishment, under the pretext of public danger and under the auspices of the President's popularity."[19] Now Hamilton was at the head of an army, and Jefferson concurred with Madison's pessimism.[20]

As the New Year came into view, Madison believed that instead of the danger decreasing, it had worsened. Within five weeks he again wrote Jefferson, counseling a mood of despair: "I am extremely sorry to remark a growing apathy to the evil and danger of standing armies. And a vote passed two days ago, which is not only an evidence of that, but if not the effect of unpardonable inattention, indicates a temper still more alarming….The debate brought out an avowal that the Executive ought to be free to use the regular troops, as well as the Militia in support of the laws against our own Citizens."[21]

FACTION DOMINATES THE
HOUSE OF REPRESENTATIVES

In the wake of this extremely pessimistic discussion, opinion had polarized within the legislative branch. The previous year had seen Jefferson's
retirement from the executive branch, and now it appeared that Madison
might be heading a losing cause. Factional differences had become so
great that no one had any idea, at least since December 1793, what course
Congress would take: compromise or greater polarization.

To another observer the longer this situation endured, the more
likely it was to have alarming consequences: "The passions of many
are so violent, and such the real diversity of views and interests, that
the prospects of tranquility and permanency in our public policy has
much diminished."[22]

The style of politics in the Congress was like that in the states:
factional and in the traditional sense. The proof of this lay in the nature of
political leadership in the House of Representatives. Madison dominated
the House to such a degree that the republicans, or *Antis,* as they were
called, were termed "Madison's party."[23]

Yet as the congressional sessions wore on, the evidence of wider
polarization became obvious, even to those who were not members of
the government. One South Carolinian wrote:

> Our Information of the proceedings of Congress is very broken
> and Imperfect. We perceive however that warmth and dissention
> prevail on almost every question.... Your Hall appears to be an arena
> where the Combattants descend to engage, not for persuasion, but
> for victory....
>
> This is a melancholy picture, but I fear it is too true.[24]

The lesson was clear to at least one writer who understood the role
of faction and party in a free society: "What caused the fall of Athens?
Faction: the spirit of discord prevailed and liberty was destroyed....The
republic of Rome experienced a similar fate. Ambitious Caesar saw the
moment when party blinded the vigilance of his country's friends, seized
it, and triumphed....This fatal shore, on which so many nations have been
stranded, is destined to produce the same fate to America, unless the spirit

of party be repressed....Party is a monster who devours the common good, whose destructive jaws are dangerous to the felicity of nations."[25]

In April 1794, John Taylor of Caroline, one of the finest philosophical minds in the South, addressed himself to the political situation in the country and attempted to analyze the causes of the increasing conflict.

He titled his examination "A Definition of Parties" and began with a general proposition: A faction will:

increase taxes and increase debts…

impose all taxes, receive most taxes, and pay no taxes

borrow for the public—making the contract for the public and with itself

renew the bank

modif[y] paper credit

raise fleets and armies to defend itself against the nation

efface the principles of republicanism, by…producing unequal wealth and by sowing partizans, in offices created for the purpose at the public expense

distract the public mind…and take advantage of the confusion generated by its own acts…under pretense of restoring order

Finally, he wrote,

A system of public plunder will plead for itself, by pretending to secure private property; and the office of an honest government will be thus assumed by a paper faction....For the truth is that a secretary of the Treasury—an incorporated bank—and a funding system, constitute substantially a phalanx of privileged orders, if they can influence the legislature. They are a correct representation of a king—lords—and commons. The first will sway the legislature, by the magic of private interest. The second is a successional body having exclusive right and legislative weight…and the third is a mode of representation, equivalent to the rotten boroughs of England.[26]

This was John Taylor's assessment of the consequences of party and faction.

The next important event that would spur the contending factions to even greater heights was the Jay Treaty. As early as April 1794, it had been rumored that an envoy would be sent to Great Britain. The rumor had it that Hamilton would "probably be appointed, unless overruled by an apprehension from the disgust to Republicanism and to France."[27]

FACTIONS USE TREATIES FOR SELFISH (AND UNCONSTITUTIONAL) ENDS

With Jefferson's and Madison's knowledge and suspicion of Hamilton's collusion with the British, this news no doubt caused them to worry about the future of American foreign policy.

Nearly the same view was expressed by John Adams when he first heard of John Jay's appointment as envoy. Adams too saw the implications of the treaty—the introduction of a standing army and monarchy—as crucial, albeit from a slightly different perspective:

> The President has sent Mr. Jay to try if he can find any way to reconcile our honour with Peace. I have no great Faith in any very brilliant Success: but hope he may have enough to keep us out of a war. Another war would add two or three hundred Millions of Dollars to our Debt: rouse up a many headed and many bellied Monster of an Army to tyrannize over Us, totally dissadjust our present Government, and accelerate the Advent of Monarchy and Aristocracy, by at least fifty Years.
>
> Those who dread Monarchy and Aristocracy and at the Same time advocate war are the most inconsistent of all Men.[28]

In fact, Adams had discovered there were politicians who would vote their special interests totally divorced from the form and the principles of a government they were elected to serve.

Fisher Ames too believed that the politics of faction had gone beyond the bounds of decency. Referring to the Jay Treaty's rough handling in Congress and in the press, he wrote, "A crisis now exists, the most serious I ever witnessed...The government cannot go to the halves. It would be another, a worse government, if the mob, or the leaders of the mob in Congress, can stop the lawful acts of the President, and unmake a treaty. It would be either no government, or instantly a government by usurpation and wrong."[29]

Ames was equating Madison and the advocates of republicanism in Congress with a mob, an indication of their status in the politics of faction.

Ames's sense of crisis was shared by President Washington, who wrote to Adams during the height of the controversy, alluding to a "pre-concerted plan." He stated, "As the ratification thereof [the Jay Treaty]… has passed from me, these meetings in opposition to the constituted authority, are as useless, as they are *at all times* improper and dangerous."[30] Thus in the midst of crisis, the chief executive naturally reprobated those in the opposition.

No clearer statement exists during this era that the non-party state could not tolerate factious opposition.

John Jay, who understood the politics of his treaty as well as anyone, had another interpretation. Writing to Washington about the difficulties in getting the treaty through Congress, he suggested, "These are political evils, which, in all ages, have grown out of such a state of things, as naturally as certain physical combinations produce whirlwinds and meteors."[31]

In short, Jay had linked the politics surrounding the Jay Treaty to the politics of faction "of all ages."

Four months later, Jefferson would lament the change in American politics that had become apparent in the aftermath of the Jay Treaty. In his depressed state, he returned to the theme that had dominated his thoughts since his return from France—the fear of counterrevolution. As his naturally conspiratorial view of politics asserted itself, he revealed an unremitting hatred for British aristocratic principles:

> The aspect of our politics has wonderfully changed since you left us. In place of that noble love of liberty and republican government which carried us triumphantly thro' the war, an Anglican monarchical and aristocratical party has sprung up, whose avowed object is to draw over us the substance as they have already done the forms of the British government.…Against us are the Executive, the Judiciary, two out of three branches of the legislature, all the officers of the government, all who want to be officers, all timid men who

prefer the calm of despotism to the boisterous sea of liberty, British merchants and Americans trading on British capitals, speculators and holders in the banks and public funds a contrivance invented for the purposes of corruption and for assimilating us in all things, to the rotten as well as the sound parts of the British model. It would give you a fever were I to name to you the apostates who have gone over to these heresies, men who were Samsons in the field and Solomons in the council, but who have had their heads shorn by the harlot England. In short we are likely to preserve the liberty we have obtained only by unremitting labors and perils. But we shall preserve them; and our mass of weight and wealth…is so great as to leave no danger that force will be attempted against us.[32]

This letter, which would play a controversial role in 1800, provided an overview of the theory of politics at the time of the Jay Treaty. Party discipline, as we know it today, did not exist.

As events shifted from the Jay Treaty to other spheres, the importance of Madison's role as the leader of the opposition faction cannot be better or more clearly demonstrated than in the politics that led to the selection of the presidential candidates in 1796. The nature of the election process, from a practical viewpoint, reflected the politics of "personal connexion" and friendships. This "old style" traditional school of politics had been known to Americans during the entire colonial period.

The old-style method produced the selection of a candidate by a few leaders who agreed on a man proven trustworthy and wise to the ways of the establishment. He would then be presented to the voters. No party primary, no truly open selection process for the highest office in the land existed. The nominating caucuses were closed affairs.

MONEY NOT AN ISSUE IN POLITICS

The principal qualifications demanded were not party loyalty or party obedience or ethnic balance or the amount of money a candidate could potentially raise—the kind we demand in the twenty-first century. The sole qualifications were leadership ability and experience.

There was also no provision made in the Constitution for a balanced party ticket or even for a party or a ticket. Instead each of the states was to submit a "List of all the Persons voted for" and the "Person having the greatest Number of Votes shall be the President...In every Case, after the Choice of the President, the Person having the greatest Number of Votes of the Electors shall be the Vice President."[33] The emphasis on choosing the president assumed that the two best-qualified men in the country would be chosen as the leaders.

This logic was so completely agreeable to everyone involved in politics at the time that no specific constitutional designation was made for the vice president either in 1796 or in 1800. Everyone simply assumed that the two men chosen would work in harmony for an efficient administration.

But what was even more characteristic of the traditional or old-style school of politics was the absence of candidates campaigning openly for office. Politicians "stood for office"; they did not actively seek it. The voters themselves, especially outside the few large cities, still maintained a "habit of subordination," and elites "managed political affairs."[34]

In the tradition of an aristocratic political society, the spectacle of a politician overtly grasping for power reflected a distasteful tendency to democracy, still considered a corrupt form of government. Politicians, of whatever persuasion, liked to believe that they were dignified and respectable. Thus it is not surprising that while electioneering and campaigning rarely entered the minds of the Founding Fathers, tight control, implicit in the machinery of the electoral college, was never very far in the back of their minds.

Washington's refusal to divulge his plans until late in the summer of 1796 was certainly part of his and his advisers' political strategy; but it also implied he did not believe that an extended party campaign, with contesting factions, was good for the country. His Farewell Address speaks eloquently to this point. Washington wished, as much as possible, to dampen the possibility of a virulent contest and in so doing was in accordance with the political theory of his time.

From the opposition's side, the theory was equally valid. For while Madison hinted, and then declared with certainty, the fact of Washington's retirement, he was faced with the problem of presenting a candidate who had the wisdom and the experience of an elder statesman yet, like the Cincinnatus of old, did not appear to be grasping for power.[35] Fortunately, Madison did not find this a serious problem. Jefferson, his closest friend and political mentor, was the ideal candidate. Retired from political life for two years, Jefferson had professed his intentions never to embark on the political high road again. He had written to Madison, "As to myself... my retirement from office had been meant from all office high or low, without exception....The question is forever closed with me."[36]

MADISON TRICKS JEFFERSON

But Madison was determined, and in the style of friendship and personal connection he simply plotted Jefferson's candidacy without gaining his consent. This first draft in American presidential politics was one in which the student turned the tables on the master.

For years Jefferson had been urging Madison to become the leader of the opposition, to take up his pen, plot the strategy, and finally direct the forces of republican interest. It was this elevation to the forefront of national politics that gave Madison the influence and the ability to decide Jefferson's fate.

Madison was not only cunning, he was wary. He knew of Jefferson's real sentiments; and although he was within a day's ride of Monticello, he avoided meeting with his mentor. He wrote to Monroe, "I have not seen Jefferson and have thought it best to provide him no opportunity of protesting to his friend against being embarked in the contest."[37] Knowingly then, Madison intended to hand Jefferson a fait accompli, thus revealing his acceptance of the time-worn method of selecting a candidate. For him the electoral process would proceed according to the style of politics that Virginians had practiced for generations: an agreement on a candidate from the gentry.

HAMILTON TRIES TO EXCLUDE JEFFERSON

On the other side, the forces marshaled by Hamilton assumed from the start a personal tone, which indicated that in 1796 the politics of faction would be intense. It was not that Hamilton had a particular candidate in mind; it was more that he simply believed *anybody* would be better than Jefferson: "'Tis all important to our country that his [Washington's] successor shall be a *safe* man. But it is far less important who of many men that may be named shall be the person, than that it shall not be

Jefferson....All personal and partial considerations must be discarded, and everything must give way to the great object of excluding Jefferson."[38]

In his search for a "safe" man, who would be "named," Hamilton was worried principally about protecting his system. The proof of this lies in a comment attributed to the new president-elect: "About the 22nd of December, 1796, John Adams spoke to a gentleman in Philadelphia, in these words: 'the Junto at New York have never wanted to make me President. They wish to get in Pinckney, that they may make an *automaton* of him.' At the head of this junto is Alexander Hamilton, and this is the way in which our Vice-President speaks of him."[39]

North and South the politics of faction reminded those who had witnessed the Revolution of 1776 that the same forms of protest and organization had reappeared. Historian Henry Cabot Lodge, later a US senator from Massachusetts, perceived the frustrations of the Federalists in this manner:

> Extra constitutional machinery, mass meetings of the people, semi-permanent committees of correspondence smacked of subversion and the spirit of subversion. When the Jeffersonian movement began to develop [George] Cabot recoiled from the form as well as the substance of its protest. "After all," said Cabot, "where is the boasted advantage of a representative system over the turbulent mobocracy of Athens, if the resort to popular meetings is necessary? Faction, and especially the faction of great towns always the most powerful, will be too strong for our mild and feeble government.[40]

What Lodge had clearly described, and Cabot certainly knew, were the revolutionary politics of the 1770s.

When the election was over, and Adams proved the victor, the nation breathed a sigh of relief while realizing that the flames of party spirit had been raised to a dangerously high level. One writer expressed his alarm in terms that everyone would understand: the contest had been carried on in a manner "very objectionable, and, if continued, seems in its tendency, not only calculated to foment and keep up heats and animosities amongst us, but in no long time…to overset our union, or split and shiver us into many governments; and if we once begin to divide, no one can foresee the end of it."

America, he continued, "seemed to split itself into two parties, through predilection for two citizens;…a Caesar and Pompey." Indeed, he hoped that the next contest would not even have the "appearance of countenancing parties." Then, to drive the main point home, the old revolutionary patriot addressed himself to the true spirit of the Constitution. He said, an "elector, who, antecedent to his appointment, has engaged to vote for any particular persons, sins…against the *spirit and vitals of the constitution.*"[41]

This was the accepted wisdom of the age, a realization that if the factious spirit continued it would destroy the Constitution.

Meanwhile, Jefferson continued, philosophically and practically, to see the politics of his time in the context of republicanism versus monarchy. He was still obsessed with the fear of counterrevolution and a reversal of those principles established in the Revolution of 1776.

His faith in the future of American independence oscillated wildly between extremes of optimism and pessimism. Thus he wrote to Aaron Burr in June, describing his lost hopes that the nation would have avoided the strife of faction. They had instead been "duped" into supporting the British faction in the executive. Indeed, Jefferson even wondered if the power of the revolutionary republican ideology was strong enough to overcome the spirit of faction and preserve the republic: "[If] you can give me a comfortable solution of them, it will relieve a mind devoted to the preservation of our republican government in the true form and spirit in which it was established, but almost oppressed with apprehensions that fraud will at length effect what force could not, and that what with currents and countercurrents, we shall in the end be driven back to the land from which we launched twenty years ago."[42]

Burr knew exactly what the old patriot wanted to hear because in his reply he suggested, "the moment requires free communication among those who adhere to the principles of our revolution."[43] This exchange between the two set the stage, as it were, for the great debate that would take place in 1800: the principles of republicanism and their preservation as the principal theme.

Jefferson would mention it time and time again, until, in the full splendor of his accession to power, he believed that that preservation had become a reality. When he had written his letter to Burr, however, his mind had been filled with doubt. One of his last lines had been totally pessimistic: "Indeed, my dear Sir, we have been but as a sturdy fish on the hook of a dexterous angler, who letting us flounce till we have spent our force, brings us up at last."[44] The "angler" was Hamilton and his British faction; and Jefferson, his optimism failing, had expressed his apprehension that the angler's counterrevolution would culminate in the restoration of the British monarchy of 1775.

Despite good intentions, however, the spirit of party and faction continued to intrude on the life of the vice president. After the publication of the Mazzei letter, Jefferson warned one of his correspondents in a special postscript: "Take care that nothing from my letter gets into the newspapers."[45] To another he imparted, "The hostile use which is made of whatever can be laid hold of of mine, obliges me to caution the friends to whom I write, never to let my letters go out of their own hands lest they should get into the newspapers."[46] It is painfully obvious that Jefferson was doing everything in his power to dampen the spirit of party, to add nothing to its fuel.

EVEN THE SYMBOLS OF MONARCHY ARE A DANGER TO THE REPUBLIC

This was one style of factional politics, and sometimes Jefferson rejected it. His reaction to the Hamilton faction ran in a somewhat different pattern. Unwilling to make his objections public, he complained to a few trusted friends, placing his comments in the context of conspiracy: "They are endeavoring to submit us to the substance as they already have to the *forms,* of the British government…the birthdays, levees, processions to Parliament, inauguration pomposities, etc."[47]

Indeed these were the symbols of monarchy that had become accepted by the Adams administration. They contradicted the republican simplicity that Jefferson wished to preserve to prevent the people from being overawed by their government. This reverence for plainness and simplicity was at the heart of Jefferson's understanding of the ethos of republicanism. And it was from this perspective that he was unable to hide his contempt for any executive who surrounded himself with the trappings of royalty and the equivalent of palace guards.

In terms of the natural divisions of Congress in 1797–98, it is clear that those which applied in 1787, during the debates over the Constitution, were, for many, still in force. Jefferson's comments on the origins of party and faction make perfectly clear his views on their significance and what they were doing to the republic:

> It is true that a party has risen up among us, or rather has come among us, which is endeavoring to separate us from all friendly connections with France, to unite our destinies with those of Great Britain, and to assimilate our government to theirs....large importations of British merchants and factors, by American merchants dealing on British capital, and by stockdealers and banking companies, who by the aid of a paper system are enriching themselves to the ruin of our country, and swaying the government by their possession of the printing presses, which their wealth commands,... not always honorable to the character of our countrymen. Hitherto their influence and their system has been irresistible, and they have raised up an Executive power which is too strong for the legislature. But I flatter myself they have passed their zenith.[48]

Whoever opposed Hamilton's factional policies was a "Jacobin," and the charge was made with effect. Eleven months later Jefferson was complaining, "Those [members of Congress] who have no wish but for the peace of their country, and its independence of all foreign influence, have a hard struggle indeed, overwhelmed by a cry as loud and imposing as if it were true, of being under French influence, and this raised by a faction composed of English subjects residing among us, or such as are English in all their relations and sentiments."[49]

When Madison retired as the leader of the opposition, Albert Gallatin took his place and the fortunes of republicanism began to decline. Illness and a paucity of speakers for the opposition caused Gallatin to say, "Our side of the House is so extremely weak in speakers and in men of business that...[George] Nicholas and myself must stay, and at all events be ready to give our support on the floor to those measures upon which the political salvation of the Union may perhaps eventually depend."[50]

Gallatin apparently believed that the pressures against the opposition had reached such heights that the future of the republic was at stake. This period of demoralization was during the XYZ Affair, the time when French diplomat Charles Maurice de Talleyrand-Périgord had imposed a number of insults on the American representatives. The reaction in America was to solidify favorable opinion of the administration and, equally, to change en masse the population's ideas about the French Revolution.

Events had changed dramatically in less than eight months. In June 1797 Jefferson had been guardedly optimistic regarding America's relations with the French republic. He had written to Madison that "nothing less than the miraculous string of events which have taken place, to wit... bankruptcy of England, mutiny in her fleet, and King's writing letters recommending peace, could have cooled the fury of the British faction. Even all that will not prevent considerable efforts still in both parties to show our teeth to France."[51] It was a prophetic letter, for with the coming of the XYZ Affair, the "British faction" and the rise of party strife would reach unprecedented heights.

In this rise of the politics of faction, Madison, like Jefferson, saw the possibilities of counterrevolution. Obviously, they believed that the British faction had gained such control that it might totally alter the principles of the government. In fact, Jefferson mentioned to Burr in June, "I consider the future character of our republic as in the air."[52]

THE MILITARY PERCEIVED AS A THREAT

In the second session, Congress passed a law for a provisional army, debated going to war with France[53] while suspending trade with that country, and made provisions for a department and secretary of the navy.[54] The consequences of these bills, especially their tone, caused Jefferson to write Edmund Pendleton: "The present period...is the most eventful ever known since that of 1775, and will decide whether the principles established by that contest are to prevail, or give way to those they subverted."[55]

These foreign measures, however, would be paled into insignificance by the domestic bills passed. Jefferson knew that the prohibitions against preparations for "war measures *externally*" meant "consenting to every rational measure of *internal* defence and preparation." This, of course, would provide one party the excuse "to make it [the military] a new source of patronage and expense."[56] To Jefferson it all appeared to be in the tradition of the British system of corruption.

During the last week of April, Jefferson, as the presiding officer of the Senate, got wind of the "war party" intentions, "in a fit of unguarded passion...[to] pass a citizen bill, an alien bill, and a sedition bill." The alien bill would be proposed in hopes of reaching Albert Gallatin, the peerless leader in the House.[57] The sedition bill had as its object "the suppression of the Whig presses," and Jefferson added, "[Richard] Bache's has been particularly named."

HAMILTON AS THE FIRST GENERAL IN AMERICA

Nothing could now ease Jefferson's apprehension. Hamilton had been named the third-leading military figure in America, behind Generals Henry Knox and Charles Pinckney. And though Washington was still nominally the commander in chief, it was acknowledged by everyone that he was too feeble to take the field. The responsibility would therefore fall on Hamilton, and neither Jefferson nor Madison believed that this line of succession had occurred accidentally.

Adams evidently believed that he had made the appointment only under pressure from Washington. In his official correspondence to the secretary of war, Adams wrote, "There has been too much intrigue in this business with General Washington and me."[58] The fear among the opposition was that Washington's commission was merely window dressing and that in the event of an emergency he would sound the alarm and then step aside for Hamilton.

For some—those who knew their English history—the fear was even greater. As George Nicholas put it:

> [In England c. 1660] Fairfax was the commander in chief of the army; he was a successful and popular general, and a virtuous man. He was kept in office until the plans of those who meditated a change in the government, were ripe for execution. They knew that he would never consent to that change, and the command of the army was then put into other hands...What has happened, may happen again; and when we are calculating on its probability, we should recollect,

that the monarchy-loving Hamilton is now so fixed, as to be able, with *one step,* to fill the place of our present commander in chief.[59]

This fear was seen not only by George Nicholas, a friend of Jefferson's and Madison's and a fervent republican philosopher; it was corroborated years later by none other than John Adams himself:

> The British faction was determined to have a war with France, and Alexander Hamilton at the head of the army and *then* Pres. of the United States. Peace with France was therefore *treason* against their fundamental maxims and reasons of State…These were their motives, and they exhausted all their wit in studies and labours to defeat the whole design. A war with France, an alliance with England, and Alexander Hamilton the father of their speculating systems, at the head of our army and the state, were their hobby-horse, their vision of sovereign felicity.[60]

Opposition to the alien and sedition bills occurred almost immediately, and Adams, as the symbolic head of the country, was confronted with the younger generation, protesting and demonstrating against his repressive legislation.

MADISON QUESTIONS ADAMS'S PRINCIPLES

James Madison too, outraged at least as much as the young people, registered his anger against the president. By the time he ended his letter, he had brought into question Adams's republican principles, even linking him with the ever-present potential for counterrevolution:

> Every answer he gives to his addressers, unmasks more and more his principles and views. His language to the young men at Pha. is the most abominable and degrading that could fall from the lips of the first magistrate of an independent people, and particularly from a Revolutionary patriot. It throws some light on his meaning when he remarked to me, "that there was not a single principle the same in the American and French Revolutions," and on my alluding to the contrary sentiment of his predecessor expressed to [Pierre-Auguste] Adet on the presentment of the Colours, added, "that it was false let who would express it." The abolition of Royalty was it seems not one of his Revolutionary principles.[61]

In addition to the Alien and Sedition Acts, the administration passed a land tax, proposed a snuff tax and a carriage tax, and seemed to be preparing the way for a salt tax. Madison, whose pristine republicanism as well as his notion of sound politics was opposed in principle to almost any kind of taxation, wondered how the administration—intent on disrupting French-American commerce—expected the average citizen to pay. His contempt for the administration and Adams took on a sinister tone.

Clearly, Madison believed that the train of legislation passed by the new administration was a blatant appeal to party violence. Adams, he believed, had gone berserk: "He is verifying completely the last feature in the character drawn of him by Dr. F. [Franklin], however his title may stand to the two first. 'Always an honest man, often a wise one, but sometimes wholly out of his senses.'"[62]

MADISON SEES POWER CONCENTRATING IN THE GOVERNMENT AS DANGEROUS

What Madison had concluded, and rather vehemently, was that the politics of faction had, by mid-1798, blurred the separation of powers. Control of the legislature by a vengeful faction had taken place; and with a sympathetic executive, they were capable of any violation of the Constitution. Not surprisingly, this was, at least in theory, the culmination of the politics of faction.

The "profound scholar and politician" of the Constitutional Convention began to see events taking the worst possible turn. Within the next six months, the rage of party and the spirit of faction would descend on the republic.

As 1799 appeared, the nation saw and heard its writers and orators proclaiming "disaster lay ahead" if the spirit of party continued unabated. Even the Almanac for 1799 predicted disaster: "On the 10th of October next, a portentous comet (which with fear of change perplexes) will approach our political hemisphere; and if it cross upon us at the same instant as the Bulam fever, the Lord have mercy on us!"[63]

New Englanders as well as Southerners reviled against party and faction. The Reverend Azel Backus thundered in his denunciation of the "wiles of faction, these depths of Satan" in the same spirit that he might have spoken of John Calvin's theory of predestination: "The perfection of a government will not save it from the evils of faction and party spirit."[64]

The implication was clear: when factions arose, the republic was inevitably doomed; and those who promoted faction and party, being equivalent to the devil, should be banished to hell.

Jedidiah Morse was more succinct regarding the political theory of his time: "A spirit of *insubordination to civil authority* is another vice which has endangered the existence of our government. Having a constitution and rulers of our own choice...there cannot be even a plausible reason alleged to justify disrespect and disobedience." He concluded, "*Faction has been bold and open-mouthed!*"[65]

These sentiments were merely reflections of a generally accepted view of civil society. Many commentators saw, amid the danger, a necessity to make a plea for unity while at the same time excoriating factions and their behavior. Generally speaking, they did not believe in an opposition party and felt that the promoters of party should be silenced. This certainly was the rationale behind the Alien and Sedition Acts.

As opposition to the administration became widespread, as the possibility of war with France heightened, as the outline of a concerted movement of factions and parties became obvious, the rhetoric of those who opposed party shifted from an emphasis on administration to an emphasis on the Constitution. A writer, calling himself "A Friend to the Constitution," declared,

> that spirit of party which generally animates an opposition, is no longer allowable when ceasing to be a mere opposition, it has become the government of the country, and has acquired the power of dictating the measures of the nation....There is much danger of being still actuated by the spirit of revenge; by the spirit of party rather than that of the nation. To guard against this danger, which in republics has often produced such calamities, *which has seldom been more imminent than in the present moment,* all those who love real liberty ought, unmindful of former distinctions or animosities, to rally together round the standard of the constitution.[66]

This shift in focus, from merely denouncing party to an argument that linked party to the certain destruction of the Constitution and the federal Union, contained a new dimension.

The analyses that developed from 1799 onward began to speculate on the potential for revolution in America. The argument that revolution was the inevitable result of faction and party maturing in the body politic became standard fare for almost everyone who commented on the political scene.

The suspicions and fears manufactured on both sides during the years leading up to 1800 were summarized by an "Impartial Citizen":

> When this idea [of party] is properly examined, it will appear to be quite unnatural to our systems of civil government, and *derogatory to all the principles, which have been advanced, in order to maintain our late glorious revolution.* It will appear to be a legitimate offspring of that tyranny which has so often deluged the world in blood. It is introduced at no other door, than that, which opens to receive the dangerous charge against the people of America, that they are incapable of preserving and enjoying a free government.[67]

The belief that revolution was in the air went beyond New England ministers and permeated the remaining states in the Union. Even in far-off Europe, the rumors of revolution had circulated in the newspapers and the dinner conversations of diplomats. In mid-1798 John Quincy Adams wrote to his mother that "*a paragraph in the* Moniteur...*says the friends of liberty* in the United States, supported by a great part of the House of Representatives, will probably not wait for the next elections, but in the mean time will destroy the fatal influence of the President and Senate *by a Revolution*."[68]

As we review these statements on the possibility of revolution, it is natural to recall Jefferson's remark immediately before the outbreak of the French Revolution: "All the world is run politically mad. Men, women, children talk nothing else."[69] A similar statement could have been made by Jefferson beginning in 1798–99. Indeed it appeared to contemporaries that a revolutionary course of events was overtaking America. Porcupine spoke for many during the quasi-war with France:

Above all, the alliance with Great Britain would cut up the French faction here. It is my sincere opinion, that they have formed the *diabolical plan of revolutionizing* (to use one of their execrable terms) the whole continent of America. They have their agents and partisans without number, and very often where we do not imagine. Their immoral and blasphemous principles have made a most alarming progress. They have explored the country to its utmost boundaries and its inmost recesses, and have left a partisan on every spot, ready to preach up *the holy right of insurrection.*[70]

ALMOST EVERYONE FEARS REVOLUTION

As we have seen, this was an almost universal sentiment. Poets, lawyers, doctors, diplomats, ministers, newspaper editors, farmers, politicians—men of every walk and run of life—saw the rise of faction and party strife surging toward one major catastrophic event. The sheer volume of such statements in the literature of the period, plus their intensity, indicates that their fears and concerns were genuine.

The real terror of faction these men experienced cannot be dismissed with the trite label "emotionalism," as has been done so frequently because their expressions did not fit into a neat pattern of a modern party structure. The fact is, their eighteenth-century historical perspective—the only one they could have known at the time—told them that the politics of faction was a prelude to revolution and, perhaps, anarchy. This was the familiar pattern the violence of faction had blocked out through history.

TERRORISM GRIPS THE MINDS OF THOSE IN POWER

Using this frame of reference, John Adams, in an argument with Jefferson, gives eloquent testimony to his genuine fears of terror and its relationship to party. In a letter to Jefferson, he describes party's vitiating influence on the body politic. He despairs of ever making himself "understood by Posterity." Yet, if the foregoing analysis has been at all successful, the reader by now should have little trouble sharing Adams's anxiety as he describes the nation tottering on the brink of disaster throughout most of the turbulent years we have examined:

I proceed to the order of the day, which is the terrorism of a former day....Upon this Subject I despair of making myself understood by Posterity, by the present Age, and even by you. To collect and arrange the documents illustrative of it, would require as many Lives as those of a Cat. You never felt the Terrorism of Chaises Rebellion in Massachusetts. I believe you never felt the Terrorism of [Albert] Gallatin's Insurrection in Pennsylvania: you certainly never realized the Terrorism of Fries's, most outrageous Riot and Rescue, as I call it, Treason, Rebellion as the World and the great Judges and two Juries pronounced it. You certainly never felt the Terrorism, excited by [Edmund] Genet, in 1793, when ten thousand People in the Streets of Philadelphia, day by day, threatened to drag Washington out of his House, and effect a Revolution in the Government, or compell it to declare War in favour of the French Revolution, and against England. The coolest and the firmest Minds, even among the Quakers...have given their opinions to me, that nothing but the yellow Fever...could have saved the United States from a total Revolution of Government. I have no doubt you was fast asleep in philosophical Tranquility, when ten thousand People, and perhaps many more, were parading the Streets of Philadelphia, on the Evening of my Fast Day. When even Governor [Thomas] Mifflin himself, thought it his Duty to order a Patrol of Horse And Foot to preserve the peace, when Markett Street was as full as Men could Stand by one another, and even before my Door; when Some of my Domesticks in Phrenzy, determined to Sacrifice their Lives in my defence; when all were ready to make a desperate Salley among the multitude, and others were with difficulty and danger dragged back by the others; when I myself judged it prudent and necessary to order Chests of Arms from the War Office to be brought through bye Lanes and back Doors: determined to defend my House at the Expense of my Life, and the Lives of the few, very few Domesticks and Friends within it. What think you of Terrorism, Mr. Jefferson? Shall I investigate the Causes, the Motives, the Incentives of these Terrorisms?...But above all; Shall I request you, to collect the circular Letters from Members of Congress in the middle and southern States to their Constituents? I would give all I am worth for a compleat Collection of all those circular Letters.[71]

In John Adams's mind, his recollections of terrorism were overwhelming. The desire for the "circular Letters" recalled to him the revolutionary impact he believed those documents had. They were the evidence he longed for to prove his case that party was synonymous with terrorism.

His assessment, moreover, leaves little doubt as to the historical perspective he places on the idea of party. In the end, speaking as an old patriot, the repository of American ideals, Adams expressed his sovereign contempt for those who would corrupt the election process in the pursuit of power. And there can be little doubt that Jefferson, Madison, Monroe, and every man of quality would have agreed.

Adams's brief survey of the old-style politics and the terror of party places this chapter's analysis of the politics of faction in perspective. In conclusion, one cannot help seeing through these statements of the most prominent men of the age—America's age of democratic revolutions—that the politics of faction and party were the most hated, detested, and feared phenomena of their times.

Thus, if we are to comprehend the meaning of Jefferson's Revolution of 1800 and its importance in the future struggles for power in America, we must view the politics of faction as the key to understanding the next stage of America's historical development: the politics of revolution.

The Kentucky and Virginia Resolutions and Threats to the First Amendment

There is in these States a faction, a numerous and desperate faction, resolved on the overthrow of the Federal Government; and the man who will not allow that there is danger to be apprehended, is either too great a fool to perceive it, or too great a coward to encounter it.

— *Porcupine's Gazette, 1799*

B Y MID-1798 THE FEDERALISTS AND JOHN ADAMS'S ADMINISTRA-tion had reached the high-water mark of their popularity. Bathed in the glow of the XYZ Affair and the enthusiastic support that incident created, the Hamiltonians and the supporters of John Adams combined to pursue a plan that, considered in its entirety, appeared threatening to anyone who opposed a consolidation of power in the national government.

A navy department had been established, the army had been expanded, a direct tax law had been passed, Hamilton was appointed inspector general of the United States Army, government loans to support the military were announced, and finally, the Naturalization Act of 1798 and the Alien Act were passed, so it was thought, to intimidate the most vocal opponents of the administration.

This spate of legislation was climaxed by a Sedition Act, which, designed to curtail the opposition presses, raised the specter of an attack on the Constitution and the fundamental liberties of the country.

The Alien and Sedition Acts were perhaps the most important bills of the Adams administration if for no other reason than that they set the tone of politics for the next two years. And because they constituted a threat to the First Amendment freedoms and constitutionalism per se, they set in motion a chain of events that consolidated opposition to the administration.

LINKING TAXES WITH THE REVOLUTION AGAINST ENGLAND

One of the most significant features of the events of July 1798 was the imposition of direct taxes by the federal government. Because the power of direct taxation was considered a primary source of revenue by the states, and because every state had a tradition of internal taxation that had begun in the colonial era, they were naturally unwilling to allow the national government to use that power. In their own experience they knew that the power to tax was the power to destroy.

And in 1798 the power of the federal government to augment its revenues beyond import duties was not universally acknowledged. Indeed, Hamilton had scrupulously avoided mentioning any such intention at the Constitutional Convention and attempted to allay all fears that the national government would impose any direct taxes on property and land.[1]

The Acts for the Assessment and Collection of a Direct Tax on Lands, Houses and Slaves passed by Congress on July 9 and 14, 1798, were thus viewed with considerable apprehension in the rural areas of the country. Alexander Graydon placed the tax issue in perspective by saying that the new taxes on houses and lands smacked of the Stamp Act: "It was a Stamp Act that first excited our displeasure with the mother country: the very name of an excise was hateful to freemen."

In Pennsylvania, which was shortly to experience a tax rebellion, Graydon reported, "the federalists…were as tyrannical as she [Great Britain] had been, and that this tax upon farms, houses and *windows*, was but the beginning of a system, which would soon extend to everything; and that we should have at length a tax on horses, wagons and ploughs." Indeed, thirty years later, Graydon stated unequivocally that "the tax on real property was the fatal blow to federalism in Pennsylvania."[2]

Jefferson knew his constituency in the southern states and especially their reluctance to pay taxes of any kind. He also suspected that the dissatisfaction would extend from Virginia to Pennsylvania and as far north as Massachusetts.

RESISTANCE TO TAXES
IS AN AMERICAN TRADITION

Jefferson's concerns were not without foundation. To collect the taxes, the federal government had to assemble in each state a vast bureaucracy of assessors plus their assistants, surveyors, commissioners, and collectors. This task force would be compounded by a national level of bureaucracy to supervise and enforce the collections. For example, in Pennsylvania alone there were 9 commissioners, 41 principal assessors, 420 assistant assessors, 4 inspectors of the revenue, 39 supervisors of the collection, 14 surveyors of the revenue, and 25 collectors—all working to execute the new tax law.[3]

As Jefferson intuited, resistance to these laws would be spontaneous and overwhelming. In Pennsylvania, Fries's Rebellion broke out in February 1799 against those who attempted to enforce the new tax law. Liberty poles sprang up over the countryside, and farmers as well as townsmen attended meetings dressed in the uniform of the Continental army and bearing arms.[4]

Nearly the same conditions applied in many other parts of the country. Little revenue was collected in the southern states of North and South Carolina, Kentucky, and Tennessee; and in western Pennsylvania the collectors never met their quotas. In the northern part of the country, Massachusetts Federalist Fisher Ames saw this resistance as potentially revolutionary: "All forces, all revenue is viewed by the factious as the power of a foe, and therefore they will try to strip the government of both, but it must have both or be a victim to the faction; and if our people cannot be brought to bear necessary taxes, and to maintain so small a force as our army, they are (and I am afraid they are) unfit for independent government."[5]

Ames, examining the government's efforts to collect taxes from a perspective of nearly two years, may have been right but for the wrong reasons. The fact that the resistance, apart from Fries's Rebellion, was not overt meant that the change was taking place in people's minds.

The conduct of the army produced outrages that were reported throughout the country. The consequence was that more animus was directed against the federal government than against those who refused to pay their taxes. Two editors, Jacob Schneider and William Duane, the latter editor of the *Aurora,* were severely beaten by the soldiers. This caused the president to write later that the "army was as unpopular, as if it had been a ferocious wild beast let loose upon the nation to devour it. In newspapers, in pamphlets, and in common conversation they were called cannibals. A thousand anecdotes, true or false, of their licentiousness, were propagated and believed."[6]

ALIEN AND SEDITION LAWS
IMMEDIATELY RAISE OPPOSITION

Passed nearly simultaneously with the tax law were the Alien and Sedition Laws. The timing of their passage more than added to the uncertainty and the suspicion of many citizens toward the federal government. In the minds of many, the two laws even raised the specter of a conspiracy against the Constitution. And their immediate effect was to polarize the national legislature.

In many states, arguments over the constitutionality of these bills became not only heated but to many the only important topics of discussion. Thus, when the Sedition Act was linked with the Alien Act, Jefferson became truly alarmed. "Both," he wrote to James Madison, "are so palpably in the teeth of the Constitution as to show they [the extremist faction] mean to pay no respect to it."[7]

The Alien Act conferred upon the president the power to remove aliens from the United States, to imprison or fine them, or both. Thus an alien who was deported as a result of the president's personal decision would be deprived of a trial by jury and his fundamental rights under the Constitution. Although the Alien Act was directed against a limited number of persons, it nevertheless caused many to become suspicious about the administration's intentions.

The Sedition Act was considered more dangerous, and therefore more volatile, than the Alien Act. Under it the federal government intended to punish any combination or conspiracy against itself with a punishment of six months' to five years' imprisonment and a fine of

$5,000. The law also gave authority to the government to punish anyone for "seditious writings." These included any writings that might, in the eyes of the administration, be "false, scandalous, and malicious" against the president, Congress, or the government. This charge was punishable "by a fine of $2,000 and imprisonment not exceeding two years." Thus while the Alien Act "was made contingent upon a declaration of war," the Sedition Act was designed "to deal with domestic political opposition in time of peace."[8]

The Sedition Law, many felt, plainly violated the First Amendment to the Constitution.

In effect, Adams and his administration were attempting to "chill" the presses.

USING A LAW TO PERPETUATE A FACTION IN POWER

Albert Gallatin, sensing this, revealed the administration's blatant use of propaganda in a speech on the floor of the House. The purpose of the bill, he said, was "to enable one part to oppress the other....Is it not their object to frighten and suppress all presses which they consider as contrary to their views; to prevent a free circulation of opinion; to suffer the people at large to hear only partial accounts, and but one side of the question; to delude and deceive them by partial information and through these means to perpetuate themselves in power?[9]

Gallatin's alarm was shared by more than a few of his fellow republicans. Jefferson saw the bill not only in terms of dividing the state legislatures but as a conspiracy against the Constitution:

> The XYZ fever has considerably abated through the country, as I am informed, and the Alien and Sedition Laws are working hard. I fancy that some of the State legislatures will take strong ground on this occasion. For my own part, I consider those laws as merely an experiment on the American mind, to see how far it will bear an avowed violation of the Constitution.[10]

When the Adams administration passed the infamous Alien and Sedition Laws in 1798, there were few men who foresaw their catalytic nature for the political upheaval that was to follow. Hamilton, who would later attempt to use the bills for his own ends, saw the consequences immediately.

Hamilton wrote to Oliver Wolcott, referring to the Sedition Law:

> I have this moment seen a bill brought into the Senate, entitled, "A Bill to define more particularly the crime of Treason etc." There are provisions in this bill, which, according to a cursory view, appear to me highly exceptionable, and such as, more than any thing else, may endanger civil war....I hope, sincerely, the thing may not be hurried through. *Let us not establish a tyranny.* Energy is a very different thing from violence. If we make no false step, we shall be essentially united; but if we push things to an extreme, we shall then give to faction *body* and solidity.[11]

Accepting the basic premise of the Sedition Law, Hamilton had, in a flash of insight, seen the danger as well as the opportunity within it. For whether pretended, imagined, manufactured, or real, the uproar surrounding the passage and the enforcement of that bill sounded an alarm that reverberated throughout the nation.

THE FIRST MENTION OF "SECESSION"

Only a few weeks before Hamilton counseled caution to his own faction, Jefferson had recorded in a highly conjectural letter an observation by John Taylor of Caroline that it would not be "unwise now to estimate the separate mass of Virginia and North Carolina, with a view to their separate existence."[12]

This was strong language; moreover, its main point—a theoretical one—indicated a willingness on the part of Taylor to destroy the Union. It is also implied that Taylor—one of Jefferson's closest friends and a brilliant constitutional theorist—had concluded that the extremists in power were willing to test the limits of the Union, to raise the violence of faction, and even precipitate a constitutional crisis, thus compelling the opposition to resort to "scission."

Assessing this grim situation, Jefferson prepared to meet the crisis in a truly revolutionary way. Working in complete secrecy, and collaborating with his closest friend, he drafted the Kentucky Resolutions sometime between July 21 and October 26, 1798.[13] His state of mind, responsible for the tone of the Kentucky Resolutions, can be seen in a letter written during those days when he was mulling over the substance and the style of that document. Referring to the Alien and Sedition Laws, Jefferson wrote: "If this goes down, we shall immediately see attempted another act of Congress, declaring that the President shall continue in office during life, reserving to another occasion the transfer of the succession to his heirs, and the establishment of the Senate for life."[14]

Goaded by fears of conspiracy, Jefferson wrote a series of resolutions that, if passed by a state legislature, would dramatize the crisis.

THE COMPACT THEORY REVOLUTIONIZES THE CONSTITUTION

These resolutions became known as the Kentucky Resolutions. Jefferson's logic, contained within the draft, was a dialectical approach to the Constitution. It gave rise to a novel theory that the states had "*by compact* under the style and title of a Constitution for the United States, and of amendments thereto…constituted a general Government for special purposes—delegated to that Government certain definite powers, reserving, each State to itself, the residuary mass of right to their own self-government; and that whensoever the general Government assumes undelegated powers, its acts are unauthoritative, void, and of no force."[15]

Jefferson was attempting here to place the focus of debate on the Constitution itself and not on the government's ability or right to construe, interpret, or assume powers from it. The same logic would follow in the Virginia Resolutions. Hence, Jefferson and Madison were both attempting to deny any construction or interpretation of the Constitution by the general government. Indeed, if there was to be any interpretation, it would be done by the states, for "each party [state] has an equal right to judge for itself, as well as infractions as of the mode and measure of redress."

This approach, if successful, would have curtailed the power of the national government and prevented any future expansion of power, especially at the expense of the states. So far as the controversy over the Alien Law was concerned, Jefferson's approach provided an example. The fourth resolution claimed it would have made "an act concerning aliens… altogether void and of no force."

USING PRINCIPLES AND RESOLUTIONS
TO AVOID ARMED CONFLICT

These arguments, we must note, were cast as "principles" in the resolutions. The reason for this was that no definite plan of *immediate* practical action was contemplated. Their main purpose contained within the third resolution was to stimulate *reflection* on the basic freedoms guaranteed by the Constitution, especially those contained within the First Amendment.

Other resolutions called attention to the Alien and Sedition Acts, the act against bank frauds, and the combination of powers vested in the president by these bills. In this manner the Kentucky Resolutions called attention to the republicans' major philosophical and constitutional concerns. The purpose of these resolutions, moreover, revealed a basic union between theory and practice in Jefferson's strategy: he was essentially beginning, for very practical reasons, a debate on the principles of constitutionalism.

Within the Kentucky Resolutions, Jefferson took extreme care to delineate *principles* of fundamental revolutionary importance. One was the right not only of the states but *of the people* to make decisions regarding the national government and the use of its power. Throughout the resolutions the term *the States, or to the people* recurs again and again. Jefferson wished the people to realize that the ultimate power in a republic lay with them and not with the government. This was consistent with his republican ideology.

According to that ideology, the people cannot divest themselves of their authority, and no governmental or legislative body can usurp it. It therefore would remain a reservoir of strength—a final appeal against tyranny and the force of government.

APPEAL OF THE NATURAL-RIGHT
THEORY FOR LIMITED GOVERNMENT

Another principle lay in Jefferson's urging the "co-states" to turn to "their natural right" in the event of disagreement with the general government on "cases not made federal." Jefferson's use of the natural-right argument against everything not delegated specifically to the federal government meant almost everything that the general government was doing.

By invoking the natural-right doctrine, he hoped the states would "concur in declaring these acts void and of no force."

It was not difficult to imagine what would follow if and when such a collision took place. The fact that the resolutions ended on a proper constitutional note (i.e., each "state requesting repeal at the next session of Congress" of the oppressive legislation) did not disguise the dialectical nature of Jefferson's ideas.

Once a citizen admitted the unconstitutionality of the Alien and Sedition Laws and then accepted the original compact theory, there was no middle ground. A citizen was either in favor of preserving the Constitution and the idea of limited government, or he must accept the growth of government's power ad infinitum.

The ninth, or final, resolution added to the dialogue the proper Socratic note that Jefferson had in mind. He purposely stated "that this Commonwealth does therefore call on its co-States for an expression of their sentiments on the acts concerning Aliens, and for the punishment of certain crimes herein before specified, plainly declaring whether these acts are or not authorized by the Federal Compact?"

The method was clear. Jefferson hoped to have a friend of republicanism introduce that question in the legislature of every state, distribute to the people printed copies of the debates in their legislatures, and print copies of the original records in the newspapers and pamphlets of all the states. The method followed was identical to that of the colonists in the 1770s and echoed precisely John Adams's prescription for revolution in America.

CONSTITUTIONAL PRINCIPLES STATED AS AN IDEA OF REVOLUTION

Through his authorship of the compact theory, Jefferson was attempting nothing less than a revival, *in principle*, of the Spirit of '76. In fact, the very day after their passage, November 16, and before a messenger could have physically conveyed the news to Monticello, he wrote to Madison the following: "I inclose you a copy of the draught of the Kentucky resolves. I think we should distinctly affirm all the important principles they contain, so as to hold to that ground in future, and leave the matter in such a train as that we may not be committed absolutely to push the matter to extremities, and yet may be free to *push as far as events will render prudent.*"[16]

Not only was the method clear but the reasoning was also: Jefferson had, in the midst of crisis, unleashed a powerful force in society. It was an *idea of resistance,* peaceful and constitutional in nature but profoundly revolutionary in purpose. And it was an idea that could be developed practically and prudently to a full revolutionary potential. In retrospect, Jefferson along with Madison had put together the first building blocks of a revolution.

As Jefferson sat brooding atop his little hill in the Virginia mountains, a new strategy began to unfold. About this time the most able republicans began writing long tracts dealing with the nature of the Constitution, expounding its principles, and attempting, in short, to make people realize that for the Constitution to be meaningful and preserve liberty it must be maintained in its purity. This, the republican strategists concluded, was the only way they could arouse public opinion.

DEFINING OPPOSITION TO STIMULATE PUBLIC DEBATE

By the second week in December, the Kentucky Resolutions had taken effect, and in Virginia the state legislature began debating its own version of the constitutionality of the Alien and Sedition Laws. As Jefferson's strategy trickled down to the county level, a fever of resolutions began to heat up the political tempo of the state.

These resolutions quickly found their way to other parts of the country in leaflets and newspapers. But the dynamic effect of the opposition's pamphlets provoked a reaction. Journalists sympathetic to the administration's policies reacted hysterically to the Kentucky statement then being printed all over the country. Peter Porcupine even made a prediction of revolution: "Now the crisis is advancing. The abandoned faction, devoted to France, have long been conspiring, and their conspiracy is at last brought near to an explosion. I have not the least doubt but they have fifty thousand men, provided with arms, in Pennsylvania alone. If vigorous measures are not taken; if the provisional army is not raised without delay, *a civil war, or a surrender of independence is not at more than a twelvemonth's distance.*"[17]

The ministry also believed that a moment of crisis had arrived. One New England minister, Jedidiah Morse, had exclaimed in April, "That our present situation is uncommonly critical and perilous, all persons of reflection agree." Hinting at the possibility of full-scale rebellion, he left no doubt as to where the revolutionary conspiracy derived its strength. It was Virginia. Then, alluding to the notorious society of the Illuminati, he said, in phrases that would become familiar to Americans nearly a century and a half later. "I have now in my possession complete and indubitable proof that such societies do exist…in the United States. I have, my brethren, an official, authenticated list of names, ages, places of nativity, professions, etc. of the officers and members of a Society of the Illuminati…consisting of *one hundred* members instituted in Virginia, by the Grand Orient of France. This society has a deputy, whose name is on the list, who resides at the mother Society in France, to communicate from thence all needful information and instruction."[18]

The ferment brought the Hamiltonians to attention. Hamilton wrote to Harrison Gray Otis that "with a view to the possibility of internal disorders alone" the army ought to be brought up to its "authorized force." He also suggested that "the act respecting the eighty thousand militia ought likewise to be revived." Thus, for Hamilton, the standing army was not enough. "In these precarious times," he asserted, the government should be "armed with the whole of the force which has been voted."[19] Hamilton was obviously worried about resistance.

CAN PRESIDENTS PROCLAIM DIVINE RIGHT?

John Taylor of Caroline, who introduced the resolutions, began his commentary against the Alien and Sedition Laws by asserting starkly: "Liberty was in danger…and every effort should be made to repel attempts to subvert it." He observed, "If once we were to permit executive power to overleap its limits, where was it to stop? And, if the executive branch exercised powers not bestowed, it overleaped the Constitution."

Taylor estimated that together the two laws were "destructive of the most essential human rights." As to the "probable effects of those laws," he believed that "they would establish executive influence, *and executive influence would produce a* REVOLUTION."

The great constitutional scholar then pointed to the immediate danger to liberty. The combined effect of these laws would beget "fear." And, "if public opinion were to be directed by government by means of fines, penalties and punishments, on the one hand, and patronage on the other, public opinion itself would be made the stepping stone for usurpation.... *The most dangerous effect of those laws would be the abolition of the right to examine public servants.*"[20]

A General Equates the Virginia Resolutions with Revolution

From the Federalist point of view, the Virginia Assembly was promoting actual revolution.

General Henry Lee, on the anti-republican side, complained that the resolutions "struck him as recommending resistance. They [the resolutions] declared the laws null and void. Our citizens thus thinking, would disobey the laws. This disobedience would be patronised by the State, and could not be submitted to by the United States. Insurrection would be the consequence. We have had one insurrection lately, and that without the patronage of the legislature. How much more likely might an insurrection happen, which seemed to be advised by the Assembly?"[21]

A Politician Sees Monarchy Ahead

James Barbour, Madison's cohort and a future senator, "believed…that in [these debates on the Alien and Sedition Acts]…might be read the destinies of America….For should so important a state as Virginia sanction the measures complained of…it would become a step-stone to further usurpation, until those great rights, which are guaranteed by nature and the Constitution, will be destroyed one by one, and a monarchy erected on the ruins thereof."[22]

There were many who spoke for or against the provocative nature of the resolutions, but Barbour's remarks pointed to the fears that Jefferson and Madison had entertained for nearly a decade. For he had addressed himself to the basic differences in ideology and principle outlined in the fourth resolution—the most oft-quoted sentence of the Virginia Resolutions, accusing the federal government of attempting to "*consolidate* the States by degrees into one sovereignty, the obvious tendency and inevitable result of which would be to transform the present republican system of the United States into an *absolute, or at best, a mixed monarchy.*"[23]

As news of the Virginia Resolutions became widespread, a sense of alarm swept over the country.

PATRICK HENRY SEES MONARCHY, TOO

Patrick Henry, as an old revolutionary, had sensed the danger in the Virginia and Kentucky Resolutions. In fact, he had lost little of his oratorical fire. In his final public speech, he displayed that, in theory at least, he still maintained his patriotic fervor. Before a group of students at Hampden-Sydney College, he said, "If I am asked what is to be done when a people feel themselves intolerably oppressed, my answer is ready: OVERTURN THE GOVERNMENT." But Henry, who would die in less than six months, was a tired and sick man. He not only disapproved of the resolutions but he feared the factional violence that any future revolutionary struggle would produce. Ironically, his fears paralleled Jefferson's and Madison's, for he warned that "if ever you recur to another change, you may bid adieu forever to representative government. You can never exchange the present government but for a monarchy."[24]

In less than a week, Henry's fears were reinforced by the one man he revered. George Washington had also seen the implications in Jefferson's and Madison's revolutionary strategy "at such a crisis as this." He wrote, "It would be a waste of time to attempt to bring to the view of a person of your observation and discernment the endeavors of a certain party among us to disquiet the public mind with unfounded alarms; to arraign every act of the administration; to set the people at variance with their government, and to embarrass all its measures. Equally useless would it be to predict what must be the inevitable consequences of such a policy, if it cannot be arrested."[25]

WASHINGTON WONDERS
ABOUT REVOLUTION, TOO

There can be little doubt that Washington believed that the resolutions were polarizing citizens against their government. And he must have known or at least suspected that the authors of the resolutions were Jefferson and Madison, for he added parenthetically: "Unfortunately... the State of Virginia has taken the lead in this opposition. I have said the State, because the conduct of its Legislature in the eyes of the world will authorize the expression; and because it is an incontrovertible fact, that the principal leaders of the opposition dwell in it."

Washington's analysis was correct in several ways. Not only was the state of Virginia taking the lead by announcing its own resolutions but its most important men were creating a dialogue that would give impetus to the revolution they believed must occur.

JEFFERSON STATES
HIS PRINCIPLES

Jefferson began the New Year by announcing the *principles* of his "political faith" to combat the anticipated "calumnies" and "falsehoods" that would be directed against him. Placing them in the context of the current political dissension, he made an effort to counter what were the inevitable consequences of the administration's policies.

The letter is a philosophical statement as well as a complete program for revolution. It is also the kind of statement that can be properly integrated with the debates over the Kentucky and Virginia Resolutions and Jefferson's struggles against the Hamiltonians for the previous eight years. As such, it deserves to be quoted at length:

> I...wish an inviolable preservation of our present federal constitution, according to the true sense in which it was adopted by the States, that in which it was advocated by its friends, and not that which its enemies apprehended,...and I am opposed to the monarchising its features by the forms of its administration, with a view to conciliate first transition to a President and Senate for life, and from that to an hereditary tenure of these offices, and thus to worm out the elective principle. I am for preserving to the States the powers not yielded by them to the Union, and to the legislature of the Union

its constitutional share in the division of powers; and I am not for transferring all the powers of the States to the general government, and all those of that government to the Executive branch. I am for a government rigorously frugal and simple, applying all the possible savings of the public revenue to the discharge of the national debt; and not for a multiplication of officers and salaries merely to make partisans, and for increasing, by every device, the public debt, on the principle of its being a public blessing. I am for relying, for internal defence, on our militia solely, till actual invasion, and for such a naval force only as may protect our coasts and harbors from such depredations as we have experienced; and not for a standing army in time of peace, which may overawe the public sentiment; nor a navy, which, by its own expenses and the eternal wars in which it will implicate us, will grind us with public burthens, and sink us under them. I am for free commerce with all nations; political connection with none; and little or no diplomatic establishment. And I am not for linking ourselves by new treaties with the quarrels of Europe; entering that field of slaughter to preserve their balance, or joining in the confederacy of kings to war against the principles of liberty. I am for freedom of religion...for freedom of the press, and against all violations of the constitution to silence by force and not by reason the complaints or criticisms, just or unjust, of our citizens against the conduct of their agents....These, my friend, are my principles; they are unquestionably the principles of the great body of our fellow citizens.[26]

This famous letter, placed in the context of the previous chapters, is a summary view of the rights of American citizens as Jefferson saw them.

JAY SEES HOPE

John Jay was another "elder statesman" who sensed the approaching crisis. While his prediction for the New Year augured ill for the country, he at least held out a ray of hope:

The seeds of trouble are sowing and germinating in our country.... Why and by whom were the Kentucky and Virginia Resolutions contrived, and for what purposes?

I often think of Pandora's box—altho' it contained every kind of evil, yet it is said that *Hope* was placed at the bottom. This is a singular fable, and it admits of many (and some of them very extensive) applications.[27]

HAMILTON SEES GANGRENE

Hamilton viewed events from such a dire perspective that he was incapable of holding out hope. He could only speak of the "signs of gangrene" that had "begun" and become more "progressive" with each passing day. Choosing his audience carefully, in this case the Speaker of the House of Representatives, he railed against the republican "faction" and accused them of preparing for revolution against the government:

> It is...apparent that opposition to the government has acquired more system than formerly, is bolder in the avowal of its designs, less solicitous than it was to discriminate between the Constitution and the administration, and more open and more enterprising in its projects. The late attempt of Virginia and Kentucky to unite the State Legislatures in a direct resistance to certain laws of the Union can be considered in *no other light than as an attempt to change the government.*

> It is stated in addition that the opposition party in Virginia, the headquarters of the faction, have followed up the hostile declarations which are to be found in the resolutions of their General Assembly by an *actual preparation of the means of supporting them by force,* that they have taken measures to put their militia on a more efficient footing—are preparing considerable arsenals and magazines... Amidst such serious indications of hostility, the safety and the duty of supporters of the government call upon them to adopt *vigorous measures of counteraction. It will be wise in them to act upon the hypothesis that the opposers of the government are resolved,* if it shall be practicable, *to make its existence a question of force.*[28]

The main point of Hamilton's plan for the nation lay in his advocacy of the use of force against the rebellious Virginians.

Within a week or two, Hamilton wrote an even stronger letter that revealed his true intentions. If ever Hamilton gave expression to his counterrevolutionary mentality, it was here: he explicitly accused Virginia of engaging in a revolutionary "conspiracy to overturn the government." Indeed had his advice to Theodore Sedgwick been taken and applied, there would have resulted immediate civil war. On February 2, 1799, Hamilton wrote,

> What, my dear sir, are you going to do in Virginia? This is a very serious business, which will call for all the wisdom and firmness of the government. The following are the ideas which occur to me on the occasion. The first thing in all great operations of such a government as ours is to secure the opinion of the people. To this end the proceedings of Virginia and Kentucky, with the two laws complained of, should be referred to a special committee. That committee should make a report, exhibiting with great luminousness and particularly the reasons which support the constitutionality and expediency of those laws, the tendency of the doctrines advanced by Virginia and Kentucky to destroy the Constitution of the United States, and with calm dignity united with pathos *the full evidence which they afford of a regular conspiracy to overturn the government....*
>
> The government must not merely defend itself, it must attack and arraign its enemies. But in all this there should be great care to distinguish the people of Virginia from their Legislature, and even the greater part of those who may have concurred in the Legislature from their chiefs, manifesting, indeed, a strong confidence in the good sense and patriotism of the people that they will not be dupes of an insidious plan to disunite the people of America, to break down their Constitution, and expose them to the enterprise of a foreign power. This report should conclude with a declaration that there is no cause for a repeal of the laws....No pains or expense should be spared to disseminate this report. A little pamphlet containing it should find its way into every house in Virginia. This should be left to work and nothing to court a shock should be adopted. In the meantime the measures for raising the military force should proceed with activity....When a clever force has been collected, let them be drawn toward Virginia, for which there is an obvious pretext, then let measures be taken to act upon the laws and put Virginia to the test of resistance.[29]

These letters to Dayton and Sedgwick reveal, in addition to the near panic that had struck the High Federalists, the true revolutionary nature of the Kentucky and Virginia Resolutions of 1798.

WHEN PHILOSOPHY AND POWER COLLIDE

By his own testimony, Hamilton viewed Jefferson and Madison as the leaders of a revolutionary faction. And Hamilton, who believed that energy and power were the main engines by which a government accomplished its aims, knew he could not compromise. This was consistent with his view that the administration of a one-party state should not brook interference by a minority faction or, for that matter, any opposition at all. Virginia and Kentucky republicans were a minority faction, or so Hamilton believed, and they should therefore be crushed. To do otherwise was to violate the principle of majority rule and run the risk of the government's becoming a cypher.

Ignoring Virginia's constitutional right to raise the militia's standards and levy taxes, Hamilton interpreted their actions as a willingness, even an intention, to use force. He thus dismissed the logic and expressed commitments to the Constitution and the Union contained within the resolutions. This pointed to an inability on Hamilton's part to distinguish between a constitutional right and Virginia's *potential* to make war against the Union. This is not to say that the author of *The Federalist* was constitutionally naïve.

On the contrary, it is a recognition that in February 1799 Hamilton's constitutional principles, contained within his theory of government and administration, simply would not allow even the germ of a spirit of resistance. We need only recall his earlier statement in 1790 regarding Virginia's protest against the assumption bill to place this in perspective: "This is the first symptom of a spirit which must either be killed or will kill the Constitution of the United States."

Jefferson, on the other hand, may have believed that Hamilton was wrongheaded about his principles of administration and view of the Constitution, but he would have agreed that in a one-party state the administration should not tolerate factional opposition.

The difference was that Jefferson believed Hamilton represented a faction himself—one that had gained control of the government and was, in addition to misusing the Constitution, failing to live up to or abide by its principles. He could not compromise, either.

Thus, while Hamilton was accusing the Virginia faction of using the resolutions to destroy the Union, Jefferson was accusing Hamilton of promoting faction to destroy the Constitution *and* the Union. Both perceptions of the Constitution and the Union could not be right; thus a dialectic between the competing factions must ensue.

LIBERTY VERSUS SECURITY: AN ONGOING TUG-OF-WAR

In addition to these, there were differences between their ideas of union and liberty. Hamilton's notion of the Constitution was that it must preserve union at all costs, even at the expense of individual liberty. Jefferson's idea was that liberty was a primary—even an absolute—value. One was a commitment to the post-revolutionary society emphasizing values of stability and order. The other was a commitment to the revolutionary society emphasizing the values of liberty and denying power to the central government. The primary concerns of the first were considerations that gave rise to empire, commerce, and security; the second were equated with the basic ideals of the American Revolution.

THE PEOPLE VERSUS THE ELITE

The role that ideology played in furthering these ever-widening divisions revealed, in an even broader sense, that the two factions were irreconcilable. Hamilton's belief in an elitist theory of government and his fear that the common people might participate in its administration were in direct opposition to Jefferson's faith in the people and what he believed was their right to direct public affairs. The lines being drawn between the many and the few indicated that the two cities of revolution had appeared.

As we have seen, this potential conflict regarding opposing factions and constitutional principles had been obvious to republicans for some time. And, as we ponder Hamilton's "plan," plus his advice to Sedgwick, we can conclude that as he looked into the future he could not help but see that Jefferson's ability to appeal to a growing constituency was in stark contrast to a dwindling Federalist elite who had contempt for the masses and the emerging forces of democracy. The future balance of power in the nation, then, was painfully obvious to Federalists who had eyes to see.

And Hamilton, whose vision was rarely clouded, perceived that the dialectical nature of the Virginia and Kentucky Resolutions was producing a revolution of opinion against the government. Unable, in his own words, to intimidate the opposition presses short of tyranny, he had begun to entertain the idea of using force to accomplish his ends.

ONE FACTION CONTEMPLATES FORCE

We must remember that Hamilton was the foremost military figure in America. His advice therefore carried considerable weight. This was especially true because there were so many in Adams's administration whose loyalties went to Hamilton rather than to the president. Keeping this in mind, we can appreciate the potential impact such a plan might have had among Adams's chief advisers.

So far as the plan was concerned, Hamilton's intuition was serving him well. His suggestion for concerted action gave truth to Madison's fears that the Constitution could be used as a mask to wreak vengeance on the friends of republicanism. Hamilton obviously wished that the committees of Congress would prejudge their deliberations and authorize the use of naked force against Virginia. Clothed with legislative respectability, Hamilton intended to turn Jefferson's strategy against him: accuse the Virginians of violating the Constitution, malign their intentions, link them with a foreign power, produce a report, and then disseminate it widely. But there was one major difference: Hamilton had regard for only one principle—power. He wished from the outset to go further than Jefferson, and his blatant advocacy of the use of "clever force" indicated that he intended to plunge the Union into a bloodbath.

RUMOR ABOUT AN
INTERREGNUM OR REVOLUTION

The fact that Hamilton could mask his plan with the legitimate organs of government came as no surprise to the republicans. They had suspected for some time that his intentions were to exacerbate the crisis; and, so far as they were concerned, it was merely a question of the particular methods he would use.

Madison believed, as early as January 1797, that there might be an interregnum declared.[30] In the ensuing two years, little had occurred to change his mind. Thus by late 1798 republican confidence had reached its nadir, and anything was possible. James Thomson Callender, the artful propagandist, raised the possibility of the administration's ending the republican experiment by simply declaring an interregnum: "The present Congress will cease to exist on the 3d of March, 1799. On the 4th Mr. Adams may get a certificate from some confidential judge that Virginia or Tennessee is in a state of rebellion. Whether the story be true or false rests entirely within his breast. He directly calls out the militia…till the first Monday of December thereafter, he and his militia are absolute masters of America…Thus nine months of a royal interregnum might readily put an end to the government."[31]

JEFFERSON STEPS UP THE PACE OF REVOLUTION BY PRINCIPLE

The first seven months of the New Year were considered crucial in the opposition's circles; and Jefferson, in the closing days of January, placed his revolutionary "engine" into high gear. Jefferson advised Madison: "This summer is the season for systematic energies and sacrifices. The engine is the press. Every man must lay his purse and his pen under contribution." Indeed he urged Madison "to set apart a certain portion of every post-day to write what may be proper for the public."[32]

This was Jefferson's method of beginning a revolution in people's minds. He had noted earlier, in a letter to Colonel Nicholas Lewis, that "reason, not rashness [was] the only means of bringing our fellow-citizens to their true minds."[33] Thus he warned Madison that the public "wish[ed] to hear *reason instead of disgusting blackguardism.*"[34]

THE LEADERS DISAVOW FORCE

Jefferson well knew that one false step toward violence, and the extremists would be able to use an equal if not greater force against him. His reasoning therefore was exactly parallel to that he had given La Fayette in France. Jefferson outlined his perceptions of what was becoming a nationwide movement:

> This State [Pennsylvania] is coming forward with a boldness not yet seen. Even the German counties of York and Lancaster, hitherto the most devoted, have come about, and by petitions with four thousand

signers remonstrate against the alien and sedition laws, standing armies, and discretionary powers in the President. New York and Jersey are also getting into great agitation. In this State, we fear that the ill-designing may produce insurrection. Nothing could be so fatal. Anything like force would check the progress of the public opinion and rally them round the government. This is not the kind of opposition the American people will permit. But keep away all show of force, and they will bear down the evil propensities of the government, by the constitutional means of election and petition. If we can keep quiet, therefore, the tide now turning will take a steady and proper direction.[35]

JEFFERSON CONNECTS HIS EFFORTS TO THE SPIRIT OF '76

The strategy was proving so potent that Jefferson's optimism was nearly euphoric. To his friend Thomas Lomax he placed the "movement" in perspective: "You ask for any communication I may be able to make, which may administer comfort to you. I can give that which is solid. The spirit of 1776 is not dead. It has only been slumbering. The body of the American people is substantially republican."[36]

The connection to the American Revolution had been made. Jefferson saw himself fighting essentially the same struggle he had twenty-five years earlier.

Now, with a more sophisticated view of revolution, he had launched a movement that had the same capacity to change society albeit peacefully "by the constitutional means of election and petition."[37]

Jefferson's success in awakening the spirit of revolution was unnerving his opponents, however. They were unwilling, even in the House of Representatives, to abide by the tenets of reason.[38] This appalled Jefferson, who described to Madison the obvious corruption of reason.

When Albert Gallatin attempted to speak against the Alien Law, "a scandalous scene" broke out. Representatives "enter[ed] into loud conversations, laugh[ing], cough[ing] etc....It was impossible to proceed."[39] Disruption of the legislative process, especially in a manner that contradicted sweet reason, revealed the low intentions of the extremists. And Jefferson, who was then presiding over the orderly conduct of the Senate, must have viewed the House's actions with contempt.

HAMILTON BLINDED BY HIS
ACCESS TO POWER

Both Hamilton and Jefferson had determined that stronger measures were called for. Hamilton wrote to the attorney general of New York, complaining that he had "long been the object of the most malignant calumnies of the faction opposed to our government through the medium of the papers devoted to their views. *Hitherto I have forborne to resort to the laws* for the punishment of the authors or abettors, and were I to consult personal considerations alone, I should continue in this course, repaying hatred with contempt. *But public motives now compel me to a different conduct.*"[40]

When we recall Hamilton's advice to Oliver Wolcott in June 1798, the "moment" he had seen the Sedition Act, it is hard to take him seriously as he complains of others maligning him. He had been for as much repression as possible, short of actual tyranny.

Hamilton's failure to connect his own ambitions with the charge of the republicans also meant that he misunderstood the nature of Jefferson's opposition and the reasons for his success. The fact that journalists were clapped into jail and the free press was threatened eluded Hamilton and his advisers. It was as if Hamilton and those around him were so blinded by power that they were unable to see that constitutional principles were involved.

USURPING THE COMMON LAW
RAISES PROSPECTS OF TYRANNY

Jefferson's attempts to promote a debate on the principles of the Constitution were trivial compared with the next shock he endured. The federal government's attempt to usurp the common law of the United States was, for him, the final blow.

Any reservations he might have had regarding the intentions of the administration and its willingness to abide by the Constitution vanished. He wrote to Edmund Randolph,

> Of all the doctrines which have ever been broached by the federal government, the novel one, of the common law being in force and cognizable as an existing law in their courts, is to me the most formidable. All their other assumptions of un-given powers have

been in the detail. The bank law, the treaty doctrine, the sedition act, alien act, the undertaking to change the State laws of evidence in the State courts by certain parts of the stamp act, etc., etc., have been solitary, unconsequential, timid things, in comparison with the audacious, barefaced and sweeping pretension to a system of law for the United States, without the adoption of their Legislature, and so infinitively beyond their power to adopt. If this assumption be yielded to, the State courts may be shut up.

Jefferson saw this alteration of the Constitution as a naked grab for power. At stake were the legal existence of the states and those systems of justice—the state courts—which they had evolved.

Moreover, if the national government made good its "new doctrine, that the common law is the law of the United States, and that their courts have, of course, jurisdiction co-extensive with that law, that is to say, general over all cases and persons,"[41] what role *would* the states have? Their ability to limit the power of government would be nonexistent.

For those who believed in the sanctity of republican government, embodied in the state governments and their constitutions, tyranny had appeared knocking at the door.

Finally, Jefferson and his colleagues realized that this attempt to destroy the independence of the states meant, for all practical purposes, the end of constitutional government. For if the extremists within the administration were successful, one of the fundamental principles of Western constitutionalism—the idea of limiting the power of government—would be destroyed.

The proposal to usurp the common law was nothing less than a systemic approach to counterrevolution—one that only incidentally set the stage for despotism. With the principle of federalism at an end, with the power of the states destroyed and in their place the erection of a Leviathan—arrogating all power to itself—the great experiment to preserve liberty would be shattered.

Frightened by this prospect, Jefferson committed to paper one of the most crucial decisions of his entire life. Everything that he had previously written regarding the administration's policies can be considered educational and politically safe, always with an eye to preserving the Union of the states. Now, and for the first time, Jefferson stated explicitly that he would destroy the Union rather than see the states become creatures of the federal government.

JEFFERSON PLANS FOR
REVOLUTION BASED ON PRINCIPLE

Writing to Madison, Jefferson stated boldly,

> Express in affectionate and conciliatory language our warm attachment to union with our sister-states, and to the instrument and principles by which we are united; that we are willing to sacrifice to this every thing except those rights of self-government the securing of which was the object of that compact; that not at all disposed to make every measure of error or wrong a cause of scission, we are willing to view with indulgence to wait with patience till those passions and delusions shall have passed over which the federal government have artfully and successfully excited to cover its own abuses and to conceal its designs; fully confident that the good sense of the American people and their attachment to those very rights which are now vindicating will, before it shall be too late, rally with us round the true principles of our federal compact; *but determined, were we to be disappointed in this, to sever ourselves from that union* we so much value, rather than give up the rights of self-government.[42]

What is remarkable about this letter, in addition to Jefferson's mood, is that it represents a departure from as well as a refinement of his strategy. It is couched in terms of pure revolutionary theory and in that sense is a sign of his deepening commitment, in principle, to the idea of revolution in America. But it is also highly practical and represents a plan of action. Perhaps this is why Madison journeyed to Monticello so hurriedly to defuse Jefferson's anger. Madison's visit resulted in a second letter, to Wilson Cary Nicholas, that less than two weeks later altered in a minor way his radical propositions.[43]

But while Madison was able to tone down Jefferson's plan by eliminating the extreme statement regarding secession, he nevertheless did not change the basic strategy. Jefferson's assertion about severing the Union would, if the federal government persisted in usurping the power of the states, naturally follow his "agreed" upon adherence to the principles of the Virginia and Kentucky Resolutions.

A strict adherence to those principles was made explicit. This is a crucial point because it means that the concessions Jefferson made to Madison were political, not theoretical. They did not compromise the aims of his movement; they merely made his principles more palatable.

The second modification in Jefferson's letter to Nicholas, after his conversation with Madison, described the above reference to the rights of the states as a "reservation." That is, it would be tantamount to saying that if the national government succeeded in destroying state governments, the states would reserve the right, in effect, to nullify their acts and secede from the Union.

While it is not stated precisely "whatever we [the States] might now rightfully do," the language carried with it a threat either to secede from the Union or to disregard the acts of the national government or both. The implications behind this strategy were twofold: to contain the power of the federal government within restricted constitutional boundaries, and to enable the states to confront a constitutional issue in such a way that they would continually educate the people regarding their rights.

In truth, however, Jefferson's "reservation" statement carried to a logical conclusion was, from a strategic point of view, academic; and from a tactical point of view it was politically wise to eliminate it and thus avoid unnecessary criticism. The subtle issues of "reservation" and those words that implied a doctrine of nullification would come up again; but for the present, Madison had convinced Jefferson that it was advantageous to delete them.[44]

While working toward revolution, it was unnecessary to state the obvious conclusion if the administration did not change its policy. And, for reasons we have already discussed, Jefferson, as well as Madison, did not wish to endanger the possibilities of a peaceful revolution. Jefferson's acquiescence indicated that he was biding his time, preparing, along with Madison and Nicholas, for the next level of the revolutionary dialectic.

Realizing the limited nature of the successful Kentucky and Virginia Resolutions, Jefferson knew that something more must be accomplished to mobilize public opinion. Accordingly, he wrote to Nicholas that the sole "object of the present communication is to procure a concert in the general plan of action, as it is extremely desirable that Virginia and Kentucky should pursue the same track on this occasion."[45]

Indeed a general plan of action was taking shape. And although it cannot be proven, because the author or authors are unknown, the "general plan" referred to by Jefferson may have included, because of the climate of opinion at the time, another set of Kentucky Resolutions.

Before the year was out, the Kentucky legislature would pass a second set of resolutions consistent with Jefferson's revolutionary strategy. Taking his advice to "answer the reasonings of such states as have ventured into the field of reason" (i.e., on the unconstitutionality of the Alien and Sedition Laws), Kentucky did just that. Castigating its "sister states" ("Virginia only excepted"), the General Assembly went on, still consistent with Jefferson's advice, to state its "attachment to the Union" and refusal to acquiesce "in the doctrines and principles advanced and attempted" by the other states.

In addition, the General Assembly made a distinction between those who administered the Constitution and the Constitution itself, stating explicitly that its co-states had accepted "in principle and in construction" an argument that would "stop nothing short of despotism."

NULLIFICATION MAKES ITS DEBUT

Asserting this dire conclusion, the Kentucky legislature then went on to announce that "a nullification" doctrine was the "rightful remedy." Reaffirming its own "principles" of 1798, the new set of resolutions expressed Kentucky's right to resist "in a constitutional manner" all further violations of the Constitution.[46] In this way the resolutions of November 14, 1799, went beyond Kentucky's principled and constitutional resistance of 1798.

Not only had the Kentucky legislators criticized their sister states for a failure to oppose the administration but they took it upon themselves to declare a nullification doctrine. This dovetailed precisely with Jefferson's plan: to consolidate opinion among the people on the idea of resistance. And indeed this had taken place.

Three weeks after the Kentucky Resolutions had passed, John Breckinridge, now the Speaker of the Kentucky House of Representatives, wrote to Jefferson regarding the nullification clause: "In the lower house, there was not a dissenting voice." And while a few state senators had voiced their "considerable division," the future would find "the great mass of the people...uncontaminated and firm" in their support.[47]

The outlines of Jefferson's strategy were becoming clearer. Finding it necessary to deal with a rapidly deteriorating national situation, he was being prodded by Madison to become more practical and less theoretical. The next ten months would see him responding to that pressure and also paying more attention to his role as a political figure. Although still maintaining the reins of leadership, he was forced to elevate himself above the rough and tumble of politics.

As a result, when Virginia's next response to the constitutional crisis was being formulated, Jefferson discovered that his closest advisers, Madison and James Monroe, were against his direct participation. Unwilling to risk even the hint of a scandal involving Jefferson in a protest against the administration, they convinced him that he had to remain silent. Yet in the month that Madison was researching and writing his famous *Virginia Report of 1799–1800,* Jefferson could not help presenting him with a set of guidelines.

KEEPING LIMITS TO FORCE IN MIND

Jefferson's guidelines revealed that he was following the advice that he had given to the French revolutionaries Moustier, La Fayette, Dumas, and Crevecoeur only ten years earlier: above all, do nothing that may cause the army to "shew" its seducing hand. Finally, he urged his friend to place his entire faith in the elective process of the Constitution. He believed that had the French abided by these basic tenets, they would have produced a successful revolution:

> Our objects, according to my ideas, should be these: (1) peace even with Great Britain; (2) a sincere cultivation of the Union; (3) the disbanding of the army on principles of economy and safety; (4) protestations against violations of the true principles of our constitution, merely to save them, and prevent precedent and acquiescence from being pleaded against them; but nothing to be said or done which shall look or lead to force, and give any pretext for keeping up the army.[48]

Madison responded to Jefferson's guidelines by writing the *Virginia Report of 1799–1800,* one of the most important papers written by an American statesman. Making a thorough analysis of the Constitution and the threats against it, Madison revealed why he was later called "the Father of the Constitution." In the first of these new Virginia Resolutions, he declared attachment to the Constitution and the Union and then proceeded to review and reaffirm the principles of the resolutions of 1798.

The third resolution elaborated on the doctrine of "interposition," claiming that the states had a "duty" to "arrest the...dangerous exercise of powers not granted" to the federal government. Madison continued that "the object of the interposition" doctrine was "to arrest the progress of usurpation, and maintain the authorities, rights, and liberties appertaining to the states."

Along with interposition, Madison validated his commitment to Jefferson's compact theory, asserting that the states "being the parties to the constitutional compact, and in their sovereign capacity...[will] decide in the last resort, whether the compact made by them may be violated; and...[whether] such questions as may be of sufficient magnitude to require their interposition."[49]

In the fourth resolution, Madison took up the question of construction, or interpreting the Constitution. He stated that "a spirit has been manifested to enlarge the powers of the federal government, by forced construction, especially of certain general phrases; of which the effect will be to consolidate the states into one sovereignty, and the result a monarchy." This "tendency" would result because it would enlarge the executive power and thus enable "the chief magistrate to secure his own re-election" as well as "regulate his successors."[50] Finally, Madison drove home his conclusion: the presidency would become such an "object of ambition as to make elections so tumultuous and corrupt, that the people would themselves demand an hereditary succession."

The prediction was clear: bring about a concentration of power in the executive branch, blatantly corrupt the election process, raise the violence of party and faction, and the people would demand a stable and authoritarian government. Indeed this was one of Jefferson's basic beliefs and a fundamental reason for adhering to a peaceful idea of revolution.

The issue of separation of powers was taken up in the sixth resolution. Making a painstaking analysis of the Alien and Sedition Laws, Madison believed that the executive's right to deport aliens "unite[d] legislative, executive, and judicial power in the hands of the President." The executive would be in a position to "define" by his own "will," "every circumstance of *danger, suspicion, and secret machination.*" He would thus "judge" and "execute his own decrees." "This union of powers," said Madison, "subverts the general principles of free government, which require the three great functions to be kept in distinct hands." The president's signing of the Alien Act thus "subvert[ed] the particular organization and positive provisions of the Federal Constitution."[51]

DEPORTING ALIENS UNCONSTITUTIONAL

Madison next attacked the Sedition Act by addressing himself to the major problem of the common law and the Constitution. Claiming that it enabled the general government to usurp falsely the common law that had been in force before the American Revolution, Madison said, "If it be understood that the common law is established by the Constitution, it follows that no part of the law can be altered by the legislature." Further, if such a law were passed by the federal government, "the whole code, with all its incongruities, barbarisms, and bloody maxims, would be inviolably saddled on the good people of the United States."

He then placed the Sedition Act in perspective by saying that it violated the principles of the American Revolution: "The fundamental principle of the Revolution was that the colonies were...united by a common executive, but not united by any common legislative sovereign."[52] The consequence of this "construction," or interpretation (i.e., "admitting the common law as the law of the United States"), was in Madison's eyes fatal to the states: "The Administration of it would overwhelm the residuary sovereignty of the states and by one constructive operation, new model the whole political fabric of the country."[53]

A LEGISLATURE CANNOT
CHANGE A CONSTITUTION

Madison's remorseless logic continued. Not only had he exposed the dangers of the administration's policies in terms of separation of powers, corruption of elections, a tendency to monarchy, the usurpation of the common law, the destruction of state sovereignty, and the violation of the principles of the American Revolution but he addressed himself to the relation of the Sedition Act to the First Amendment.

The act, especially where freedom of the press was concerned, "abridged" the First Amendment. By recognizing no "material difference between a previous restraint, and a subsequent punishment" of a writer for his article, Madison accused the administration of going beyond the British in an attempt to crush freedom. "It would be a mockery to say that no law should be passed, preventing publications from being made, but that laws might be passed for punishing them in case they should be made." Nor, he continued, would the press be the only victim. "The freedom of conscience, and of religion, are found in the same instruments which assert the freedom of the press. It will never be admitted that the meaning of the former, in the common law of England, is to limit their meaning in the United States." The great constitutional genius was saying that attacking one of these freedoms, for example, "chilling the press," was the same as attacking them all.[54]

Without an uninterrupted flow of critical ideas in the only media that existed—the newspapers—the free society could not survive. The people, denied access to information, would not be able to make intelligent decisions.

MADISON ARGUES THAT WE MUST
PROTECT THE FIRST AMENDMENT

In sum, all the First Amendment freedoms were subtly related. Indeed the administration's passage of the Sedition Law, which attempted to stifle criticism of government policy, was highly ironic. The determination to enjoy freedom of speech, press, assembly, conscience, and religion had been the main object of the American Revolution.

Upon the exercise of these freedoms, especially where they involved criticism of the government, Madison was explicit: "As respects our Revolution,…[it] was promoted by canvassing the measures of government."[55]

Madison revealed the administration's greatest fear: it was afraid of those very principles of freedom that had given rise to revolution in the first place. But more to the point, it was determined that it would not be overthrown by a similar process.[56] Placing his faith in the language of the First Amendment and in the text of the Virginia ratifying convention, Madison repeated the statement: "The liberty of conscience and freedom of the press cannot be cancelled, abridged, restrained, or modified, by any authority of the United States."

Thus, by passing the Sedition Law, the administration's policies contradicted Madison's understanding of the theory of the Constitution. Plainly, the executive and legislative branches were in direct violation of the Constitution.

For Madison and Jefferson, this was a dangerous situation; and Madison, speaking for his committee, concluded his resolution by saying, "The unconstitutional power exercised over the press by the Sedition Act ought, more than any other, to produce universal alarm."

MADISON ATTACKS SECRECY IN GOVERNMENT AND DEFENDS THE INTEGRITY OF ELECTIONS

Knowing the damage that would be done to a free society as the result of a government attack on First Amendment freedoms, Madison reaffirmed the tenets of a free society. There was, he stated, no way in which "the responsibility of officers of government…[could] be secured without a free investigation of their conduct and motives." It was therefore "the right and duty of every citizen to make such investigation, and promulgate the results."[57] Thus any administration that would deny information to the people or their representatives in order to shield its "machinations" from their eyes was in violation of the Constitution. It constituted, in other words, a threat to the stability, harmony, and freedom of the society.

The consequences of this administrative mentality, basically repressive in nature, were so obvious that Madison, without mentioning any names, revealed the motives of the extremists within the administration:

"In the several elections, during the continuance of the Sedition Act, it would tend to screen the incumbents of office from inquiry....The right of election [which depends on full information] is the essence of a free government...[and] is impaired by the Sedition Act....Competitors against incumbents in office have not an equal chance, the latter being shielded by the act" and "the people [could] not fully discuss and ascertain the relative merits of such competitors and incumbents."[58]

The truth about faction in power had now been revealed. The extremists did not care about ethics, principles of government, honest elections, or the Constitution. They were concerned solely with power, and the people be damned. Indeed as Madison's description cut through the rhetoric of the High Federalists, it appeared that the politics of faction had come home to roost.

Thus did Madison outline the administration's attempt to undermine the Constitution through its attack on the First Amendment. By choking off the free flow of ideas—many of them critical of Federalist policies—the administration was not merely laying the groundwork for victory in successive elections but was destroying the foundations of a free society.

Both Madison and Jefferson knew that to command the respect and the trust of the citizenry, integrity in government must be absolute. And the electoral process was where these values were put to the test. Clearly, then, the Virginia Resolutions of 1799–1800 were an attempt to expose the High Federalists and their efforts to corrupt both elections and, more subtly, the values that underlay them.

Realizing that the danger to the Constitution had increased, Madison renewed the dialectic that Jefferson had begun. There was, however, one major difference, and that was a detailed analysis of the administration's attack on the First Amendment. By doing this, Madison indicated a slight change in strategy. No longer was it necessary to stress the right of the states to protest. After a fourteen-month debate on the compact and states' rights theories, the point had been made. He was now placing the burden of proof on a corrupt administration.

This is not to say that Madison had abandoned the doctrine of states' rights. Indeed, in the closing words of the *Report*, he said he viewed the states as the "intermediate" between the people and the government. This meant that Madison was taking his bearings from the period of the formation of the government, about which no one knew more.

It also meant that, in the dispute over the role that states would play in the future federal government, he placed his faith in the rights they established at the time of ratification. His entire essay, then, reinforced that final point: the states had the responsibility to "descry the first symptoms of usurpation…and sound the alarm to the public." And he concluded, if "this argument…was a proper one then…it must be a proper one now."[59]

Madison had accomplished a Herculean task. His essay on the First Amendment was now in the hands of legislators who could educate the people. And no one realized more than Jefferson how crucial it was to go beyond this and actually place Madison's *Report* in the hands of the people themselves.

Nor was there a single person in America who better understood that the critical problem of revolutionary education was time, in addition to timing. In the battle between the factions, if any revolution were to enjoy even the limited possibilities of success, both of these imperatives must be closely adhered to. Thus by April 1800, with Madison's help, Jefferson had met his schedule and the revolution was proceeding apace.

Indeed it was essential in Jefferson's drive for power that Madison's scholarly analysis have the ability to reveal the ambitions of the extremists within the administration. His *Report*, a forceful argument against the consolidation of power in the federal government, would cause those who read it to turn against the administration if they wished to preserve free government.

For, as Madison so ingeniously put it in the last pages of his *Report*, "These declarations…are expressions of opinion, unaccompanied with any other effect than what they may produce on opinion by *exciting reflection.*"[60]

Indeed, if revolution begins in the mind, as both Madison and Jefferson (and, incidentally, John Adams) knew, there was now no turning back. The Virginians had committed themselves, for the second time, to an idea of revolution.

7

The Politics of the Revolution of 1800: Prelude

No measures will be too intemperate that tend to make the citizens revolutionary enough to make the man of 1775 the man of 1800.

— Fisher Ames, 1800

S THE YEAR 1800 ARRIVED, ALEXANDER HAMILTON SKETCHED a political portrait of the republic in starkly prophetic terms. Addressing himself to the problem of faction, he lamented the loss of George Washington, expressed his pique with the president, assessed the condition of Federalist political disorganization, and then, announcing that the administration would ultimately prevail, proceeded to draw a specter of revolution:

> At home every thing is in the main well; except as to the Perverseness and capriciousness of one and the spirit of faction of many....
>
> The spirit of Faction is abated nowhere. In Virginia it is more violent than ever. It seems demonstrated that the leaders there, who possess completely all the powers of the local Government, are resolved to possess those of the National, by the most dangerous combinations, and, if they cannot effect this, to resort to the employment of physical force."[1]

This was the mood of High Federalism in the wake of Washington's death. Somber, slightly confident but wary were the prevailing attitudes. But this mood would change rapidly as the political realities of the coming months crashed down upon fond hopes. For the emergence of a full-scale theory of revolution based on the principles of the Declaration of Independence would confront almost everyone who had expressed confidence in the spring of 1800.

THE POLITICAL SITUATION IN JANUARY 1800

The Virginia and Kentucky Resolutions of 1798 and 1799 had drawn the battle lines, and those who were commentators on public affairs sensed the mood of the nation. Almost everyone believed that the political skirmishes that had dominated the country for the previous decade threatened to erupt into a full-scale war.

At stake were not simply a few offices or senatorial seats but a collision between two conflicting ideologies: democracy and republicanism versus aristocracy and a consolidating power that bore a striking resemblance to monarchy. These themes would be referred to again and again by adherents of both sides. To be decided in "this contest over principles," as Thomas Jefferson noted, was a choice between two systems of administration, two interpretations of the Constitution and the power of the government, and two views of society and the way in which it would develop.

The economic arrangement of society into two competing groups— one industrial with shipping and mercantile interests, the other reflecting a basic agricultural interest—could not help but translate itself into the politics of the young republic. Individual liberty was equated with one of those interests; power, influence, empire, and even a return to a form of mixed monarchy were associated with the other.

One view represented the "principles" of Jefferson, the other the "system" of Hamilton.

To Jefferson's supporters, as well as many who opposed him, the contest was simply the American Revolution continued to its final resolution. And this theme, above all others, dominated the political literature of the day. Appeals were made to the "Whigs of '76"[2] and those who had fought in the Revolution, who had "distinguished themselves throughout life in advancing the rights of man and particularly the preservation of our Republican Government."[3] The contest was seen as a life-or-death struggle for the new republic; a continuation of Federalist rule was equated with a return to monarchy.

Their opinions also reflected a degree of political organization that had been unknown since the earliest days of the Revolution.

REVOLUTIONARY ACTIVITY BECOMES VISIBLE

Referring to the Jeffersonians in standard revolutionary terms, one Federalist wrote, "The Jacobins appear to be completely organized throughout the United States....Their exertions are bent to introduce into every department of the State governments unprincipled tools of a daring faction."[4]

Another Federalist confessed that he was as occupied "writing letters" as any "member of a *revolutionary* committee."[5]

Josiah Quincy remarked that "a degree of organization has been effected in the opposite party unexampled, I suspect, in this country, since the revolutionary committees of 1775."[6]

By April 1800 the committees of correspondence, societies, and clubs, so feared by the British in the 1770s and by the Federalists in 1793 and 1794, began to make their appearance across the nation.

JEFFERSON IDENTIFIED AS THE CENTER OF OPPOSITION

As early as February 1798, Federalist John Nicholas had written a note to Washington on his birthday: "The opposition to the government…is here 'systematized'—regular plans are formed, and correspondences… commenced against the unsuspecting…friends of government." The words carried a meaning fraught with danger. Jefferson, "the great man on the Hill," he said, was "the very 'centre' of opposition, the 'rallying point,' the head quarters, the everything, of the enemies of the government."[7]

Indeed, this emerging opposition to the administration was looked upon as something more than subversive. And when the same organizational activity followed the Kentucky and Virginia Resolutions, they were considered, as we saw in chapter 6, revolutionary. This was plain evidence that the Virginia faction meant to overthrow the government.

Hamilton at least believed this and had good reason for doing so. The Federalists' memories were not short. They recalled the Democratic societies that had flourished in 1793 and 1794 and had been so roundly condemned by the president. A writer in the *Gazette of the United States* noted,

> Nobody will deny the usefulness of popular Societies, in cases of revolutions. The reason is obvious. By forming people together into clubs, and giving to all those clubs, a central point of union, a bad government may be shaken down: for it has to oppose not scattered and dispirited complainers, who may be kept under the harrow of the law, and demolished as fast as they show themselves, but it has to oppose an organized body, acting in phalanx, thus tyranny is pulled down because it is overmatched, and perhaps there is no other way to pull it down.[8]

Now, six years later, the same phenomenon had appeared. The preparations that took place in Virginia were nearly exact duplications of the revolutionary committees of correspondence with but one difference: they were peaceful in nature.

VIRGINIA'S ELECTORAL POLITICS BECOMES REVOLUTIONIZED

Their organization was identical as was their intended purpose: to provide information to as many citizens as possible.[9] These committees took their guidance from the major figures in Virginia politics—James Madison, James Monroe, and Thomas Jefferson, the leaders who defined the strategy of political opposition. In the tradition of the old-style factional politics of the preceding generations, these leaders were ensured election. For example, in Virginia's bid for electoral votes, while it was decided to change the mode of election (i.e., to vote by a "ticket" instead of by districts), the outcome was the same. With great names like George Wythe, Edmund Pendleton, James Madison, and William Giles, the republican faction could expect to win handily.

Similar efforts took place in New York, Pennsylvania, and New Jersey. The object of the committees in all the states was the same. In Virginia, Nicholas to wrote Jefferson, "We have begun our correspondence with the subcommittees and mean to keep up a regular intercourse upon the subjects which may seem to require it."[10]

The functions of these committees and subcommittees on the state, county, and local township levels were the same: to facilitate the exchange of information; to print newspapers, circulars, pamphlets, and handbills; and to hold meetings.

As resolutions were passed, issues decided, and candidates chosen by the various committees and cliques, the results were communicated to the people in the most expeditious fashion. It was indeed the standard decision-making process of the old school of politics: control rested in the hands of a few, and the voters were presented with their choice. Individuals nominated themselves through advertisements in the newspapers; but almost exclusively, and in the southern states especially, it was the old family patriarchs, like the Pinckneys, men of established wealth and position, who dominated political affairs and won elections.

Revolutionary patriots, like Christopher Gadsden, may have called themselves Federalists, but their allegiance was to the nation. They resented "faction," "party," "cabal," and any interference with their right to vote for the individual of their choice.

Gadsden denounced party spirit in traditional terms: "No directions can be preferable to those in General Washington's farewell address, which cannot be too much attended to." Reiterating his desire for the states to maintain their own independence, he remained "convinced that [if] each state had an equal right to vote as it pleased,…the cant names of federalist, anti-federalist, aristocrat, democrat, Jacobin, etc., etc. [would] be heard no more."[11]

Two other similarities to the revolutionary era that one might note in 1800 are the post office and the press. The Jeffersonian faction had systematically refused to use the mails for important personal messages since May and June 1797.

To Madison, Jefferson would write, "I shall trust the post offices with nothing confidential, persuaded that during the ensuing twelvemonth they will lend their inquisitorial aid to furnish matter for new slanders. I shall send you as usual printed communications, without saying any thing confidential on them. You will of course understand the cause."[12] And as late as August 1800, he was warning his correspondents to let no letter "go out of your own hands, lest it should get into the newspapers."[13]

Jefferson indicated by his caution that he knew the Federalist faction was not above an invasion of privacy.

POSITIVE VIEW OF THE PRESS

But while this form of political espionage placed limitations on his ability to communicate with his important advisers, he compensated by making greater use of the press.[14] He knew from his earlier revolutionary experience in both America and France that no true change in a people's sentiments or opinions could take place without its aid.

This was a perception also shared by his adversaries, albeit late. Fisher Ames wrote in 1801, "The newspapers are an overmatch for any Government. They will first overawe and then usurp it. This has been done; and the Jacobins owe their triumph to the unceasing use of this engine; not so much to skill in the use of it, as by repetition."[15]

But the fact that the Federalists had overplayed their hand, had failed to account for the powerful engine of the press, and had even gone beyond the rules of the system and intimidated editors was not lost on Jefferson and his followers. Their efforts to establish printing presses "in almost every town and county of the country" was reported by a Federalist at the height of the contest.[16]

Indeed this was what Jefferson had in mind when months before the campaign he had done everything in his power to enlist the aid of Edmund Pendleton, Madison, Monroe, and others to write letters, contribute funds to establishing newspapers, and in general begin a coordinated information system.

The lessons he had learned in France and America during the 1770s were yet in his mind. Revolution took place, after all, "in the minds…of… people," and no one knew this more profoundly than Jefferson. Accordingly, he staked nearly everything on the "engine of the press."

ROLE OF THE
REVOLUTIONARY CAUCUS

Another revolutionary device that became part of the contest of 1800 was the caucus. On the state and local levels, it was used to prevent the fractionalizing of supporters and to produce consensus. It also preserved the continuity of leadership and produced local and regional strategies.

One might argue that Jefferson, Madison, Monroe, John Taylor of Caroline, and others had already caucused, planned their strategy, and were producing a consensus by early 1800. The decisions made on the Kentucky and Virginia Resolutions had been in the hands of a few men who agreed on policy objectives and were united. By comparison, the members of the administration hardly spoke to one another.

A CONSERVATIVE CRISIS

The fact that the Federalists were in the midst of a "conservative crisis" had become apparent to a few of the far-seeing Federalists as early as 1797. Ames had summed up the sad state of affairs to Hamilton: "We are broken to pieces."[17]

By January 1800 Hamilton admitted that "vanity and jealousy [have] exclude[d] all counsel....The leading friends of the government are in a sad dilemma."[18]

The previous three years had seen the Federalists warring among themselves, splitting off into personal cliques and factions and creating a situation that one of their more astute members called a state of "anarchy." Gouverneur Morris wrote to Rufus King, "But the thing, which, in my opinion, has done most mischief to the federal party, is the ground given by some of them to believe, that they wish to establish a monarchy."[19]

Morris had accurately described the malady as well as the cause: between the statements attributed to John Adams regarding his affinity to British institutions and the actual tendency of the policies of Hamilton and those loyal to him in the cabinet, the tone of the administration had become increasingly arrogant and authoritarian. As this impression was relayed successively by republican editors after the Whiskey Rebellion, the direct tax, and the Alien and Sedition Acts, as well as the Virginia and Kentucky Resolutions, citizens began to wonder if there might be some truth to their assertions. As these charges were repeated, the burden of proof weighed more heavily on the administration with each successive crisis.

SPLIT BETWEEN ADAMS AND HAMILTON REVEALS THE LATTER'S POWER

The split between the Adams and Hamilton factions within the administration can be traced to the period immediately following the election of 1796.

As we have seen, Hamilton's power was near absolute in the waning days of Washington's administration, and he brought under his influence a majority of cabinet members in the new administration.

For almost three and a half years, Hamilton was to exert an influence from outside the government that would ultimately destroy the president's confidence in his closest advisers. Oliver Wolcott was secretary of the treasury and, more than any other man, owed his position to Hamilton. James McHenry was secretary of war and the least competent member of Adams's cabinet. Unfortunately, McHenry's lack of abilities caused him to defer to the inspector general, thus giving Hamilton hegemony over military as well as civil affairs.

Timothy Pickering was a secretary of state who disagreed with the most crucial part of the president's foreign policy—the US attitude toward France. From the outset he took advice from Hamilton, even assisting him in 1800 by providing evidence to attack the president on his conduct of public affairs.

ADAMS STRIKES BACK

This state of affairs piqued John Adams, and when he began to make decisions that he believed were in the national interest without consulting his High Federalist advisers, the Hamiltonians were outraged. By mid-May 1799, Adams took several steps at once—all of which could not help but anger his antagonists.

Within a period of a few weeks, Nathaniel Ames reported that he "turn[ed] out Tim[othy] Pickering from the Secretary of State's office, disband[ed] in concurrence with Congress the standing Army, and... retract[ed] from high-handed explosions against France and Democracy."[20] This was one of the first signs that Adams was asserting his independence even though he believed it might tear the administration apart. When he attempted to avoid war with France by sending three envoys on a peace mission, he was rebuked by nearly the entire Federalist faction.

Theodore Sedgwick immediately saw the consequences: "A total loss of confidence [has occurred] among the best friends of the government, in the wisdom and prudence, of the P——T...It is also expected that an irreconcilable division will in consequence of this state of things take place among the federalists."[21]

That division by June 1800 was known to a few leaders only. But as the summer wore on, the complex intrigues led by Hamilton and others, behind Adams's back, had made it obvious to everyone. The only difference now was that the president began to force the issue. More and more he aligned himself with the Jeffersonians and recalled his earlier days in the Revolution.

To Timothy Pickering, Fisher Ames had previously written of Adams, "He is a revolutionist from temperament, habit, and, lately, what he thinks policy. He is too much irritated against many, if not most, of the principal sound men of the country even to bestow on them his confidence or retrieve them. In particular, he is implacable against a certain great little man whom we mutually respect [i.e., Hamilton]."[22]

George Cabot complained to King that Adams's behavior had changed: "He sometimes praises us in strong terms; at others he denounces us in a manner that outrages all decency."[23]

Thus, as Joseph Charles suggests, it would appear that the key to understanding this period is the struggle that was "taking place in Adams's mind as to how far he would go with the High Federalists." Adams's idea of an equilibrium, in terms of both the Constitution and the factions in society, seems to have asserted itself here.

As we have seen, Adams had contempt for party intrigue, and it is logical that he would have been disgusted with Hamilton. It is also logical that as Adams revived his revolutionary ideals, at least in terms of rhetoric, he would move closer to the Jeffersonians and bridge the gap between himself and the hated Jacobins.[24] Indeed the possibility of such a coalition was not only real but had been maintained, at least in theory, in Jefferson's mind. Before Adams had even taken office, Jefferson had informed him of the attempts that would be made to separate the two. He warned the incoming president that "the public and the public papers have been much occupied lately in placing us in a point of opposition to each other. I trust with confidence that less of it has been felt by ourselves personally."[25]

JEFFERSON'S VIEWS OF THE PRESIDENT'S ACTIONS

Adams and Jefferson had every reason to believe that they could cooperate fully in the new administration. Together they shared the ideals of the Revolution, distrusted power, regarded the Constitution and a republican form of government as essential for the liberty of the country, detested factions, wanted peace with France, and despised Hamilton while recognizing his growing influence in the government. Thus it is inconceivable that in their common quest for fame—which both identified with the success of the American Revolution—either would wish to see it and the republic it had produced fail.

On the contrary, both would cooperate to ensure its success. Despite Adams's signing of the Alien and Sedition Acts, Jefferson wrote fifteen years later,

> In truth, my dear Sir, we were far from considering you as the author of all the measures we blamed. They were placed under the protection of your name, but we were satisfied they wanted much of your approbation. We ascribed them to their real authors, the Pickerings, the Wolcotts, the Tracys, the Sedgwicks, *et id genus omne* ["and all of their kind"], with whom we supposed you in a state of Duresse. I well remember a conversation with you, in the morning of the day on which you nominated to the Senate a substitute for Pickering, in which you expressed a just impatience under "the legacy of Secretaries which Gen. Washington had left you" and whom you seemed therefore to consider as under public protection. Many other incidents shewed how differently you would have acted with less impassioned advisers; and subsequent events have proved that your minds were not together. You would do me great injustice therefore by taking to yourself what was intended for men who were then your secret, as they are now your open enemies. Should you write on the

subject, as you propose, I am sure we shall see you place yourself farther from them than from us.[26]

With this perspective in mind, it is possible to view the events leading up to the election of 1800 in a different manner than has been formerly related. The focus of the political struggle is not between two embryonic political parties—Federalist and Republican—which exist almost exclusively in the minds of twenty-first-century historians.

We should realize instead that Adams had been abandoned by many, if not most, of the prominent Federalists and that he was expected to repel the attacks of Jeffersonians and Hamiltonians alike while maintaining national unity in a period of crisis. We can now better understand Adams's rapidly changing behavior and his reversion to two themes he knew would have broad popular support and undercut the strength of the extremists: the republican ideology of the American Revolution and the danger of faction.

A FEDERALIST ATTEMPT AT A COUP D'ETAT

These were two well-chosen themes, especially the latter. The degree to which intrigue, manipulation, and outright attempts to deny the people's will dominated the elections of 1800 had become apparent at both the state and national levels. To many observers it was a sign that the republic was breaking down.

Perhaps more important, it gave credibility to the opposition's charges that the Constitution was a dead parchment in the hands of the Federalists. This, more than anything else, tended to force both Federalists and Jeffersonians to consider extreme measures.

The first of these attempts was by James Ross of Pennsylvania, a senator who introduced a bill designed to secure the electoral votes of Pennsylvania for the Federalists. Ostensibly entitled a "Bill Prescribing the mode of deciding disputed Elections, of President and Vice President of the United States," it was a blatant attempt to corrupt the electoral process. The *Kentucky Gazette* described it accurately:

> A bill is now under consideration in the senate, and which I have no doubt will pass through that branch of the legislature, calculated

to do much mischief, and finally to set aside the Constitution so far as relates to the election of the President. It proposes that each house of Congress shall by ballot elect six members who shall form a committee [6 from the Senate; 6 from the House] with the Chief Judge of the US their chairman, for the purpose of examining and deciding on all contested elections, and with closed doors shall examine all the returns, and determine on the legality of any of the state proceedings as respects their mode of appointing electors. I think this the most alarming feature which has been exhibited from that quarter at any time heretofore.[27]

The arch-conservative William Cobbett had strong words for it: "This Bill was a sweeper. It would, had it passed into a law, have, in reality, placed the election of the President *in the hands of the Senate alone....* To lead the sovereign people through the farce of an election, when the choice was finally to be made by thirteen men, *seven* of whom were to be nominated by the Senate, was a departure from the *frankness,* which has been said to be the characteristics of republicans."

NEWSPAPER REACTIONS TO THE COUP ATTEMPT

When Senator Charles Pinckney released the text of the bill "to the Printer of the [*Philadelphia*] *Aurora,*" the editor

published it with very severe...remarks. The Senate summoned the man before them. He attended, and, after certain interrogatories, was ordered to attend on a subsequent day to receive his sentence. He asked for counsel, which was granted him, with the proviso, that the [legal] counsel should *not be permitted to question the jurisdiction of the Senate,* nor to urge any matter but *in mitigation.* The counsel, with the approbation of their client, refused to appear thus shackled, and their letters of refusal, being published in the newspapers, produced great effect.[28]

The consequences were that the Senate had effectually deprived the editor of his civil liberties, combined the functions of a judge and jury, and raised the specter of legislative tyranny.

MADISON'S AND JEFFERSON'S
REACTIONS TO THE COUP ATTEMPT

Madison, always noting the subtleties of any legislative or constitutional maneuver, was outraged. He saw the Ross bill "bid[ding] defiance to any possible parchment securities against usurpation." "Should the spirit of the Bill be followed up," he wrote, "it is impossible to say, how far the choice of the Executive may be drawn out of the Constitutional hands, and subjected to the management of the Legislature....If this licentiousness in constructive perversions of the Constitution, continue to increase, we shall soon have to look into our code of laws, and not [to] the Charter of the people, for the form as well as the powers of our Government."[29]

Jefferson's reaction to this crisis was similar to Madison's: "The enemies of our Constitution are preparing a fearful operation; and the dissensions in this State are too likely to bring things to the situation they wish, when our Bonaparte, surrounded by his comrades in arms, may step in to give us political salvation in his way. It behooves our citizens to be on their guard, to be firm in their principles...We are able to preserve our self-government if we will but think so."[30]

A DECLARATION OF PRINCIPLES
TO POLARIZE THE ELECTORATE

Addressing himself to the urgency of the national crisis that both he and Madison perceived, Jefferson fell back on an old revolutionary strategy: the announcing of a declaration that, in rhetorical form, would parallel the Declaration of Independence. He thus wrote to Philip Nicholas, "It is too early to think of a declaratory act as yet, but the time is approaching and not distant....As soon as it can be depended on, we must have 'a Declaration of the principles of the Constitution' in nature of a Declaration of rights, in all the points in which it has been violated."[31]

The conversion of this revolutionary device to an elective situation was interesting; and from an ideological standpoint, it would have split the national Congress (where Jefferson wished it to take place) into two major factions: one for the principles of republicanism, the other against them. It was an inflammatory suggestion, one that would polarize the legislature; and if it trickled down to the state legislatures, it would polarize the society as well. But this suggestion reveals Jefferson's revolutionary state of mind before he knew the outcome of the presidential primary election in New York.

Preparations for the election in New York City had been from the start almost totally in the hands of Aaron Burr, "a man whose intrigue and management [was] most astonishing."[32] In the typical old-style politics of faction, Burr had personally assembled the republican slate and called together a meeting to support it. Burr's one-man show was the essence of a personal faction. In his own words, he directed the nominating process thus:

> As soon as the room begins to fill up, I will nominate Daniel Smith as chairman, and put the question quickly. Daniel being in the chair, you must each nominate one member, I will nominate one...and others...and, in this way, we will get them nominated. We must then have some inspiring speeches, close the meeting, and retire. We must then have a caucus and invite some of our most active and patriotic Democrats, both young and old, appoint meetings in the different wards, select speakers to address each, and keep up frequent meetings at Tammany Hall until the election.[33]

Indeed, as Jefferson had noted, the slate consisted of the most famous and distinguished revolutionary figures that could be found to lend their name to the republican cause. Thus the republican strategy in New York was to field a group of candidates so illustrious that the average citizen would vote for long-familiar names.

The strategy worked, and in addition to surging republican fortunes, Burr emerged as one of the foremost political figures in the nation.[34]

The impact of republican success was anathema to the Federalists. Repudiated at the polls and sensing the disaster that lay ahead if the verdict was not reversed, the Federalists immediately held a "select and confidential federal caucus." Matthew Davis, one of the most active participants on the republican side, stated that the purpose of the caucus was "to solicit Governor [John] Jay to convene the existing legislative forthwith, for the purpose of changing the mode of choosing electors for president, and placing it in the hands of the people by districts. The effect of such a measure would have been to neutralize the State of New

York, and…would have secured to the federal party their president and vice-president."

The news of the caucus was relayed to William Duane, editor of the *Aurora,* who promptly published an account of the meeting. The Federalists immediately denounced the author as a "Jacobin calumniator, and the whole story was pronounced a vile fabrication. One of the New York City papers reprinted the letter, and thus close[d] its commentary on it: 'Where is the American who *will not detest the author of this infamous lie?*"[35]

HAMILTON'S ILLEGAL SCHEME TO CHANGE NEW YORK'S VOTE

The effort was worthy of a twenty-first-century public relations expert crassly manipulating primary elections. The "infamous lie" turned out to be the truth. None other than the intellectual leader of the Federalists had stooped to such a low level that he was willing, through force and through fraud, to subvert the sanctity of the constitutional process.

Hamilton set the wheels of faction in motion by writing a letter to John Jay, the governor of New York:

> You have been informed of the loss of our election in this city…

> The moral certainty therefore is, that there will be an anti-federal majority in the ensuing Legislature; and the very high probability is that this will bring *Jefferson* into the chief magistracy, unless it be prevented by the measure which I shall now submit to your consideration, namely, the immediate calling together of the existing Legislature.

> I am aware that there are weighty objections to the measure, but the reasons for it appear to me to outweigh the objections; and in times like these in which we live, it will not do to be over-scrupulous. *It is easy to sacrifice the substantial interests of society by a strict adherence to ordinary rules.*

Then Hamilton, completely overlooking the fact that he had requested Jay to commit an immoral act against law and the Constitution (i.e., those "ordinary rules"), alluded to the integrity of the governor and artfully suggested, "I shall not be supposed to mean that any thing ought to be done which integrity will forbid." The constitutional rules, he suggested, "ought to yield to the extraordinary nature of the crisis. They ought not to hinder the taking of a *legal* and *constitutional* step," he said, which would not be in accordance with the Constitution.[36]

Hamilton had concluded that the ends justified the means, and in the following sentence he told why: "[We must] prevent [Jefferson] an atheist in religion, and a fanatic in politics, from getting possession of the helm of state." Reasoning "from indubitable facts," he lectured Jay on his naïveté and led the governor to believe that the consequences of *not* taking his advice would be revolution: "You, sir, know in a great degree the anti-federal party; but I fear you do not know them as well as I do. It is a composition, indeed, of very incongruous materials; but all tending to mischief—some of them, to the OVERTHROW of the GOVERNMENT, by stripping it of its due energies; others of them, to a REVOLUTION, after the manner of BONAPARTE. I speak from indubitable facts, not from conjectures and inferences."

Following this attempt at intimidation, Hamilton softened his language and appealed to Jay's political constituency. Calling the legislature into session would "be approved by all the federal party" and be "justified by unequivocal reasons of PUBLIC SAFETY."

Hamilton went on to rationalize his suggestion for all mankind: "The reasonable part of the world will, I believe, approve it. They will see it as a proceeding out of the common course, but warranted by the particular nature of the crisis and the great cause of social order." Blinded by his fury, his hatred of Jefferson and Burr, and the prospects of losing power, Hamilton had gone so far as to accept a version of Jefferson's and Madison's "interposition theory" in the Virginia and Kentucky Resolutions. Then, being so bold as to instruct Jay in minute detail as to how to corrupt the electoral process, he wrote:

> In your communication to the Legislature they ought to be told that temporary circumstances had rendered it probable that, without their interposition, the executive authority of the general government would be transferred to hands hostile to the system heretofore pursued with so much success, and dangerous to the peace, happiness, and order of the country; that under this impression, from facts

convincing to your own mind, you had thought it your duty to give
the existing Legislature an opportunity for deliberating whether it
would not be proper to interpose, and endeavor to prevent so great
an evil by referring the choice of electors to the people distributed
into districts.

Finally, Hamilton revealed his contempt for popular government
by describing the violence of party, incidentally accepting Jefferson's idea
in nearly identical language of why party must be suppressed. He then
noted with condescension the inevitable cycle of revolutions to which he
believed republican (i.e., popular) governments were subject.

At this point it is obvious that Hamilton perceived that Jefferson's
Revolution of 1800 had already begun:

> In weighing this suggestion you will doubtless bear in mind that
> popular governments must certainly be overturned, and, while
> they endure, prove engines of mischief, if one party will call to its
> aid all the resources which vice can give, and if the other (however
> pressing the emergency) confines itself within all the ordinary forms
> of delicacy and decorum.

> The Legislature can be brought together in three weeks, so that there
> will be full time for the object; but none ought to be lost.

> Think well, my dear sir, of this proposition—appreciate the extreme
> danger of the crisis.[37]

JAY: A PRINCIPLED POLITICIAN

The "crisis" was one of magnitude, and as rumors filled the air as well
as the newspapers of the nation, many believed the republic was on the
brink of civil war. Cobbett was one of those who, ordinarily supporting
the High Federalists in every undertaking, nevertheless drew the line. His
confidence in Jay proved worthy: "It was said that Mr. Jay, the governor
of New York, foreseeing that the legislature of that state would choose
electors favorable to Mr. Jefferson, was resolved not to call a session,
and thus deprive the state of its voice in the election. But, so bold, and,
indeed, so unlawful a measure, is not to be expected from Mr. Jay, who,
though he might prevent the election of Jefferson, would certainly stain

his own character, and very probably plunge the country into an immediate civil war."[38]

In fact, much to his credit, Jay did not even send a reply. He scrawled
across the top of Hamilton's "proposition" the most succinct condemnation of party and faction penned by an American statesman: "Proposing
a measure for party purposes which it would not become me to adopt."[39]

ANOTHER HAMILTON SCHEME
TO SABOTAGE THE PRESIDENT

Next, Hamilton initiated a change in strategy that was disastrous in
its implications. Knowing that he could not simply ignore Adams and
jettison him without atomizing the Federalist organization, he suggested
to Theodore Sedgwick: "To support *Adams* and [General Charles Cotes-
worth] *Pinckney* equally is the only thing that can possibly save us from
the fangs of *Jefferson*."[40]

Thus Hamilton began his attack on the president. Claiming "most
of the most influential men of that party [the Federalist] consider him as
a very *unfit* and *incapable* character," Hamilton began sowing the seeds
of doubt. He subtly initiated a link between Adams and Jefferson in the
minds of the hardcore Federalists:

> If we must have an *enemy* at the head of the government, let it be one
> whom we can oppose, and for whom we are not responsible, who will
> not involve our party in the disgrace of his foolish and bad measures.
> Under *Adams,* as under *Jefferson,* the government will sink....

> The only way to prevent a fatal schism in the federal party is to
> support General Pinckney.[41]

After making up his mind to abandon Adams, Hamilton conceived
a new treachery: political espionage! He would steal the president's
papers to discover evidence to use against him. Informed in advance that
Timothy Pickering and James McHenry were about to resign from the
cabinet, Hamilton wrote a confidential message to the secretary of state:
"I perceive that you as well as McHenry are quitting the administration....
Allow me to suggest that you ought to take with you copies and extracts
of all such documents as will enable you to explain both *Jefferson* and

Adams. You are aware of a very curious journal of the latter when he was in Europe—a tissue of weakness and vanity."[42]

This eighteenth-century equivalent of a modern-day "bugging operation" found Hamilton's clique inside the highest circles of government and in a position to convey any and all secrets to which they might have access.

ADAMS OUTMANEUVERS HAMILTON

The fact that Adams had refused to appoint him commander in chief and had actually "argued the propriety of changing the commander-in-chief every year" had galled Hamilton.[43]

Adams's pardon of John Fries had appeared to Hamilton a contemptible bid for popularity, as did the president's sending of William Vans Murray to reopen negotiations with France. All were against the advice of Hamilton and his supporters. Finally, when Adams dismissed the secretaries of state and war and supported the disbanding of the army in quick succession, he struck a blow so hard that Hamilton felt compelled to hit back.[44] Retaliation took the form of a direct letter to the president, a prelude to the pamphlet that Hamilton was preparing. Thus Hamilton, attempting to engage the president in a polemic, accused Adams of asserting "the existence of a British faction in this country…and that you have sometimes named me."[45]

Adams, of course, was too shrewd a politician to rise to Hamilton's provocation. Hamilton had literally accused the president of having his friends attack him for "electioneering purposes." In every other way, however, the president's charges denouncing Hamilton were beginning to take hold if for no other reason than they substantiated what the Jeffersonians had been saying all along.

HOW ADAMS'S ENEMIES SAW HIS FRIENDSHIP WITH JEFFERSON

Not only was Adams openly hostile to Hamilton but he was aiding the hated Jefferson.

Fisher Ames implied as much when he remarked that Adams, for what he considered the good of the country, or a spirit of "revenge," was willing to abandon the Federalist faction with whom he had been identified since the first Washington administration. In a long letter to Rufus King, outlining the domestic political situation, Ames described the mutual admiration that had sprung up between Jefferson and Adams and the latter's identification with the principles of the American Revolution:

> I think there is rather too much complacency on the part of our man [Adams] towards his antagonist [Jefferson]…This proceeds from several causes—but chiefly from the lofty idea he [Adams] entertains of his own superior wisdom and greatness which disdains to have either for a second or a successor any less personage than the *first* of the other side. He has also a strong revolutionary taint in his mind, admires the characters, principles and means which that revolutionary system exacts and for a short period seems to legitimate, and as you know holds cheap any reputation that was not *then* founded and top'd off. Accordingly he respects his rival and the *Gazette* here, absolutely devoted to him and in the hands of his personal friends exclusively, is silent and has been for some months in respect to that rival. His irreligion, wild philosophy and gimcrackery in politics are never mentioned. On the contrary the great man has been known to speak of him with much regard, and an affected indignation at the charge of irreligion, asking what has that to do with the public and adding that he is a good patriot, citizen and father. The good Lady his wife has been often talkative in a similar strain, and she is as complete a politician as any Lady in the old French Court.[46]

It seemed inconceivable to Ames that the president would hold himself above the Hamiltonian faction and jeopardize Federalist unity. As early as July, George Cabot had expressed the opinion "I have no doubt Mr. A[dams] will favor the election of Jefferson in preference to a federal Rival, as far as he dares."[47]

The fact that Adams had gained control of the *Gazette of the United States,* which was silent as to Jefferson, was indicative that a change in policy and attitude had been adopted. And knowing Abigail Adams's fondness for Jefferson throughout a lifetime's correspondence, Ames's assessment of her political acumen would increase rather than decrease that possibility.

"SHADOWS, CLOUDS, AND DARKNESS"
IN THE FEDERALIST FACTION

In sum, Adams had personally destroyed whatever unity the Federalists might have enjoyed. Sedgwick, one of the most astute observers among the arch-Federalists, remarked to King:

> He [the president] every where denounces the men, and almost all the men in whom he confided, at the beginning of his administration, as an oligarchish faction, who are combined to drive him from office, because they cannot govern him...[with] Hamilton its head, the country is to be driven into a war with France and a more intimate, if not an indissoluble, union with Great Britain. In consequence of these representations by him, which are diffused thro' this state by his friends, and more by the indefatigable industry of his enemies the jacobins, the federal party *here* has been disorganized, and every where thro' the nation its energies are paralized.[48]

The president's decision to destroy the power of the Hamilton faction within his administration had been devastating. Through his masterful understanding of the arts and the machinations of politics, Adams had engineered the total collapse of Federalism.

Robert Troup, writing to King, put it starkly: "I cannot describe to you how broken and scattered your federal friends are! At present we have no rallying point; and no mortal can divine where or when we shall again collect our strength!...Shadows, clouds, and darkness rest on our future prospects. My spirits, in spite of all my philosophy, cannot maintain the accustomed level."[49]

The Politics of the Revolution of 1800: Revolution

*"The progress of the horseman can only be proportioned to the speed of his horse." Had Hamilton, the "commander-in-chief" of both houses of Congress, of all the five heads of departments of General Washington, and consequently of the President of the United States, been aware of your principle, and acted upon it, **the revolution of 1801 would not have happened**. There is...no exaggeration...in this language...it is strictly true.*

> —John Adams to James Lloyd
> April 24, 1815 (emphasis added)

T HE COLLAPSE OF THE FEDERALISTS' FAÇADE OF UNITY IMPROVED the republicans' situation immensely. Yet it would be months before they realized their gain, and in the interim their opponents would be compelled to play out their intended roles. Generally recognizing their shared prospect for a dismal political future, the supporters of Alexander Hamilton appeared paralyzed. But the leader of the arch faction was determined to do something—anything—to revive his flagging power base.

Accordingly, Hamilton refined his attack on President John Adams and released it to a number of the Federalist leaders. He seemed to ignore and discount the clouded prediction of what such an attack would mean. His correspondence indicates that nearly every adviser disapproved. They appeared, almost to a man, to reflect the opinion of Fisher Ames, who believed that Adams had decided to aid Jefferson and scuttle the Federalists' ambitions. Reinforcing Ames was George Cabot, who wrote early in August that "if Adams prevails," it will be by his "sacrificing the old federal cause and all its advocates."[1]

Be that as it may, by September Hamilton had become desperate. To Oliver Wolcott he reiterated his concern: "You may depend upon it, a very serious impression has been made on the public mind, by the partisans of Mr. Adams, to our disadvantage; [and these people] for want of information, are disposed to regard his opponents as factious men. If this cannot be counteracted, our characters are the sacrifice."

HAMILTON'S PAMPHLET
ATTACKING THE PRESIDENT

Decrying "anonymity," the leader of the High Federalist faction was anxious to get a rebuttal into print for the eyes, at least, of Adams's supporters. Not wishing to implicate the source of his information, Hamilton was willing to "stand upon the credit of [his] own veracity." Thus seeking Wolcott's approval, Hamilton sent him a draft of the pamphlet, asking him to "say quickly what is to be done, for there is no time to spare."[2] Again he wrote Adams, virtually demanding a confrontation.[3] When the president maintained his silence, Hamilton released his essay titled *A Letter from Alexander Hamilton concerning the Public Character of John Adams, Esq.; President of the United States.*[4] It was Hamilton's intention that the circulation be private, but Aaron Burr obtained a copy and proceeded to have extracts printed in the *Aurora* and the *New London* (Connecticut) *Bee.*[5]

The publication of Hamilton's essay caused an immediate sensation, and the result was the complete disintegration of the Federalists, destroying any possibility of solidarity in the coming election. Instead of "sound[ing] the tocsin about Jefferson," as Ames had advised Wolcott,[6] it appeared that the campaign, so far as the Federalists were concerned, centered around a controversy between the president and Hamilton.

The pamphlet was in many ways a series of accusations and personal innuendos, all calculated to bring into disrepute the four years of Adams's presidency. Hamilton's personal attack not only succeeded in throwing the Federalists into consternation but alienated many of his closest friends. Evidently, Hamilton had been so disposed to vent his anger against

Adams that he refused to listen to his counsel. Ames had argued against it, albeit indirectly.

Robert Troup, one of Hamilton's closest confidants, expressed his dismay less than two weeks after its publication: "The general impression at Albany among our friends was that it would be injurious and they lamented the publication of it. Upon my return home I find a much stronger disapprobation of it expressed every where. In point of imprudence it is coupled with the pamphlet formerly published by the General respecting himself; and not a man in the whole circle of our friends but condemns it."[7]

Hamilton, however, was glorying in the furor that the letter had created and was oblivious to the defections of his friends. To Timothy Pickering he wrote, "You no doubt have seen my pamphlet respecting the conduct and character of President Adams. The press teems with replies, and I may finally think it expedient to publish a second time."[8]

JEFFERSON'S SUPPORTERS ANSWER HAMILTON

But try as he might, Hamilton would not be able to keep up with the rising sentiment his attack had provoked. Adams's supporters made replies, and the republicans published excerpts in all the states that had not chosen their electors. One of these, *An Answer to Alexander Hamilton's Letter Concerning the Public Conduct and Character of John Adams, Esq.,* was particularly devastating.

James Cheetham turned Hamilton's logic against him and accused him of making "ambition the principle lever of all [his] actions." In a series of questions directed at Hamilton himself, Cheetham asked, "Who controuled the New York elections, and represented himself the umpire and leader of the federal party, it was a gentleman by the name of EGO, so notorious in every page of your pamphlet."

Cheetham made a succinct review of Hamilton's role in the New York elections and then portrayed the Federalists as every republican saw them and, indeed, as many Federalists had now begun to view themselves:

> British agents...united in your plans, and enjoyed the pleasing
> dreams of monarchy...The points you had gained by such base and

dishonorable means gave you a majority in congress, and saddled the country with alien and sedition laws…laws for which public necessity never called, but which served to shade and protect the follies and vices of administration; laws that were intended…to restrain the liberty of the press, the only certain guarantee of public freedom and national happiness…but all your projects have proved abortive, and those connected with you are sinking into irretrievable disgrace.[9]

HAMILTON'S MISGUIDED STRATEGY

It was as Richard Stockton had told Oliver Wolcott six months before. What was the reason for the abandonment of Adams, asked Stockton. "These men [the leaders of the Hamiltonian faction] have for four years been holding up Mr. Adams as one of the wisest and firmest men in the United States. What reason could be given for so sudden a change of sentiment?"[10] Stockton's query was never answered, and Adams's place in the hearts of his countrymen remained firmly fixed. He was, said George Cabot, somehow "interwoven with the web of national government."[11]

The policy of Hamilton's support for Charles Pinckney had been attacked on several grounds. Theodore Sedgwick placed his finger on the main problem when he stated that the president himself had implied the reason for Pinckney's advancement: "because he could be more easily influenced."[12]

Many simply resented Hamilton's attempt to draw a parallel between Pinckney and George Washington. Pinckney was, in fact, little known compared with Adams and Jefferson. He had none of the glamour that surrounded Burr, and his one claim to statesmanship had been during the XYZ Affair.[13] Tunis Wortman, one of the ablest spokesmen for the Jeffersonians, put the candidacy in perspective: "I know not Mr. Pinckney, politically speaking, he is a man whom nobody knows, but it is perfectly understood that he is contemplated as a second Bibulus who permitted Caesar to govern. We can judge of the individual from the character of the party by whom he is supported…C. C. Pinckney is now the candidate of the exiled members of the present administration."[14]

None of the republican critics, however, could deter Hamilton from his dream that supporting Pinckney would ultimately prove successful.

Hamilton, in attempting to manipulate the choice of a president, had, in six short months, tried to destroy the election laws of the state of New York, committed an act of political espionage, alienated a vast number of Federalist supporters by unnecessarily attacking the conduct of the president, and lost sight of his original goal: the defeat of Jefferson. By December 1800, on the eve of the presidential election, he was truly a desperate man. His stranglehold on the Federalist faction had been broken, and he faced the inescapable probability that he had committed political suicide.

What was even worse was the prospect that he had driven Adams into the arms of the republican faction.

As Hamilton's friends were now saying to one another, their leader's strategy had culminated in uniting the two men he hated most: for nearly a decade both Adams and Jefferson had been his bitterest enemies.

THE HIGH FEDERALISTS SEE REVOLUTION COMING

A writer in the *Salem* (Massachusetts) *Gazette* commented, "There is now on foot a plan of the Jacobins, which they are pursuing everywhere with the most indefatigable industry, to have a majority in our next legislature, who will favour the views of France, and the Virginia and Kentucky Resolutions…and there is much fear they will…accomplish their ends.[15] As we have seen, in May 1799 New York politico Robert Troup realized that Aaron Burr had "done a great deal towards *revolutionizing* the State."

New York congressman William Bingham noted, "The Party which is attached to them [the Jacobins] have a better System and more Industry than their opponents and…make a *greater impression on the lower Class of People.*" Bingham was describing a popularly based revolutionary movement, in complete contrast to the elitism of the Federalists.[16] Hamilton wrote that Burr was "intriguing with all his might in New Jersey, Rhode Island, and Vermont, and there is a possibility of success in his intrigues."[17]

Finally, the *Connecticut Courant* stated in late September, "There is scarcely a possibility that we shall escape a civil war."[18] But it was already too late. By June 1800, Gideon Granger had written to Jefferson that "as it respects New England,…a mighty revolution in opinion has taken place within one year."[19]

JEFFERSON'S STRATEGY CONFIRMED

That was the kind of news calculated to lighten Jefferson's heart. The changing of men's minds was his principal aim, and the fact that this could be accomplished through the engine of the press while still keeping an eye on the elections was proof that a revolution could remain peaceful. It also reflected the wisdom of placing the locus of opposition in the state governments.

The sixteen states were the units that could cut into the strength of the Federalists by degrees. One would not have to confront a national government on every issue, a national army, or administration. It was possible to gain control of those states that were already republican in sentiment, neutralize others, and isolate the few that were intransigent.

Ames saw this strategy at work and was frightened. His knowledge of the past told him that a violent revolution was in the making: "The rival state governments are organized factions, and I have long seen, are systematically levying the force to subvert their common enemy....I see the great states leaguing together under democratic governors; Jefferson and Co., at the head of a stronger faction than any government can struggle with long, or prevail against at last, unless by military force; for it is obvious to me, that all other modes of decision will be spurned as soon as the anties think they have force on their side."[20]

A FEDERALIST EDITOR PROPOSES ABOLISHING THE STATES

John Ward Fenno noticed as much when he wrote a political tract against the Jeffersonians. Seeing the state governments falling increasingly into the hands of the opposition, he wrote, "Those pestiferous incitements to demagogy, the State Governments, might be abolished and their offices rendered dependent as they ought to be on the Government of the United States, instead of having it in their power as at present, to *organize revolts against that government.*"[21]

Fenno, editor of the *Gazette of the United States*, saw the implications of the opposition's political organization.

His criticism of Adams's lack of "prudence" in the face of revolution was the difference between the two Federalist factions: one would in defiance of the Constitution abolish the state governments; the other was determined to maintain a respect for federalism and the Constitution. Indeed when John Adams gave his fourth annual address in November 1800, he asserted that Americans should "fortify and cling to those institutions" and criticized those who would promote "dangerous innovations which may diminish their influence."[22]

But a recognition that revolution was occurring in their midst would simply not have taken place if the rhetoric of politics had not reached the fundamentals of society. The opposition that had merely "whisper[ed] against government" in 1799 had by 1800 increased its decibel level to a clamor that was now a constant din in the ears of Federalists.

The Virginia and Kentucky Resolutions had spoken to the basic social contract, a certain sign that government was breaking down. And the rhetoric of those resolutions had taken a form that set the stage as well as the tone for 1800: opposition to government based on principle and not party.

A RETURN TO MONARCHY

One writer remarked succinctly, "We have seen old Tories, the enemies of our revolution, recommended as the guardians of our country."[23]

Even Jefferson was writing on the theme as late as December 1800: "The Constitution to which we are all attached was meant to be republican...Yet we have seen it so interpreted and administered, as to be truly what the French have called, a *monarchie masque*." If we cannot restore true republican principles, he asserted, "we shall be unable to realize the prospects which have been held out to the people, and we must fall back into monarchism."[24]

Another writer simply stated, "There is a monarchical party in the United States, and...Mr. Hamilton and Mr. Adams belong to that party."[25]

The charge of monarchy was even more effective when it was linked to the system of administration and finance that had characterized England for the past two centuries. One author noted that the national debt had accumulated to "eighty millions of dollars....But why was this done?" He continued:

> The answer is obvious; Mr. Hamilton and his party, knew very well that the people would never consent to a monarchy, and that his only chance was to introduce it by degrees; it was therefore necessary to

assimilate the measures of administration as nearly as possible to those of a monarchy, and the funding system was one of the first steps. The genealogy of the business will stand briefly thus: the funding system begets and perpetualizes debt; debt begets intrigue, offices and corruption; those beget taxation; taxation begets the treasury; the treasury begets a swarm of Pickerings and Daytons; Pickerings and Daytons beget a standing army, and a standing army begets monarchy, and monarchy begets an enslaved and impoverished people.[26]

HAMILTON'S SPEECH AT THE CONSTITUTIONAL CONVENTION

Thus in Marcus Brutus's mind, the economic system introduced by Hamilton led straight to a reimposition of monarchy. Citing his reverence for the "course dictated by the spirit of our revolution," another writer referred to the federal convention and then warned those who failed to take the subject seriously:

> Are such suggestions to be lightly regarded when it is now known that a number of men, who have been our political leaders, were holding their meetings in the year 1787 to contrive ways and means for the establishment of what they termed, *A Confederate Monarchy?* When we read the speech of General Hamilton in the Federal Convention, and now find him at the head of our army? When we hear our leading men avow that this country can never be governed without an *Hereditary Monarch?* When we see the appropriate plans of *Monarchy* adopted by administration? When we read the federal papers filled with reflections on liberty and republicanism, and with praises of *Monarchial* government? When Fenno, the mouth-piece of the federal party has just published a scheme of a *Federated, Presidential, Monarchial Aristocracy?*

The author closed with the admonition "If one half of my positions and conclusions be just, *A Monarchy is decidedly before us!*"[27]

The rhetoric implicit in these political writings led to a sense of crisis, an inescapable feeling that in the results of this election hung the fate of popular government.

Every politician of national standing had been assessing the outcome of the election. By August, Hamilton had begun to speculate on the possibility of Pinckney and Adams losing and Jefferson or Burr becoming president. If it were the latter, Hamilton suggested, Burr "will certainly attempt to reform the government *à la Bonaparte*. He is as unprincipled and dangerous a man as any country can boast—as true a Catiline as ever met in midnight conclave."[28] Hamilton was describing nothing less than a conspiracy against the republic.

JEFFERSON WINS, BUT THEN HE DOESN'T

When the presidential electors were known, Jefferson's supporters were ecstatic: "Our Electors are chosen,..." wrote Peter Freneau, "rejoice and let the good news be known. Our country is yet safe. The vote tomorrow will be Jefferson 8; Burr 7; Clinton 1. This I am told—it is not the wish to risque any person being higher than Jefferson."[29]

But the country was far from safe, and the results of the election were to presage the results in the other states as well. For it was soon realized, even before the results from all the states were in, that the Jeffersonians had carried the election.[30] In the final tally, the vote stood Jefferson eight and Burr eight. It was a tie that indicated a lack of foresight on the part of the republicans for which they might pay dearly.

Jefferson immediately sensed the danger. He wrote to Burr, discreetly informing him of his plans for the new administration. Lamenting the fact that Burr would not be in his cabinet, Jefferson implied that Burr must now act out his role as the vice president—a role Jefferson believed to be severely limited. By instructing Burr in this manner, Jefferson also implied that he had expected to emerge as the clear presidential choice. The reason he had not was only thinly veiled. The contest, he said, "was badly managed," and it was unfortunate "not to have arranged with certainty what seems to have been left to hazard."

Then, alluding to the problem that was uppermost in his, and by now everyone else's mind, he wrote, "It was the more material, because I understand several of the high-flying federalists have expressed their hope that the two republican tickets may be equal, and their determination in that case to prevent a choice by the House of Representatives, (which they are strong enough to do) and let the government devolve on a President of the Senate."[31]

Thus Jefferson had joined Hamilton in imagining his own version of a conspiracy against the republic.

RUMORS OF CATILINE
AND BONAPARTE

By the second week of December, it was realized that a tie between two republican candidates had occurred. Rumors and speculations filled the air, of which Jefferson's was only one. No one knew what was going to happen. Hardly anyone even knew how to proceed. The Constitution, by failing to make a distinction between a president and a vice president in the electoral votes, had failed to "enounce precisely the true expression of the public will."[32] And while it gave limited guidelines as to how a successor would be chosen, it was nevertheless an unprecedented state of affairs in the political history of the Western world.

One thing had become obvious to Jefferson and Madison, though, as it had to the more perceptive Federalists: their strategy of revolution had been a resounding success. More than any other measure, the elections in the states had validated Jefferson's idea of the possibility of a permanent, peaceful, constitutional revolution in a republic.

His idea of progressively organizing the states to obtain majorities in their legislatures, until a majority of the Union had been accomplished, was now a fact. Suddenly, for want of a single electoral vote, the entire political strategy of peaceful revolution was in jeopardy.

Jefferson's and Madison's faith in the constitutional process and the limits to which they were willing to go to preserve republican government would now be put to the test. Would the House of Representatives honor its constitutional obligation and elect a new president? Or would faction rear its head and plunge an orderly constitutional process into an abyss of violence and intrigue? Hamilton had predicted a "revolution" if Pinckney was not elected. He had also predicted a conspiracy "*à la Bonaparte*" if the Federalists adhered to Burr.

That event, fresh in everyone's minds, had seen General Napoleon Bonaparte drive the legislature from its halls at the point of a bayonet, dismiss the Directory, and, after overturning the constitution of the republic, declare himself emperor. Hamilton had in the same connection alluded to the sinister conspiratorial mentality of the Roman Catiline (Lucius Sergius Catilina). There was no mistaking his meaning: Burr would become Catiline if he were ever elevated to the presidency.

STRETCHING THE CONSTITUTION

With these thoughts Jefferson wrote to his most trusted political adviser that "the federalists...openly declare they will prevent an election, and will name a President of the Senate, *pro tem* by what they say would only be a *stretch* of the Constitution."[33]

Meanwhile, Madison, struggling with a sick father at his home in Orange, had written to Governor James Monroe of the "inquietude prevailing in this quarter as to the precise issue of the election."[34] Unaware of the final election returns or the uproar that was being fomented in the new capital city, Madison next wrote to Jefferson matter-of-factly: in case of a tie electoral vote, the choice for a president would "devolve on the House of Representatives...There can be no danger, I presume." Madison, whose blind instincts were also constitutional, naturally assumed that the next level of decision making would automatically take over. But others did not necessarily see the same sequence.

Already Madison alluded to a development responsible for the nightmare that would follow for the next two months. Madison's advice, that it would be "desirable" to preclude a tie vote "by the foresight of some of the Electors," came approximately one month too late.[35]

This was a crucial issue and would cast its pall over events for the next four years. Jefferson had, in an earlier letter to Burr, disclaimed any intention of reducing Burr's total number of votes. This avowal was designed to serve a dual purpose: to gain Burr's personal confidence and to indicate to him that a repetition of the events of 1796, when Burr had received merely one vote from Virginia, had not occurred. Burr, however, was suspicious of Virginia's intentions; he had expressed his suspicions to Maria Gallatin, wife of the Pennsylvania congressman.[36]

Despite this background of mutual assurance amid mutual suspicion, it was apparent that something had gone wrong. Within a week the inner circle of the Virginia clique began to suspect that a new Federalist intrigue was commencing. Jefferson summed up the situation:

> The federalists…propose to prevent an election in Congress, and to transfer the government by an act to the C. J. (Jay) or Secretary of State, or to let it devolve on the President *pro tem* of the Senate, till next December, which gives them another year's predominance, and the chances of future events. The republicans propose to press forward to an election. If they fail in this, a concert between the two higher candidates may prevent the dissolution of the government and danger of anarchy, by an operation, bungling indeed and imperfect, but better than letting the legislature take the nomination of the Executive entirely from the people.[37]

In the last two weeks of December, Jefferson communicated with his major advisers, Madison and Monroe, on the emergence of the crisis. His correspondence indicates that despite his disappointment over the failure to arrange the electoral votes and avoid a tie, he nevertheless did not suspect, or at least say he suspected, Burr of intriguing with the Federalist faction.

His main preoccupation was with a Federalist faction turning the government over to the chief justice or the president of the Senate. At best he hoped to proceed with the election with the belief that he and Burr would be able to make an amicable arrangement between themselves over a future republican administration. He was thus willing to sacrifice his personal ambition and serve as the vice president for another four years. At worst he saw the emergence of a legislative tyranny and a usurpation of the Constitution that would still have a constitutional solution after a year.

An observation one cannot help but make is that Jefferson, faced with the possible destruction of nearly five years of hard political labor, was still willing to seek a solution through the constitutional and legislative machinery. Perhaps his mind was reminiscing on the scenes he had witnessed in France when the factions abandoned the constitutional process for a trust in force.

This was not so on the part of the Federalists. On the contrary, the extremists, with the exception of Hamilton, were more than willing to cabal in an attempt to resurrect their fleeing fortunes. George Cabot observed to a friend abroad in the closing days of December that despite the "remarkable calm here...some of the Jacobins are afraid... Burr will be Chief."[38]

Joseph Hale, a Federalist, noted it had become "fashionable with feds to declare in favor of Mr. Burr."[39]

Oliver Wolcott, referring to the Federalists' choosing between Jefferson and Burr, noted simply: "There will be intriguing here through the winter on a high scale."[40] Uriah Tracy, an arch-Federalist, wrote to the former secretary of war, indicating that perhaps all was not lost: "Burr is a cunning man. If he cannot outwit all the Jeffersonians, I do not know the man."[41]

From republicans came similar observations. Two weeks later Stevens Mason wrote to a Jeffersonian leader that "the desperate Feds, are hope[ful] of throwing things into confusion by defeating an election altogether, and making a President for us by act of Congress. This project has been the subject of much caballing and caucusing."[42]

One writer in the New York *Gazette and General Advertiser* said Burr would become president by "forming a faction among the dregs—the refuse of both parties."[43]

The truth was, several factions had now developed and were contending against one another: Jefferson, Hamilton, Burr, and Adams supporters often found themselves in violent disagreement. It thus appeared to many that the politics of faction had plunged the country into a constitutional crisis.

On the same day that Jefferson wrote to Madison of the Federalist plan to deny the election, Hamilton appealed to his faithful friend Wolcott: "Jefferson is to be preferred...as to *Burr*, there is nothing in his favor. His private character is not defended by his most partial friends. He is bankrupt beyond redemption, except by the plunder of his country. His public principles have no other spring or aim than his own aggrandizement, *per fas et nefas.* If he can, he will certainly disturb our institutions, to secure to himself *permanent power,* and with it *wealth.* He is truly the Catiline of America."

With deadly calculation Hamilton continued, denoting his sense of urgency:

> But early measures must be taken to fix on this point the opinions of the Federalists....Burr will find partisans. If the thing be neglected, he may possibly go far.

> Yet it may be well enough to throw out a lure for him, in order to tempt him to start for the plate, and then *lay the foundation of dissension between the two chiefs.*"[44]

Thus, in the midst of an emerging constitutional crisis, Hamilton was not above attempting still another devious strategy: paralyzing the new administration and ultimately producing deep divisions within it.[45]

The following day Hamilton gave a justification for his opposition to Burr: it would injure the Federalists generally by acquiring the "animosity" of Jefferson if they failed; and if they succeeded, placing a man in power who could give "success to the Jacobin system." Hamilton believed that the Federalists deluded themselves if they thought they could win Burr to accept "federal views."

He then described Burr's character by charging that once Burr was in power, he would do anything, and use anyone, good or bad, "to accomplish his ends." "Every step in his career proves that he has formed himself upon the model of *Catiline,* and he is too cold-blooded and too determined a conspirator ever to change his plan."

He finally alluded to the fact that Burr had publicly toasted "Bonaparte" within the "last three or four weeks." The Federalists, he concluded, might as well bid "adieu to the Federal Troy, if they once introduce this Grecian horse into their citadel."

Following this warning, Hamilton announced the stipulations that the Federalists ought to extract from Jefferson. They were to be important, so much so that in the end they would decide whether the nation would be plunged into civil war. Hamilton laid down these propositions:

1st   The preservation of the actual fiscal system.

2d   Adherence to the neutral plan.

3d   The preservation and gradual increase of the navy.

4th   The continuance of our friends in the offices they fill, except in the great departments, in which he ought to be left free.[46]

Within one short week, Hamilton had attempted to alert those few leaders among the Federalists he could yet trust. His credibility as a political leader had been undermined by the attack on Adams,[47] yet he was able to make his case to Oliver Wolcott, Gouverneur Morris, James A. Bayard, Robert Troup, Timothy Pickering, Theodore Sedgwick, and others of influence.[48]

Urging Morris to use his "opinion…freely," Hamilton had begun a desperate campaign to gain control over what he saw was an inevitable but dangerous process.[49]

To James A. Bayard of Delaware, he sounded the depth of the constitutional crisis: "Several letters to myself and others from the city of Washington, excite in my mind extreme alarm on the subject of the future President." Then, waxing hotly about Burr's character and abilities, Hamilton hit upon the arguments that he believed would cause the most sensible Federalists to think twice before supporting Burr: Burr wanted permanent power, and he would destroy "the system":

> The maintenance of the existing institutions will not suit him; because under them his power will be too narrow and too precarious. Yet the innovations he may attempt will not offer the substitute of a system *durable* and *safe,* calculated to give lasting prosperity, and to unite liberty with strength. It will be the system of the day, sufficient to serve his own turn, and not looking beyond himself. To execute this plan, as the good men of the country cannot be relied upon, the worst will be used. Let it not be imagined that the difficulties of execution will deter, or a calculation of interest restrain. The truth is, that under forms of government like ours, too much is practicable to

men who will, without scruple, avail themselves of the bad passions of human nature.[50]

JOHN QUINCY ADAMS IDENTIFIES THE CONSEQUENCES OF FACTION

As the old year ended with the election in doubt and the prospect of a violent factional dispute on the horizon, John Quincy Adams summed up for many the mood that must have dominated the traditional Christmas spirit. Willing to admit that he might be in error, he nevertheless stated to his younger brother, Thomas Boylston Adams,

> It is impossible for me to avoid the supposition that the ultimate necessary consequence, if not *the ultimate object of both the extreme parties which divide us, will be a dissolution of the Union and a civil war.* Your father's policy was certainly to steer between the shoals on one side, and the rocks on the other. But as both factions have turned their arms against him, and the people themselves have abandoned him, there is too much reason to expect that the purpose common to the two opposite factions will be effected.[51]

A HIGH FEDERALIST CHOOSES BURR OVER JEFFERSON

Gouverneur Morris had estimated at one point, "It seems to be the general opinion that Colonel Burr will be chosen President by the House of Representatives. Many of them [the Federalists] think it highly dangerous that Mr. Jefferson should, in the present crisis, be placed in that office. They consider him as a theoretic man, who would bring the National Government back to something like the old Confederation. Mr. Nicholas comes to-day, and to him I state it as the opinion, not of light and fanciful but of serious and considerate men, that Burr must be preferred to Jefferson."[52]

The republicans attempted to stem the rising tide of doubt by sending Samuel Smith to meet again with Burr and obtain a declaration that he had no ambitions for the presidency and "to say he would not serve if elected."[53] Smith ended his interview with the opposite impression. Burr was not only willing to serve as president but had intimated the next morning that his republican "friends must join the federal vote" and vote him into the presidency, and Jefferson would then become vice president.[54]

Not only was the republican leadership repudiated by Burr himself but overtures were made to loyal Jeffersonians to gain their support. Jefferson recorded one incident that may have been made to others as well. Matthew Lyon of Vermont was approached by John Brown of Rhode Island, who, "urging him to vote for Colonel Burr," used these words: "What is it you want, Colonel Lyon? Is it office, is it money? Only say what you want, and you shall have it."[55] And while there was no direct connection proven between Burr and the solicitation, many republicans might draw an inference.

By the second week in January even the normally calm and unruffled Madison had begun to contemplate the excesses of the politics of faction. Writing to Jefferson, he avowed, "Desperate as some of the adverse party there may be, I can scarcely allow myself to believe that enough will not be found to frustrate the attempt to strangle the election of the people, and smuggle into the Chief Magistracy the choice of a *faction.*"

**MADISON FEARS
AN "INTERREGNUM"**

But his next thoughts bore directly on the crisis, suggesting several constitutional ways that it might be headed off. His first was to remind Jefferson that the president had it in his power to "appoint…as early a day as possible…for the succeeding House to meet and supply the omission." Then he proceeded to the possibility that appeared to everyone who was aware of the consequences of the scene being played before them: "On the supposition of either…*an interregnum* in the Executive, or of a surreptitious intrusion into it, it becomes a question of the first order, what is the course demanded by the crisis?" Madison's answer revealed his pessimism of what the future would hold. He began by raising two more questions. The first dealt with his fear of a usurpation of executive authority and the vacuum that would be created by that act. He had little doubt, as we have seen, to what that might lead. The second dealt with a more subtle problem and, so far as he was able to envision it, might provide a way to legitimate the constitutional will of the majority. Thus Madison believed that his second suggestion would enable the young nation to at least maintain an attachment to the principles of constitutionalism:

> Will it be best to acquiesce in a suspension or usurpation of the Executive authority till the meeting of Congress in December next, or for Congress to be summoned by a joint proclamation or recommendation of the two characters having a majority of votes for President? My present judgment favors the latter expedient. The prerogative of convening the Legislature must reside in one or other of them, and if both concur, must substantially include the requisite will. The intentions of the people would undoubtedly be pursued. And if, in reference to the Constitution, the proceeding be not strictly regular, the irregularity will be less in form than any other adequate to the emergency, and will lie in form only, rather than substance; whereas the other remedies proposed are substantial violations of the will of the people, of the scope of the Constitution, and of the public order and interest.[56]

Madison's suggestions were an indication that he had fully understood the dangerous game being played by the legislators in Washington. Indeed, in the days immediately preceding the election, the situation had become grave and finally desperate. Two days before the balloting, Gouverneur Morris captured the tension and the uncertainty that gripped the members of every faction: "It is impossible to determine, which of the two candidates will be chosen President. Rumors are various and intrigues great."[57]

Evidence of increasing support for Burr made Federalists like Hamilton shrill in their fulminations against Burr.[58] The *Philadelphia Aurora* on February 6 printed a letter stating, "We are credibly informed [from] Mr. Bayard of Delaware...that it is the intention of the Federalists *at all hazards* to attempt the defeat of Mr. Jefferson's election. This information the Editor had direct two days ago."[59]

Republicans were equally determined. Congressman Joseph H. Nicholson wrote to a constituent that in the event of a usurpation, "Virginia would instantly proclaim herself out of the Union."[60] George Erving wrote to James Monroe that the Federalist extremists, men like

"Harper, Otis, Rutledge, etc....flatter themselves that they can bring their federal troops to act as heretofore in a united Phalanx."[61]

**GALLATIN'S LAST-DITCH
STRATEGY AGAINST USURPATION**

But the supporters of Jefferson were also forming a phalanx. Albert Gallatin, the Jeffersonian floor leader, conceived of a "plan" and with the consent of his fellow republicans presented it to Jefferson.

In it he stated the objectives of the extremists:

1. To elect Mr. B[urr].

2. To defeat the present election and order a new one.

3. To assume *executive* power during *interregnum*.

Noting that any effort on the extremists' part to assume power was "clearly unconstitutional," he asked,

> If they shall *usurp*, for unconstitutional assumption is usurpation, are we to submit or not?...

> Any assumption on their part is usurpation. Usurpation must be resisted by freemen whenever they have the power of resisting. To admit to a contrary doctrine would justify submission in every case, and encourage usurpation for ever hereafter. The mode of resisting seems to be the only question.

Gallatin went on to note that in the states controlled by the republicans it would be possible to resist and not risk civil war "by refusing to obey only those acts which may flow from the usurper as President."

The wily Gallatin, who had "clogged the wheels of government" before, now revealed why he was so feared by the Federalists. He outlined a plan whereby republicans would themselves consider "preventing every partial insurrection, or even individual act[s] of resistance,...refusing to obey every order from the usurper, such as a call for militia, etc.; declaring our intention to have the usurper punished according to law as soon as regular government shall have been re-established."

As an alternative to this plan, Gallatin suggested simply that the republicans not risk civil war and the ruin of republican institutions and "assume the executive power either by a joint act of the two candidates, or by the relinquishment of all claims by one of them."

Next Gallatin submitted an "outline of our [republican] conduct":

1. Persevere in voting for Mr. J[efferson].

2. Use every endeavor to defeat any law on the subject.

3. Try to prevail on Mr. A[dams] to refuse his assent to any such law, and not to call the Senate on any account if there shall be no choice by the House.

4. The Republican Senators to secede from any illegal meeting of the Senate…in case of no choice being made by the House.

5. To have a meeting, either self-created or of delegates appointed by the Legislatures of the Republican States, or only by the House of Representatives of those States where we have but one branch (viz., New York, Pennsylvania, Maryland, and South Carolina), in order to form an uniform plan of acting both in relation to a new election and to the usurpation if attempted.

Gallatin had considered every constitutional subtlety available. If that new election occurred, as suggested by the extremists, the republicans could protest it or let matters take their course and hope to duplicate their success; or they could leave the entire situation up to the next Congress, which would be republican controlled.

Another tack was to call a new national election. By another strategy the republicans agreed to refuse to obey all orders of the usurpers and obey only those they believed "should continue in operation."

Still other options were open: attempting to persuade John Adams to call on Congress "to put an end to the interregnum, or to propose passing a law for that purpose"; "to hasten the elections of Tennessee and Kentucky"; and to ask the legislatures of New York and Pennsylvania to appoint special electors. In all of their strategies, Gallatin noted, "the meeting [which would choose one of them] to be constituted and to act so as not to be considered as the result of an unconstitutional compact between the States." The consequences of each of these strategies were then hypothesized in detail.

The main consideration throughout the long list of options was the determination on the part of the republicans to do nothing that might endanger republican institutions. Specifically, Gallatin stated that the republicans should do anything to prevent "an assumption of power not strictly warranted by the forms and substance of our constitutions being adopted, and adopted by *us* in any one case."

While recognizing "the remedy [was so]…dangerous," they were determined to adhere to their principles and maintain the inviolability of the Constitution.

Everything depended on whether a "usurpation" took place. If it did, the Jeffersonians were prepared to go to desperate lengths.[62]

REPUBLICAN POLITICS EQUATED WITH TERROR

Such was the air of expectation that hung over the capital city when the new Congress convened. Fisher Ames, addressing himself to the state of the nation during this period, summed up the mood. He wished, of course, to describe only the Jeffersonians, but he was, in truth, describing the partisans of Burr and Hamilton, as well:

> A FACTION, whose union is perfect, whose spirit is desperate, addressing something persuasive to every prejudice, putting something combustible to every passion, granting some indulgence to every vice, promising those who dread the law to set them above it, to the mean whispering suspicion, to the ambitious offering power, to the rapacious, plunder, to the violent, revenge, to the envious, the abasement of all that is venerable, to innovators, the transmutation of all that is established, grouping together all that is folly, vice, and passion in the state, and forming of these vile materials another state, *an imperium in imperio*—Behold this is our condition, these our terrours. And what are the resources for our safety?[63]

No one at this point could or would tell. As John Vaughan had written to Jefferson, "Our political destiny is suspended by a slender thread."[64]

PENNSYLVANIA TAKES A STAND
AND MOBILIZES ITS MILITIA

The House of Representatives was in session on February 9 amid confusion and alarm. It was rumored that Governor Thomas McKean of Pennsylvania had declared that he would issue an executive order for all state officials to refuse to obey federal laws if Jefferson were not elected. For "Pennsylvania will *protest* against the proceeding, and will refuse to obey any laws that may be sanctioned by a President in whose election she has had no share."[65]

A Jeffersonian supporter had proclaimed to "the assembled Congress of America": "Dare to designate any Officer whatever, even temporarily, to administer the Government, in the event of a non-agreement on the part of the House of Representatives, and we will march and dethrone him as a Usurper."[66]

This was a threat that, if it meant anything at all, raised the specter of civil war.

A series of resolutions had been passed relating to the election. On the final resolution, an amendment was passed, stating, "All elections shall be considered as *incidental* to the main power of voting by states, that each State shall have a vote. This was opposed by Messrs. Gallatin, Randolph, Nicholas and Macon." This raised the question of a new strategy pursued by the Federalists on the eve of the election.

DEADLOCK MEANT
AN "INTERREGNUM"

Samuel Tyler spoke for nearly everyone when he said, "It gave rise to very uneasy sensations not only with myself but those with whom I associate. In a word, the opinion as far as it can be formed by the most intelligent is—that they will unquestionably pursue precisely the same system of policy that the Senate of Pennsylvania did [i.e., deadlock] and that, in a caucus, which they held last night, it was resolved to put everything to the hazard."[67]

Thus the strategy of the Federalists, it appeared, also had their own fait accompli in mind.

But neither Gallatin, McKean, Tyler, nor anyone else knew what the outcome would be. Morris had been accurate in his assessment: no one had any idea who would win the election. The delegates knew that the Jeffersonians controlled a majority of the states but that they would fail to attain the necessary number prescribed by the Constitution. Thus the first order of business was to reveal what everyone already knew: Jefferson and Burr were tied with 73 electoral votes apiece. With this formality over, the delegates began the serious balloting by states.

On the first ballot Jefferson received 55 votes and Burr 49. An eyewitness recalled, less than a week after the election, "It was necessary to recommence the balloting, which was repeated up to 28 times with the same result throughout the day and night of the 11th."[68] Jefferson received 8 electoral votes, Burr 6. By the evening of the first day's voting, the tension reached a breaking point.

Governor Monroe's courier, dating his dispatches by the hour, waited until 5 p.m. before he sent a description of the first day's balloting. On the first round, Jefferson had received 16 electoral votes from Virginia. On the second he lost ground and dropped to 14.

Samuel Tyler then reported that the Federalists had made an attempt to "set aside the vote of Georgia on the ground of some informality." It was "rejected," but Jefferson's loss of votes and an attempt by the Federalists to nullify a state whose vote was obviously for Jefferson was an ominous trend.

Tyler then gave his opinion that "the Republicans will remain firm and never relinquish…and that they will put everything to the hazard; the fact is this opp[osition] cannot elect Mr. Burr."

Tyler then went on to report the fulfillment of Gallatin's plan, which had been carried many steps further. "In the event of extremities," he reported, "Penn[sylvania] has her courier here and the report is that she has 22,000 prepared to take up arms." Virginia also had twelve thousand militia mobilized and a courier going from Richmond to Washington and back every four hours.

Events looked so critical that Tyler recommended to Monroe an emergency session of the legislature. That "the Ass[embly] of Virginia should be convened if things remain in S[tatus] quo for this week I should decide as prudent."[69]

Finally, Tyler, whose judgment both Jefferson[70] and Monroe respected, submitted a plan that portended civil war: "Pennsy[lvania] and Virg[inia] should clasp hands, N[ew] York would join, and that a Congress composed of these States and all South of the Poto[mac] ought to be recommended; yet I would be understood to mean that this should be adopted only in last extremities: for I am clear the Feds will yield."[71]

Not only did the republicans agree on what should be done if the Federalists should resort to usurpation but they also had troops. Pennsylvania with her thousands of militiamen and Virginia with her militia, supported by all the states "south of the Potomac," would be a force that would overawe the federal government. This was especially true, as Adams had so fortuitously "disbanded" the army a few months earlier.

But what was more important was the fact that the republicans had informed the Federalists of their intentions. This was no empty threat. And while it came close to violating Jefferson's concern not to allow the army to "shew its force" in the midst of a constitutional revolution, it did intimidate the opposition forces and make them respect the sanctity of the electoral process.

In addition, the suggestion reflected Jefferson's thinking in that it combined the implicit threat of force with the revolutionary idea of calling a congress, the process that would automatically give constitutional legitimacy to a burgeoning revolution. It was, in fact, how the American Revolution began in 1774.

The first day's balloting saw the members vote a recess without suspending session. February 12 saw the same procedure repeated with the results unchanged: "8 votes for Mr. Jefferson—6 for Mr. Burr—Maryland and Vermont divided."

HOUSE MEMBERS DISREGARD THEIR DUTY TO REMAIN TOGETHER

When the second day's balloting broke up, it had become apparent because of the "determination of both sides to adhere to their man, they [the Representatives] have *done away* the resolution which required them to remain together, and adjourned to meet to-morrow at 11 o'clock."[72] The policy of stalemate had made its formal appearance.

A Federalist member of the House of Representatives from Maryland wrote, "Both parties appear determined to hold out. I think we shall succeed."[73] Each side believed it would persevere, despite the fact that the votes representing the states remained the same. But a subtle change had taken place. In the individual electoral votes, Burr had forged ahead. He now had fifty-four votes to Jefferson's fifty-one.

Thus, while Jefferson had control of the states, it was clear that a majority of those voting favored Burr. The psychological trend was toward Burr; and the Jeffersonians, knowing the consequences of a slow loss of yet a few more votes, became desperate.

100,000-PLUS PROTESTORS CONVERGE ON WASHINGTON

The deadlock of the third day had raised the tension beyond the confines of the House of Representatives. "Persons whom curiosity had brought to Washington, *more than a hundred thousand of them,* began to get impatient and to mutter at the obstinacy of the Federalists, saying that the representatives of that party were voting for Burr only to throw the country into confusion and to see if they could retain, in their own hands,...*power.*"[74]

Among them were many Federalists from the neighboring counties who "presented addresses to their representatives [John C.] Thomas and [William] Craik, instructing them to vote for Jefferson; but as yet they are far from having complied with this request—nevertheless, such is the scandalous conduct of certain members, that were the Federalists themselves to disapprove of it...this will be the result of the election." With an eye toward their future prosperity, these "Washington locals" put pressure on Congressman John Chew Thomas "not to oppose the election of Mr. Jefferson." They were "damnably afraid that there will be no President, and consequently a *dissolution of the government, and then to Hell goes the Federal City.*"[75]

RUMORS OF CIVIL WAR

While those may have been the sentiments and the fears of a limited few, a greater number realized the consequences of further obstruction. The eyewitness noted that most of these hundred thousand or more people "feared, and rightly, that with the exercise of presidential and vice-presidential functions expiring on March 3, the United States would find itself without a government on the 4th...and therefore if the Federalists continued to ballot in the same manner until March 4, the federal government would see itself threatened by a dissolution that must inevitably produce civil war."[76]

Despite the fears and the remonstrances, however, the vote of Maryland remained split, and the tally continued to show Jefferson eight and Burr six. The Maryland voters were both frustrated and shaken. A writer in the *American* wrote, "Let the Republicans wait patiently, till the 3d of March—If the *spirit of faction* shall then, by its opposition to the voice of the majority of the people and the states, put the Constitution afloat, God send them safe out of the storm they may raise."[77] By Saturday the Federalists were "charged with threatening war," and rumors were to the effect that "the people of Philadelphia had seized upon the public arms."[78]

The politics of faction threatened to escalate into a violent revolutionary situation.

Nothing offered greater proof of this than the ultimatum the republicans presented to the obstructionists. Jefferson wrote to James Monroe on Sunday, describing the course of events thus far. He revealed the intentions of the faction that opposed his election: "If they could have been permitted to pass a law for putting the government into the hands of an officer, they would certainly have prevented an election." Knowing this the republicans had made the ultimate threat: dissolution of the Union, revolution, and civil war.

JEFFERSON CALLS FOR AN IMMEDIATE CONSTITUTIONAL CONVENTION

Jefferson's own measured words corroborate Samuel Tyler's suggestion as well as Albert Gallatin's plan; and his use of the plural indicates that a consensus had been gained: "We thought it best to declare openly and firmly, one and all, that the day such an act was passed, *the Middle States would arm,* and no such usurpation, *even for a single day, should be submitted to.* This first shook them; and they were completely alarmed at the resource for which we declared, to wit, a *convention to reorganize the government, and to amend it.* The very word convention gives them the horrors,…in the present democratical spirit of America."[79]

Indeed Jefferson and his colleagues had thrown the fear of revolution into the minds and the hearts of the Federalists: "In the present democratical spirit of America" was nothing less than a recognition that the spirit of revolution, like that of 1776, had come alive.

The threat was as desperate a gamble as men might make with their security and the peace of the body politic. It was not a statement that could be made and then abandoned. Its very logic meant that, once uttered, the republicans must be willing to see it through to the end. But it had become necessary, even more so because of John Adams's seeming indifference to the plight of the nation.

JEFFERSON CONFRONTS ADAMS OVER A RESORT TO FORCE AND AN INTERREGNUM

Jefferson had found the situation so desperate the day before that he personally "called on Mr. Adams." He recorded in *The Anas,*

> I observed to him, that a very dangerous experiment was then in contemplation, to defeat the Presidential election by an act of Congress declaring the right of the Senate to name a President of the Senate, to devolve on him the government during any interregnum; that such a measure would probably produce resistance by force, and incalculable consequences, which it would be in his power to prevent by negativing such an act. He seemed to think such an act justifiable, and observed, it was in my power to fix the election by a word in an instant, by declaring I would not turn out the federal officers, nor put down the navy, nor spunge the national debt. Finding his mind made up as to the *usurpation* of the government by the President of the Senate, I urged it no further, observed the world must judge as to myself of the future by the past.[80]

Like Hamilton, Adams was intent on gaining assurances from Jefferson that he would protect "the system." Jefferson in his turn was determined to not be bound by any agreement whatsoever. He had at about the same time made similar declarations to Dwight Foster of Massachusetts and to Gouverneur Morris, both of whom had presented him with Hamilton's original conditions.

HIGH FEDERALISTS AGREE
TO RISK CIVIL WAR!

Thus a consensus among the Federalists seemed to have been arrived at for the first time in more than a year: unless Jefferson agreed to their three basic conditions, they were willing to risk plunging the country into civil war.

In the maneuvering that had taken place since the beginning of the election, Jefferson and his colleagues had done everything in their power to convince the Federalists that their opposition to the government had been based on principles—and they were not about to change that ground. But as the balloting continued day after day and the tension grew, solicitations were made to Jefferson and his colleagues with increasing fervor.

With Jefferson spurning offers of compromise by the president, Dwight Foster, and Gouverneur Morris, a solution had to be found that was independent of the solid phalanxes of both republican and Federalist factions. Hamilton had written to James A. Bayard of Delaware a long and devastating letter regarding the character and the diabolical intentions of Burr.[81] Thus, Bayard, even though he may have been disposed toward his Federalist colleagues and their attempt to gain concessions from Jefferson, probably did not wish to see Burr elevated to the presidency. A mutual friend of Bayard's and Jefferson's had written to the latter in late December:

> I do not know what intrigues under various shapes may be going on at headquarters [Washington] or what influence...the Federal Partizans, may have on the mind of my friend Bayard (I call him my friend, widely as we differ in our political course, with a great truth and justice for in private life I have never met with a better) when he arrives, but I have lately heard him say repeatedly and in company, that in case of an equality of votes between yourself and Col. Burr he should not hesitate to vote for you and he has spoken frequently of the dignified impartiality observed by you in your conduct as President of the Senate with much approbation.[82]

At the same time that the republicans were entertaining their hopes for his eventual defection, Bayard was apparently making overtures to Edward Livingston and General Samuel Smith to gain the states of New

York and Maryland. Despite this, Bayard had become the one person in whom the Jeffersonians believed they might place some hope. But Bayard had voted with the obstructionists for the first five days of balloting, and there was little sign that he would change. The republicans' hopes were revived on Saturday the fourteenth, when it was rumored that Bayard had informed his colleagues that he intended to break the tie and vote for Jefferson. The intrigue had deepened.

BAYARD AND THE REPUBLICANS BOTH PLAY A "DOUBLE GAME"

Sometime on Friday Bayard "applied to" John Nicholas of Virginia to gain assurance for "certain points of the future administration [that] could be understood and arranged with Mr. Jefferson." Bayard "proposed" that Nicholas "consult Mr. Jefferson. This he declined, and said he could do no more than give the assurance of his own opinion as to the sentiments and designs of Mr. Jefferson and his friends. I told him that was not sufficient—that we should not surrender without better terms. Upon this we separated; and I shortly after met with General Smith."[83]

Despite Bayard's refusal to surrender, a door had been opened. It was obvious that Bayard had now placed himself in a position to bargain with the opposition. In addition to the conditions originally laid down by Hamilton, he had asked for the continuance of two men in federal offices.[84] These were points of negotiation which, it seemed, Jefferson would never accept. Realizing this, one of Jefferson's supporters took it upon himself to tip the balance of power.

That evening (Friday), General Samuel Smith of Maryland added to the confusion and, by a strategy that smacked of not a little deception, initiated a new round of negotiations with Bayard. Speaking, as he claimed, in Jefferson's name,[85] he led the Delawarean to believe he would speak to the leader of the republicans and gain assurances on each of his points. "The next day (Saturday) [I] told him that Mr. Jefferson had said he did not think that such offices ought to be dismissed on political grounds only." This seemed an adequate assurance to Bayard, who then replied, according to Smith, "We will give the vote on Monday."[86]

But the republicans were destined for disappointment, for on Monday the sixteenth, Bayard maintained the solid front of the Federalist faction.[87]

TOTAL CONSTITUTIONAL CRISIS!

The situation over the weekend had thus become one of total constitutional crisis. With more than a hundred thousand people in the capital city and rumors flying to the effect that others from major cities were preparing to march on Washington—and rifles in the federal armories in Charleston, Philadelphia, and New York City taken over by Jefferson's supporters—it was expected that the government might fall at any hour.

> As the news of what was happening in the capitol spread through the country, the discontent of the moderates of both parties increased with rumors spreading that the Federalists' tenacity was aimed at some act of violence or usurpation such as using their 22-to-12 majority in the Senate to name a Federalist member of that body President ad interim, which would have been a violation of the Constitution—began to arm and organize themselves into companies for the purpose of marching on Washington to seize it from those who proposed the usurpation of government, as well as from the usurpers.
>
> Within a few days, they formed a very numerous body at Baltimore. The same movement took place in Virginia and in the more distant cities, like Philadelphia and New York.[88]

A sense of deep crisis gripped the capital. On Monday the specter of violence appeared: "The lobby of the chamber of the House of Representatives was cleared in consequence of the threats of some violent person who had been stationed there."[89] Yet even this failed to deter the Federalists, who again voted for Burr. At the close of the balloting on Monday evening, the tally remained Jefferson eight, Burr six.

Bayard's failure to respond to Smith's solicitation had shaken the republicans, and they became grim. Amid the confusion it was learned that "two Federalist members of the House received notes threatening them with death if they did not vote according to the will of the people. During the night, stones were thrown against the houses where other representatives of the same party were living, and there is no doubt whatsoever that their lives [were] in danger."[90]

The mad confusion that followed these events created panic among the Federalists. One element that added to their uncertainty was the location of Burr. No one had seen him, talked to him, or even knew if he was still in Baltimore, where he had allegedly gone. Bayard had called a caucus earlier that weekend to inquire if anyone knew when Burr might arrive.

THE INTERREGNUM IS INEVITABLE

When no one replied, Bayard made a statement that "the opposite party [the Jeffersonians]—would persevere to the 4th of March…undismayed by whatever disasters might result." Therefore, without the personal assurance or even the knowledge of the intentions of the man he was supporting, "he could not consent that the 4th of March should arrive without a chief magistrate."[91] Burr's failure to appear on the scene the following day increased the Federalists' apprehensions. It was not certain that he would ever appear.

But what was becoming a virtual certainty was the dissolution of the government.

The republicans had successfully convinced the Federalist faction that they would not relent and would see a dissolution of the government before conceding to their demands. This, coupled with their own threats of organizing a revolutionary convention, made the more rational members among them realize that continued opposition meant the Constitution would be destroyed.

The pressures that built up within the Federalist ranks were described by the one man who, having done everything in his power to maintain his loyalty to party, finally cracked under the strain. In what was a revelation of the lengths to which faction would go in destroying the republic, Bayard described the last-minute pandemonium that gripped the extremists when he finally decided to change his vote.

ONE MAN'S DESCRIPTION OF PARTY AND FACTION GONE MAD

Bayard's rationale was a devastating blow against the excesses of party and faction and a tribute to what Jefferson and his fellow republicans had been claiming all along: the Constitution, the republic, and republicans were inseparable. Bayard thus writes,

> When it was perfectly ascertained that Burr could not be elected I avowed that the only remaining object was to exclude Jefferson at the expense of the Constitution. According to an arrangement I had made with Maryland I came forward and avowed my intentions of putting an end to the contest. The clamor was prodigious. The reproaches vehement. I procured a meeting—explained myself and declared an inflexible intention to run no risk of the constitution. I told them that if necessary I had determined to become the victim of the measure. They might attempt to direct the vengeance of the Party against me but the danger of being a sacrifice could not shake my resolution. Some were appeased: others furious, and we broke up in confusion. A second meeting was no happier in its effect.[92]

The end came amid a tremendous amount of confusion. The Federalists, frenetic in their desire to achieve agreement, held several caucuses that saw their unity shattered. By two o'clock on the afternoon of the seventeenth, they could no longer sustain their support for Burr. Bayard, sensing that the danger of delaying even one more ballot might plunge the nation into violence, declared his intentions of changing Delaware's vote.

"The manner of the last ballot was arranged but a few minutes before the ballot was given."[93] The final vote was Jefferson ten, Burr four, and two states, Delaware and South Carolina, abstaining. Thomas Jefferson had finally acquired the necessary number to become president *constitutionally.*

Thus ended the deadlock and the threat of civil war.

PARTY AND FACTION DEFEATED

In the words of the eyewitness, "Such has been the last effort of a faction which has governed the United States since Gen. Washington retired from office."[94] The Revolution of 1800 had been achieved without the violence and the bloodshed that appeared to engulf it.

Jefferson's and Madison's theory of revolution had been validated in the final outcome of the election.

Through their own form of "electoral Caesarism" (i.e., the peaceful organizing of a constitutional majority of the people), they had achieved what no other group of revolutionaries had gained in the entire course of Western political history: a change in the power of government, from one party to another, without a tremendous cost in violence and bloodshed.

Indeed they had set a precedent that could be followed by the world as well as their own nation for all generations to come: the possibility of a permanent, peaceful, constitutional revolution.

IN THE MOMENT OF TRIUMPH:
THE AMERICAN REVOLUTION PRESERVED

But what was just as important, at least to Jefferson and the members of his generation, was that the American Revolution of 1776 had finally been consolidated. Fifteen days after the nearly catastrophic election in the House, Jefferson gave his Inaugural Address. Referring to the principles of the American Revolution, he said,

> These principles form the bright constellation which has gone before us and guided our steps through an age of revolution and reformation. The wisdom of our sages and blood of our heroes have been devoted to their attainment. They should be the creed of our political faith, the text of civic instruction, the touchstone by which to try the services of those we trust; and should we wander from them in moments of error or of alarm, let us hasten to retrace our steps and to regain the road which alone leads to peace, liberty and safety.[95]

Certainly, Jefferson had regained the road by retracing the steps of the American Revolution and resurrecting the Spirit of '76. By appealing to the people, he had literally renewed its promise.

Indeed he would later claim, and justly so, that "the Revolution of 1800 was as real a revolution in the principles of our government as that of 1776 was in its form; not effected indeed by the sword, as that, but by the rational and peaceable instrument of reform, the suffrage of the people."[96]

Afterword

by Thom Hartmann

Y OU HAVE JUST READ ABOUT THE EARLY AMERICAN REVOLU-
tionary experience that *consciously* brought together form and
principle in the midst of revolution for the first time in Western history.
Defined largely by Thomas Jefferson and James Madison, it is a major
contribution of political thought to the world. And, apart from the gift
of liberty, it may be our most important legacy.

Jefferson realized that since ancient times all societies had gone
through what Polybius called "the cycle of revolutions." In that cycle
social, political, and economic changes would inevitably force society
to accept, without question, that different types of regimes will always
control society.

Some members of society would encourage liberty and freedom
under a legal-constitutional form; others would accept a tyrannical or
oligarchic form and concentrate all power into the hands of elites—who
would make the lives of the vast majority of citizens miserable.

Still other elites would mask their power under a form, for example,
with a patina of what appears to be democracy, to create an *illusion* of
freedom while they exploit the masses. But upon examination the total
contradiction between their principles and true democracy is revealed.

Jefferson, Madison, Albert Gallatin, and their allies were determined
to break that cycle and prevent the worst effects of the different forms from
happening. And the way they would do this was to elect representatives
who would examine the principles of the powerful—both economically

and politically—and analyze how the policies those powerful members and factions within society espoused and acted on would affect the majority of citizens.

Most importantly, these representatives would scrutinize the laws that determined justice and the distribution of wealth. For example, if taxes were unjustly imposed on the many while the few were exempted, they would change the tax laws in favor of the majority.

An example in modern society would be if wages were so low that the majority were economically desperate, laws would be passed to pay a living wage. If banks and wealthy corporations cheated homeowners in their loans, laws would be passed to prevent the abuses and to punish the abusers with "a long train of et ceteras."

To ensure that democracy and a republican form of government would remain stable, the representatives had to make choices for the many, not just the few. But if the people cannot be informed because the media is corrupt and owned by the very few, then, lacking information, citizens will not know how to vote for candidates or support laws that would restore a balance between form and principle.

This Jeffersonian system of governing society requires constant attention by the voters and their representatives to demand that the *principles of democracy*—equality, privacy, the right to vote, the rights of individuals, access to courts of law—be respected to guarantee that democracy has integrity and is not an illusion.

This is the true meaning of the connection between form and principle in Jefferson's revolutionary ideas. It is a system based on common sense that requires constant attention—hence the observation of one of Jefferson's close friends, Thomas Paine: "Eternal vigilance is the price of liberty."

Our condition has not changed since those words were uttered more than two hundred years ago, save for a few instances: too many of our citizens are ill-informed, our wealth is concentrating in the hands of fewer and fewer people, our middle class is shrinking, and our representatives, by and large, no longer represent the people but the special interests of the rich.

This is why it is so important for us, today, to examine our current situation in light of Jefferson's idea of the role of *principles* in bringing about revolutionary change, remembering when doing so that principles opposed to liberty and justice—if they become the gradual norm—will have a chilling, if not permanent, effect on the form.

Consider our current moment in the context of Jefferson's perspective on revolution. He believed—asserted—that regular revolutions were *necessary* for a nation and that there were definite signposts signaling a revolution's imminence. Each of these conditions represented a certain type of pressure within society, and the way the nation responded to that pressure would determine what kind of revolution was going to occur. Would it be at the ballot box, or would it be like the French Revolution— violence in the streets, leading to a time of terror and guillotine?

DANGER

If these conditions were not addressed head-on and in a way satisfactory to the people, a nation would be condemned to a perpetual cycle of either political or actual violence—what Jefferson called "force."

He wrote, "If this avenue [of periodic revolution] be shut to the call of sufferance, it will make itself heard through that of force, and we shall go on, as other nations are doing, in the endless circle of oppression, rebellion, reformation; and oppression, rebellion, reformation, again; and so on forever."[1]

So, to determine if such a thing is possible today, let us examine Jefferson's time-tested formula for the things that would keep a society— including our nation—stable and politically healthy through generational revolutions. Because if it is not possible for us to have a ballot-box-driven revolution in our era, the pressures will build to a dangerous point and undermine the integrity of our republic.

SMARTS AND MEDIA

Jefferson's first and second conditions for a developing revolution, as mentioned earlier in the book,[2] were that the general populace of the nation possess the intellectual potential to become aware of a political crisis and—because the press would play such a large role in providing that intellectual potential—that the role of the press in shaping public opinion is operated for the interests of the democratic republic rather than the parochial or business interests of the press itself.

The last truly significant "revolution" in modern American politics was the Reagan revolution, when two ideas became dominant:

- ☙ That there was virtually nothing government could do as well as the private sector (this led to massive outsourcing)

- ☙ That government interference in private-sector activity would inevitably gum up the works and lead to an inefficient economy (this led to massive deregulation)

One result of this was the end of any meaningful enforcement of antitrust laws, leading in the early 1980s to a mergers-and-acquisitions (M&A) mania. The big companies got bigger, the medium-sized companies were bought up or pushed out of business, and the ability to pull off a "garage startup" type of company has almost vanished. One easily visible example of the result of this is that in 1980 most downtowns and malls were filled with local companies (mostly retail establishments and restaurants). Today they are almost entirely giant national chains.

This has also happened in our media. Prior to the Reagan revolution, newspapers, radio stations, and television stations across the country were owned by tens of thousands of individuals and small companies. Today fewer than a dozen companies own or control well over 80 percent of all our national and local media in all three categories.

And these very large companies, while being in the media business, have also learned that by becoming major players in our national politics they can get tax and regulatory laws and rules that make them continuously more and more wealthy and powerful.

They have also learned that it is profitable to be politically active, so they spend hundreds of millions of dollars to hire tens of thousands of lobbyists and consultants to monitor and influence politicians and regulators from the federal level all the way down to the city and county levels.

They also know that it is *not* to their advantage for the average person to have a similarly sophisticated political understanding.

The upshot of this last point is that major political issues that have very real and significant impacts on the lives of average citizens—from trade policy to education policy to Internet policy and more—get virtually no coverage in what has become derisively known by those on both the left and the right as the "mainstream media."

One of the things that most amazed the French aristocrat Alexis de Tocqueville, when he visited America in 1834 and subsequently wrote his famous book *Democracy in America,* was how the average farmer working in his fields could engage de Tocqueville in a thoughtful and sophisticated conversation about the politics of the day, both nationally and internationally. The press was broad and diverse and saw its job as informing the populace.

In the early decades of the twentieth century, as radio and television became major national parts of our media landscape, Congress and the Federal Communications Commission (FCC) wanted to make sure that the "informed populace" that Jefferson said was so necessary to a functioning democratic republic was maintained.

The FCC wrote a rule—the Fairness Doctrine—that required radio and television stations to "program in the public interest." The result of this rule was that every year when a radio or TV station's license was up for renewal, its programming was examined in that context.

The main way that radio and TV stations proved to the FCC that they were in fact "programming in the public interest" was to run both national and local news every hour.

During the early 1970s, I worked in the newsroom of one of the largest radio stations in Lansing, Michigan, the state's capital. That radio station had a five-person local news staff and also carried national network news at the top of each hour. Every station of any substance did the same, and the smaller stations subscribed to local or statewide news services so that they could provide local news content.

These stations all lost money on their news operations, as did the "big three" television networks. But by producing a genuine newscast every day, they satisfied the FCC requirement that they program in the interests of an informed and educated electorate.

In 1976 Dan Sisson ran for the US Congress in California's 19th District (Santa Barbara–Ventura). Although he did not win, he made the race interesting and, for a while, even competitive. He could not have done so without the Fairness Doctrine then enforced by the FCC. That law enabled Dan access to free radio and TV coverage as often as ten times a day. Eleven years later, even the idea of "running" would have been unthinkable without vast amounts of money in a "war chest."

Over the ensuing three decades, there has been a steady chipping away of media regulations aimed at the public interest.

- In 1982 President Ronald Reagan functionally stopped enforcing the Sherman Antitrust Act and its heirs. Media properties were swept up in the M&A frenzy, although the FCC kept on the books a number of rules that limited media ownership by very large corporations.

- In 1987 the Reagan administration stopped enforcing the Fairness Doctrine.

- And in 1996 Congress passed and Bill Clinton signed into law the Telecommunications Act. It was a deregulation of the media of historic proportions.

- In 2012 the Obama administration deleted the Fairness Doctrine from FCC regulations altogether.

The net effect of all this is that our political dialogue has become narrowed. Our political debates are neither deep nor well informed, and personality has surpassed policy in terms of electability.

As a result, it is reasonably safe to assert that we have failed to meet Jefferson's first test for a republic capable of refashioning and reforming itself purely by candidates educating voters through the electoral process.

ECONOMIC CRISIS

Jefferson's third criterion for provoking revolution was that a nation must be experiencing the political pressure that an economic crisis would provoke, particularly one tied into taxes.

Although there was no income tax during his time—remember, we are living in Hamilton's America, not Jefferson's, at least with regard to economics—we know now that income tax policy in a highly industrialized and finance-driven nation like ours has a significant impact on producing economic crises.

The simple explanation for how this works is that when there is a lot of hot money flying around in an economy, that economy tends toward "bubbles" and "frenzies." These bubbles eventually pop, usually within a decade, sometimes within two; and when they pop, we call that a "crash," which typically leads to a recession or depression. An emphasis on using the tax code to preserve wealth accumulation for the rich— "Reaganomics" in our era—rather than balance wealth inequalities has been shown again and again to cause trouble.

Not surprisingly, today's thirty-plus-year era of Reaganomics has been characterized by a progressive series of small bubbles and bursts, with a larger pop in 2008.

It is slowly dawning on American working people that Reagan's promise—that when taxes were cut on the very rich, the wealth would "trickle down" to everybody else—was hollow. Instead wealth accumulated at the very top. And the release of presidential candidate Mitt Romney's income tax data during the 2012 election cycle awakened working people to the fact that the very rich pay virtually nothing in income taxes.

Indeed as the rich have become richer, working people's wages and wealth have gone down. And, if you draw a paycheck—no matter how little it is—it is impossible to avoid the payroll tax. The economic crisis this has provoked, caused in large part by Reagan's changes to our income tax code, seem to pretty clearly satisfy Jefferson's suggestion that an economic crisis associated with a tax issue could push a nation toward revolution.

SOCIAL MOBILITY DIES

Jefferson's fourth and fifth conditions for a revolution were the rate of nonviolent change and the differences between the newly emerging and the past forms of government. In American politics today, that is the difference between an emerging oligarchy and a true democracy.

If the rate of change met the desires of the people, and the consequences of that change—the newly emerging changes in government— met the needs of the people, revolution would be unnecessary.

These are both problematic today.

Two previous generations saw dramatic and, to their minds, *desirable* rates of change in our form of government—in the New Deal era from the 1930s to the 1960s and the Great Society era of the 1960s. The New Deal produced a dramatic rise in the white middle class. The Great Society cut American poverty in half in less than a decade, continued the growth of that white middle class, and passed civil rights laws that helped bring about a substantial Black middle class while also bringing women into the working mainstream.

But the Reagan revolution of the 1980s brought to a rapid stop the continued flow of working people into the middle class; and, as Reagan's policies have continued into the twenty-first century, many in both the White and Black middle classes have fallen to the status of the working poor.

In other words, the rate of nonviolent change for the vast majority of Americans has been either zero or negative. And the newly emerging forms of government—conservative policies that have actually rolled back large parts of the American social safety net and reduced the rights and the power of working people in state after state—have been the *opposite* of those policies that so satisfied preceding generations. This is called *emerging oligarchy:* rule by the few in the interests of the few. (And indeed the very, very wealthy have done well and appear to be quite happy, although history tells us that this is bound to be an illusion and will last but a short time.)

Probably the best indicator of this radical, negative change in the state of life for the majority of the American electorate is seen in social mobility—the ability of people to move up through the economic quintiles during their lifetimes.

When Reagan came to power after fifty years of New Deal policies, America was among the most socially mobile of all the world's developed nations. After thirty years of Reaganomics, the United States is among the *least* socially mobile nations in the developed world. All of this suggests a revolution could be brewing.

Jefferson's final two criteria for a revolution were the people's understanding of their relation to the constitutional powers present in the government of the day and even of the hour, and the degree of liberty expressed in a declaration of rights toward which the revolution aims.

Once again we find the vast majority of the people frustrated.

In 1976 in the Supreme Court case *Buckley v. Valeo*, the Court discovered in the First Amendment an explicit protection for money and its uses, particularly with regard to politics. Two years later, in the case of *First National Bank v. Bellotti*, the Court found that the Fourteenth Amendment was passed after the Civil War to give equal protection rights to corporations.

Most Americans had never noticed the word *money* in the First Amendment or, indeed, anywhere in the Constitution itself. And most Americans thought the Civil War was fought largely to free the slaves, not the transnational corporations.

But there it was, and the Supreme Court brought these two decisions together in a big way in 2010 in its *Citizens United v. Federal Election Commission* ruling. Corporations are now "persons," even "humans," and money is no longer property but has become "free speech."

To add insult to injury, both major political parties have spent much of the past thirty years promoting so-called free-trade deals that have added vast powers to corporations to not only send American jobs overseas but to even sue individual states or cities that might act in ways to prevent it.

And the revelations by Edward Snowden and others that the US government was treating its citizens' privacy with contempt has revealed most of all how much our Constitution has eroded. Many Americans are asking, What happened? Without privacy how can one have private thoughts? How can democracy even exist? These were what the First and Fourth Amendments were supposed to protect and guarantee.

Throughout the 1980s and 1990s, those Americans who sounded the tocsin about rising inequality, the loss of manufacturing jobs, and disappearing civil liberties were largely regarded as the "fringe," although

Ross Perot, running on these "fringe" issues, captured nearly 20 percent of the presidential vote in 1992. People were starting to wake up.

Americans began to see, as corporations and the very wealthy acquired increasing powers and rights, that their own individual rights under the Constitution were actually being diminished, and the degree of liberty they experienced was in a downward spiral, both politically and economically.

REVOLUTIONARY TIMES

Today the rise of grassroots movements on both the right and the left—the Tea Party and Occupy—are ample evidence of revolutionary pressures. Jefferson's observations have been borne out over and over again throughout American history and the history of the world, and now his prescience about revolution confronts us.

Not only have political parties sealed their lock on America's political system, but the power of faction—the faction of corporate and multigenerational wealth—has been cemented into place by our Supreme Court.

Meanwhile the founding notion that our government was to be a force of good, fully representing the will and the needs of We the People, is ridiculed as a matter of policy by one of our two national parties. The ideals of majority rule, principled compromise, and collaboration and cooperation have been discarded in favor of a relentless effort to destroy the opposing party and its standard-bearer.

James Madison must be rolling over in his grave, and Thomas Jefferson, were he alive today, would be saying, "I warned you." Even the High Federalists like John Adams and John Marshall—and that fervent mercantilist Alexander Hamilton—would be shocked by the state of our nation today.

One of the most important lessons of the Revolution of 1800 was that when a nation has gone astray, it can be brought back to its senses with a revolution at the ballot box.

Once again we can see the connection between Jefferson and our time by recalling one of his most quoted sentences, the one that circles the dome of the Jefferson Monument in Washington, DC. Uttered in frustration over lies spread during the campaign by extremist religious factions, it stands as the remedy for a free society to rebut the allegations made in our time. Jefferson's rebuttal two hundred years ago still stands. He said: "I have sworn upon the altar of God eternal hostility against every form of tyranny over the mind of man."

The "tyranny" over the minds of men today continues to include that of the religious zealots, but to this faction has been added the factions of transnational corporations and billionaires.

In sum, our Congress is looking more like the High Federalist–dominated legislature on the eve of Jefferson's Revolution of 1800: polarized and paralyzed by factions within parties that ignore the vast majority of working people in America.

In a very real sense, we are still, in 2014, confronting the choice between Hamilton's vision of society—an elitist government owned by the wealthy and "bottomed on corruption"—or Jefferson's: liberty, freedom, economic equality, and democracy in the interests of the common man.

One is the illusion of freedom in a false democracy; the other is the promise of our Declaration of Independence, our Constitution, and the Revolution of 1800.

We present this historical account of the Revolution of 1800, first exhaustively researched and written by Dan Sisson more than forty years ago, in the hope that it can help ensure that the next American revolution will similarly take place at the ballot box and not, as it did during the era of Abraham Lincoln, on the battlefield.

Tag, *you're* it.

Notes

An online version of these notes with clickable hyperlinks is available at
http://bkconnection.com/book-resources/revolution-of-1800

Introduction

1. Thomas Jefferson to John Adams, October 28, 1813, in *The Adams-Jefferson Letters: The Complete Correspondence between Thomas Jefferson and Abigail and John Adams,* ed. Lester J. Cappon, 2 vols. (Chapel Hill: University of North Carolina Press, 1959), vol. 2, 387–92.

2. Thomas Jefferson to George Washington, November 14, 1786, in *The Papers of Thomas Jefferson,* ed. Julian P. Boyd (Princeton: Princeton University Press, 1950), vol. 10, 532–33 [hereafter, *Papers of Jefferson*].

3. Thomas Jefferson to James Madison, September 6, 1789, *Papers of Jefferson,* vol. 15, 395–97.

Chapter 1

The Idea of a Non-party State

1. "Caesarism is the classic maneuver employed by the disaffected or thwarted members of a ruling class. Their response to being thwarted is to capitalize on the grievances of the subject population. The people are promised reforms in return for their aid in overthrowing the elite. The Gracchi initiated this maneuver in ancient Rome, but Julius Caesar made it successful." See Harvey Wheeler, *Democracy in a Revolutionary Era: The Political Order Today* (New York: Center for the Study of Democratic Institutions, 1968), 16.

2. Douglass Adair, "The Intellectual Origins of Jeffersonian Democracy" (unpublished PhD dissertation, Yale University, 1943), 1 (summary).

3. Richard Hofstadter has come closer than any other American historian, but for unknown reasons failed to follow his research to its logical conclusions. Perhaps the title of his book *The Idea of a Party System: The Rise of Legitimate*

Opposition in the United States, 1780–1840 (Berkeley: University of California Press, 1969), explains the failure, for to do so would have invalidated his thesis insofar as it applied to the period 1790 to 1801.

4. *A New English Dictionary on Historical Principles* (later the *Oxford English Dictionary*) (Oxford, 1901), vol. 4, s.v. "party," "faction," "sedition."

5. Nathan Bailey, *An Universal Etymological English Dictionary* (Edinburgh, 1800), s.v. "party," "faction."

6. Samuel Johnson, *A Dictionary of the English Language* (London, 1799), vol. 1. Dr. Johnson's combination of the two words can also be seen in the subsequent use of the derivative terms *factious* ("in a manner criminally dissentious or tumultuous"), *factiously* ("loud and violent in a party"), and *factiousness* ("violent clamorousness for a party").

7. Thomas Hobbes, *Leviathan* (New York: Great Books of the Western World, 1952).

8. *New English Dictionary on Historical Principles,* vol. 4, 12.

9. Hofstadter, *Idea of a Party System,* 11.

10. Noah Webster, *An American Dictionary of the English Language* (New York, 1828), vol. 1, s.v. "faction."

11. *Memoirs of the Life and Ministerial Conduct of the Late Lord Visc. Bolingbroke* (London: R. Baldwin, 1752), 41–42. An e-version is available at http://books.google.com/books?id=fq31NMx984wC&printsec=frontcover&source=gbs_ge_summary_r&cad=0#v=onepage&q&f=false.

12. David Hume, *The History of England,* 6 vols. (London, 1841), vol. 6, 163–64. An e-version is available at http://www.econlib.org/library/LFBooks/Hume/hmMPL8.html.

13. *The Works of the Right Honorable Edmund Burke,* 5 vols. (Boston: Little, Brown, 1865), vol. 1, 460–64 [hereafter, *Works of Burke*]. An e-version is available at http://www.econlib.org/library/LFBooks/Burke/brkSWv1c1.html.

14. *Works of Burke,* vol. 2, 95–96 ("Speech to the Electors of Bristol"). An e-version is available at http://press-pubs.uchicago.edu/founders/documents/v1ch13s7.html.

15. James Madison, Alexander Hamilton, and John Jay, *The Federalist Papers,* ed. Clinton Rossiter (New York: Penguin Putnam, 1961), No. 10, 77–84 [hereafter, *Federalist*] (italics added). The Library of Congress e-versions are available at http://thomas.loc.gov/home/histdox/fedpapers.html.

16. *Federalist,* No. 10, 82.

17. *Federalist,* No. 1, 34.

18. *Federalist,* No. 9, 71

19. *Federalist,* No. 21, 139–40 (italics added).

20. *Federalist,* No. 77, 462

21. Clinton Rossiter, *Alexander Hamilton and the Constitution* (New York: Harcourt, Brace, World, 1964), 148.

22. Hofstadter, *Idea of a Party System,* 18. "All these anti-party manifestos by party leaders can be set down, if we like, to hypocrisy…" Then, after adroitly stating this theme, Hofstadter has it both ways and says, "the only justification of any party…was to eliminate all parties."

23. Fisher Ames, "Laocoon No. 1," in *Works of Fisher Ames* (Boston: T. B. Wait, 1809), 107. An e-version is available at https://archive.org/details/works fisheramesooamesrich.

24. Ibid., 110.

25. John Jay to Thomas Jefferson, October 27, 1786, in *The Papers of Thomas Jefferson,* ed. Julian P. Boyd (Princeton: Princeton University Press, 1950), vol. 10, 489 [hereafter, *Papers of Jefferson*]. An e-version is available at http://jeffersonpapers.princeton.edu.

26. "Dissertation on First Principles of Government" (July 1795), in *The Life and Writings of Thomas Paine,* ed. Daniel Edwin Wheeler, 10 vols. (New York: Parke, 1908), vol. 9, 273 [hereafter, *Paine*] (italics added). An e-version is available at http://books.google.com/books?id=0RaFAAAAMAAJ& authuser=2&source=gbs_navlinks_s.

27. Thomas Jefferson to Spencer Roane, September 6, 1819, in *The Writings of Thomas Jefferson,* eds. Andrew A. Lipscomb and Albert Bergh, 20 vols. (Washington, DC: Thomas Jefferson Memorial Association, 1903), vol. 15, 212 [hereafter, *Writings of Jefferson*]. The Library of Congress offers e-versions of Jefferson's papers at http://memory.loc.gov/ammem/ collections/jefferson_papers/mtjprov.html.

28. James Monroe to Thomas Jefferson, March 3, 1801, *The Writings of James Monroe,* ed. Stanislaus M. Hamilton, 7 vols. (New York: G. P. Putman's Sons, 1900), 263.

29. *Patrick Henry; Life, Correspondence and Speeches,* ed. William Wirt Henry, 3 vols. (New York: Charles Scribner's Sons, 1891), vol. 2, 609–10. An e-version is available at books.google.com/books?id=yx5CAAAAIAAJ.

30. *A Compilation of the Messages and Papers of the Presidents, 1789–1897,* ed. James Daniel Richardson (Washington, DC: Bureau of National Literature

and Art, 1897), vol. 1, 209–11 [hereafter, *Messages and Papers*] (italics added). An e-version is available at https://archive.org/details/acompilation mes63richgoog.

31. John Adams to Jonathan Jackson, October 2, 1780, in *The Works of John Adams,* ed. Charles Francis Adams (Boston: Little, Brown, 1851), vol. 9, 511 [hereafter, *Works of Adams*]. An e-version is available at http://oll.liberty fund.org/titles/adams-the-works-of-john-adams-10-vols.

32. *Messages and Papers,* vol. 1, 221.

33. John Adams to Thomas Jefferson, December 25, 1813, in *The Adams-Jefferson Letters: The Complete Correspondence between Thomas Jefferson and Abigail and John Adams,* ed. Lester J. Cappon, 2 vols. (Chapel Hill: University of North Carolina Press, 1959), vol. 2, 412 [hereafter, *Letters*].

34. Thomas Jefferson to Francis Hopkinson, March 13, 1789, *Papers of Jefferson,* vol. 14, 650–51.

35. Thomas Jefferson to John Taylor, June 1, 1798, in *The Works of Thomas Jefferson* (Federal edition), ed. Paul Leicester Ford, 12 vols. (New York: G. P. Putnam's Sons, 1904), vol. 8, 430–433. An e-version is available at http://oll.libertyfund.org/titles/jefferson-the-works-of-thomas-jefferson-12-vols.

36. *Messages and Papers,* vol. 1, 310.

37. *The Anas, Writings of Jefferson,* vol. 1, 282.

38. *Messages and Papers,* vol. 1, 312.

39. Thomas Jefferson to Henry Knox, March 27, 1801, *Writings of Jefferson,* vol. 10, 245–46.

40. Thomas Jefferson to John Adams, June 27, 1813, *Letters,* vol. 2, 335–38.

41. Thomas Jefferson to Marquis de La Fayette, May 14, 1817, *Writings of Jefferson,* vol. 15, 115–16 (italics added).

CHAPTER 2

The Idea of Revolution

1. That Adams considered himself a student of revolutions as well as constitutions is borne out in a letter he wrote late in life. And though he may have viewed them more skeptically than Jefferson, he nevertheless saw them much in the same light. Here he recounts his involvement:

> I had been plunged head and ears in the American revolution from 1761 to 1798 (for it had been all revolution during the whole period). Did [anyone]…think that I had trod upon feathers, and slept upon

beds of roses, during those thirty-seven years? I had been an eye-witness of two revolutions in Holland; one from aristocracy to a mongrel mixture of half aristocracy and half democracy, the other back again to aristocracy and the splendid restoration of the Stadt-holder. Did [anyone]…think that I was so delighted with these electric shocks, these eruptions of volcanoes, these *tremblements de terre,* as to be ambitious of the character of the chemist, who could produce artificial ones in South America? I had been an ear-witness of some of the first whispers of a revolution in France in 1783, 1784, and 1785, and had given all possible attention to its rise and progress, and I can truly say, that it had given me as much anxiety as our American revolution had ever done. The last twenty-five years of the last century, and the first fifteen years of this, may be called the age of revolutions and constitutions. We began the dance and have produced eighteen or twenty models of constitutions, the excellences and defects of which you probably know better than I do.

John Adams to James Lloyd, March 29, 1815, in *The Works of John Adams,* ed. Charles Francis Adams (Boston: Little, Brown, 1851), vol. 10, 148–49 [hereafter, *Works of Adams*].

2. John Adams to Thomas Jefferson, May 18, 1817, in *The Writings of Thomas Jefferson,* eds. Andrew A. Lipscomb and Albert Bergh, 20 vols. (Washington, DC: Thomas Jefferson Memorial Association, 1903), vol. 15, 120 [hereafter, *Writings of Jefferson*].

3. John Adams to Thomas Jefferson, August 24, 1815, in *The Adams-Jefferson Letters: The Complete Correspondence between Thomas Jefferson and Abigail and John Adams,* ed. Lester J. Cappon, 2 vols. (Chapel Hill: University of North Carolina Press, 1959), vol. 2, 455 [hereafter, *Letters*]. See also John Adams to Dr. Jedidiah Morse, December 29, 1815, *Works of Adams,* vol. 10, 182; and John Adams to Thomas McKean, November 26, 1815, *Works of Adams,* vol. 10, 180.

4. Nathan Bailey, *An Universal Etymological English Dictionary* (Edinburgh, 1800), s.v. "revolution."

5. Noah Webster, *An American Dictionary of the English Language* (New York, 1828), vol. 2, s.v. "revolution," "revolutionized."

6. John Quincy Adams to William Vans Murray, January 27, 1801, in *The Selected Writings of John and John Quincy Adams,* ed. Adrienne Koch and William Peden (New York: Alfred A. Knopf, 1946), 257–58 (italics added).

7. John Adams to Thomas Jefferson, May 11, 1794, *Letters,* vol. 1, 254.

8. *Autobiography, Writings of Jefferson,* vol. 1, 180.

9. Thomas Jefferson to James Currie, September 27, 1785, in *The Papers of Thomas Jefferson,* ed. Julian P. Boyd (Princeton: Princeton University Press, 1950), vol. 8, 558 [hereafter, *Papers of Jefferson*].

10. Thomas Jefferson to Hilliard d' Auberteuil, February 20, 1786, *Papers of Jefferson,* vol. 9, 290–91.

11. "Address to the General Assembly of Virginia" (February 16, 1809), *Writings of Jefferson,* vol. 16, 333.

12. Thomas Jefferson to Joseph Priestley, June 19, 1802, *Writings of Jefferson,* vol. 10, 324.

13. "To the Citizens of Washington" (March 4, 1807), *Writings of Jefferson,* vol. 16, 347–48.

14. Thomas Jefferson to John Adams, September 12, 1821, *Letters,* vol. 2, 574–75.

15. Thomas Jefferson to John Adams, September 4, 1823, *Letters,* vol. 2, 596.

16. Harvey Wheeler, *The Politics of Revolution* (Berkeley, CA: Glendessary Press, 1971), vii.

17. Thomas Jefferson to John Adams, September 4, 1823, *Letters,* vol. 2, 596–97.

18. Thomas Jefferson to William Smith, November 13, 1787, *Papers of Jefferson,* vol. 12, 356 (italics added).

19. Thomas Jefferson to James Madison, January 30, 1787, *Papers of Jefferson,* vol. 11, 93.

20. Thomas Jefferson to James Madison, December 20, 1787, *Papers of Jefferson,* vol. 12, 442.

21. Thomas Jefferson to St. John de Crevecoeur, August 9, 1789, *Papers of Jefferson,* vol. 13, 485.

22. *Papers of Jefferson,* vol. 17, 63. See editor's comment.

23. See the explanatory notes in *The Anas, Writings of Jefferson,* vol. 1, 265–66.

24. *Autobiography,* in *The Life and Selected Writings of Thomas Jefferson,* eds. Adrienne Koch and William Peden (New York: Modern Library, 1944), 108–9 [hereafter, *Autobiography*]. An e-version of *Jefferson on Jefferson* is available at http://books.google.com/books?id=q7e8zI3QwY8C&lpg=PP1&pg=PP1#v=onepage&q&f=false.

25. Thomas Jefferson to John Jay, May 4, 1787, *Papers of Jefferson,* vol. 11, 340–41.

26. Thomas Jefferson to John Adams, May 17, 1818, *Letters,* vol. 2, 524.

27. Thomas Jefferson to Elénor-François-Elie, Comte de Moustier, March 13, 1789, *Papers of Jefferson,* vol. 14, 652.

28. Thomas Jefferson to Thomas Paine, March 17, 1789, *Papers of Jefferson*, vol. 14, 671.

29. Thomas Jefferson to George Washington, May 2, 1788, *Papers of Jefferson*, vol. 13, 126.

30. Thomas Jefferson to Edward Rutledge, July 18, 1788, *Papers of Jefferson*, vol. 13, 378.

31. Thomas Jefferson to David Humphreys, March 18, 1789, *Papers of Jefferson*, vol. 14, 676–77.

32. Thomas Jefferson to Gilbert du Motier, Marquis de La Fayette, April 2, 1790, *Papers of Jefferson*, vol. 16, 293.

33. *Autobiography*, 38–47.

34. Thomas Jefferson to C. W. F. Dumas, September 10, 1787, *Papers of Jefferson*, vol. 12, 113.

35. Thomas Jefferson to David Humphreys, March 18, 1789, *Papers of Jefferson*, vol. 14, 678.

36. Ibid.

37. Thomas Jefferson to James Madison, September 6, 1789, *Papers of Jefferson*, vol. 15, 395–97.

38. Wheeler, *Politics of Revolution,* 9.

39. Robert R. Palmer, *The Age of Democratic Revolution: The Challenge* (Princeton: Princeton University Press, 1959), vol. 1, 21.

40. Jacques Ellul, *Autopsy of Revolution* (New York: Knopf, 1971), 79.

41. Thomas Jefferson to David Humphreys, March 18, 1789, *Papers of Jefferson*, vol. 14, 679 (italics added).

42. Thomas Jefferson to Thomas Lomax, March 12, 1799, *Writings of Jefferson*, vol. 10, 123–24.

CHAPTER 3

The Idea of Revolution: Conspiracy and Counterrevolution

1. Bernard Bailyn, *The Ideological Origins of the American Revolution* (Cambridge, MA: Harvard University Press, 1967), 94. The most informative treatment on the fears of conspiracy in early American politics can be seen in Bailyn's book. See especially chapters 3 and 4 and "A Note on Conspiracy."

2. John Adams to Thomas Jefferson, November 15, 1813, in *The Adams-Jefferson Letters: The Complete Correspondence between Thomas Jefferson and Abigail*

and John Adams, ed. Lester J. Cappon, 2 vols. (Chapel Hill: University of North Carolina Press, 1959), vol. 2, 400 [hereafter, *Letters*] (italics added).

3. "The Vindication No. 1," in *The Papers of Alexander Hamilton,* eds. Harold C. Syrett and Jacob E. Cooke (New York: Columbia University Press, 1961), vol. 11, 463 [hereafter, *Papers of Hamilton*]. Though this essay was never published, it was written May–August 1792.

4. *The Journal of William Maclay: United States Senator from Pennsylvania 1789 to 1791,* ed. Charles A. Beard (New York: Albert & Charles Boni, 1927), 11–12.

5. Thomas Jefferson to George Washington, November 14, 1786, in *The Papers of Thomas Jefferson,* ed. Julian P. Boyd (Princeton: Princeton University Press, 1950), vol. 10, 532–33 [hereafter, *Papers of Jefferson*].

6. *The Anas,* in *The Writings of Thomas Jefferson,* eds. Andrew A. Lipscomb and Albert Bergh, 20 vols. (Washington, DC: Thomas Jefferson Memorial Association, 1903), vol. 1, 267 [hereafter, *Writings of Jefferson*].

7. *The Anas, Writings of Jefferson,* vol. 1, 267. Years later William Branch Giles would say on the floor of Congress (November 19, 1794) that "there existed a self created society, that of the Cincinnati, the principles of which were…hereditary succession." William Cobbett, *Porcupine's Works,* 12 vols. (London: Cobbett and Morgan, 1801), vol. 2, 177 [hereafter, *Porcupine's Works*]. An e-version is available at http://books.google.com/books/about/Porcupine_s_Works.html?id=LtgFAAAAIAAJ. "Porcupine" is Cobbett, a journalist whose *Porcupine's Gazette* was one of the most vitriolic and partisan papers of the era.

8. *The Anas, Writings of Jefferson,* vol. 1, 266.

9. Thomas Jefferson to John Langdon, September 11, 1785, *Papers of Jefferson,* vol. 8, 512.

10. Thomas Jefferson to John Page, May 4, 1786, *Papers of Jefferson,* vol. 9, 446.

11. Thomas Jefferson to Charles W. F. Dumas, May 6, 1786, *Papers of Jefferson,* vol. 9, 462–63.

12. Thomas Jefferson to John Adams, September 28, 1787, *Papers of Jefferson,* vol. 12, 190.

13. John Adams to Thomas Jefferson, October 9, 1787, *Papers of Jefferson,* vol. 12, 220–21. Less than two years later, Adams would flabbergast Jefferson by requesting the Senate and the House of Representatives to address the president with a royal title. See Thomas Jefferson to James Madison, July 29, 1789, *Papers of Jefferson,* vol. 15, 315. Madison, meanwhile, pushed through the lower House a resolution that "formally and unanimously condemned" Adams's suggestion. "This," said Madison, "will show to the friends of

Republicanism that our new Government was not meant to substitute either Monarchy or Aristocracy, and that the genius of the people is as yet adverse to both." James Madison to Thomas Jefferson, May 9, 1789, *Papers of Jefferson*, vol. 15, 115.

14. David Ramsay to Thomas Jefferson, April 7, 1787, *Papers of Jefferson*, vol. 11, 279.

15. Thomas Jefferson to Benjamin Hawkins, August 4, 1787, *Papers of Jefferson*, vol. 11, 684.

16. Thomas Jefferson to George Washington, May 2, 1788, *Papers of Jefferson*, vol. 13, 128.

17. *The Anas, Writings of Jefferson*, vol. 1, 269.

18. David Humphreys to Thomas Jefferson, November 29, 1788, *Papers of Jefferson*, vol. 14, 500.

19. *The Anas, Writings of Jefferson*, vol. 1, 270–71.

20. *The Anas, Writings of Jefferson*, vol. 1, 271.

21. *Jefferson: Political Writings*, eds. Joyce Appleby and Terence Ball (Cambridge, UK: Cambridge University Press, 1999), 158.

22. *The Reports of Alexander Hamilton*, ed. Jacob E. Cooke (New York: Harper & Row, 1964), 1–45.

23. See "Editor's note on Arrearages in Soldier's pay, 1790," *Papers of Jefferson*, vol. 16, 455–62.

24. *The Anas, Writings of Jefferson*, vol. 1, 272.

25. "Editor's Note," *Papers of Jefferson*, vol. 16, 460.

26. *The Anas, Writings of Jefferson*, vol. 1, 271.

27. John Marshall, *The Life of George Washington*, 4 vols. (Philadelphia, 1804; rev. ed. 1831), vol. 2, 182–83.

28. *The Anas, Writings of Jefferson*, vol. 1, 276.

29. Thomas Jefferson, *Memorandum on the Compromise of 1790*. An e-version is available at http://oll.libertyfund.org/pages/1790-jefferson-memorandum-on-the-compromise-of-1790?q=memorandum+on+the+compromise+of+1790.

30. Thomas Jefferson to George Mason, February 4, 1791, *Papers of Jefferson*, vol. 19, 241–42.

31. *The Anas, Writings of Jefferson*, vol. 1, 277.

32. *The Works of Thomas Jefferson* (Federal edition), ed. Paul Leicester Ford, 12 vols. (New York: G. P. Putnam's Sons, 1904), vol. 6, 198 [hereafter, *Works of Jefferson* (Federal ed.)]. An e-version is available at http://oll.libertyfund.org/titles/jefferson-the-works-of-thomas-jefferson-12-vols.

33. Jared Sparks, "Life of Gouverneur Morris," *American Quarterly Review* 11 (June 1832): 454.

34. *The Anas, Writings of Jefferson,* vol. 1, 278–79.

35. Others too had tasted the fruits of Hamilton's corruption, and one John F. Mercer became embroiled in a controversy with Hamilton over his conduct of administration. Mercer accused Hamilton of "increasing your own influence and attaching to your administration a Monied Interest as an Engine of Government." See Alexander Hamilton to John Mercer, September 26, 1792, *Papers of Hamilton,* vol. 12, 575. See editor's note on the details of the dispute, 481–90.

36. Samuel F. Bemis, *Jay's Treaty: A Study in Commerce and Diplomacy* (New York: Macmillan, 1924), 41–48.

37. Thomas Jefferson to George Washington, September 9, 1792, in *Works of Jefferson* (Federal ed.), vol. 7, 140.

38. There is enough of a parallel between English and American politics, of which Hamilton was a particularly keen student, to suggest that he might have, in the spirit of the times, believed he was "managing" the government in the personal and factional style of Robert Walpole. William L. Smith, one of Hamilton's supporters, noted that after the establishment of the funding and assumption plans, "the Secretary of the Treasury acquired a well-earned Fame and general popularity; his reputation traversed the ocean and in distant climes his Name was mentioned among the great ministers of the age." *The Politicks and Views of a Certain Party Displaced* (n.p., 1792), 12.

Indeed it is possible that Hamilton, with his admiration for the British system, knew people still alive who had witnessed the great minister Walpole, and his administration, firsthand. A description of Walpole's life by a contemporary author, Tobias Smollett, reads like a miniature biography of Alexander Hamilton.

39. *The Anas, Writings,* vol. 1, 284. Entry date August 13, 1791 (italics added).

40. *The Anas, Writings,* vol. 1, 298. Julian P. Boyd brought out the truth of Jefferson's suspicions in the full light of day. Boyd's *Number 7: Alexander Hamilton's Secret Attempts to Control American Foreign Policy* (Princeton: Princeton University Press, 1964) implicated Hamilton as aiding Major George Beckwith, the British representative in 1790. Boyd proved that Hamilton revealed secret information to the British minister and was ready

to engage in deceit and intrigue (a conspiracy?) to such a degree that it endangered American foreign policy.

41. George Washington to Thomas Jefferson, October 20, 1792, in *The Writings of George Washington from the Original Manuscript Sources 1745–1799,* ed. John C. Fitzpatrick, 39 vols. (1931–1944), vol. 32, 187. An e-version is available at http://etext.virginia.edu/washington/fitzpatrick.

42. Leonard D. White, *The Federalists* (New York: Macmillan, 1948), 228.

43. *Gazette of the United States* (Philadelphia), October 24, 1792, Metellus. See *Papers of Hamilton,* vol. 12, 613–17.

44. Alexander Hamilton to Colonel Edward Carrington, May 26, 1792, in *The Works of Alexander Hamilton,* ed. Henry Cabot Lodge, 10 vols. (New York, 1886), vol. 8, 248–65 [hereafter, *Works of Hamilton*]. An e-version of the Federal Edition is available at http://oll.libertyfund.org/titles/hamilton -the-works-of-alexander-hamilton-federal-edition-12-vols. Five months later Hamilton would reveal his uncanny foresight in intuiting Jefferson's becoming president. Hamilton seemed to believe that any serious rival was guilty of excessive ambition. In addition to his attack on Jefferson, his rival in New York, Aaron Burr, was caricatured as "the worst sort," "determined to climb to the highest honors of the State," and caring "nothing about the means of effecting his purpose." "In a word," said Hamilton, *"if we have an embryo-Caesar in the United States, it is Burr."* His use of the word "Caesar" in this instance had all the dangerous connotations of one ready and willing to overthrow the republic. Alexander Hamilton to [unknown], September 26, 1792, *Works of Hamilton,* vol. 10, 22.

45. *The Anas, Writings of Jefferson,* vol. 1, 317.

46. Ibid., 318. Entry date October 1, 1792. This was a topic of long debate and resulted in a combined strategy by Jefferson and William Giles in the House.

47. *The Anas, Writings of Jefferson,* vol. 1, 332. Entry date February 7, 1793.

48. Alexander Hamilton to Colonel Edward Carrington, May 26, 1792, *Works of Hamilton,* vol. 8, 252.

49. Alexander Hamilton to Colonel Edward Carrington, *Works of Hamilton,* vol. 8, 264. William Cobbett raised a point that bears on Hamilton's remark and throws light on the relationship between conspiracy and revolution. Given the administrative theory of the time, wherein opposition to government was considered intolerable, Porcupine defined the struggle between the factions, with their conspiratorial mentality, as an idea of revolution. And revolution, we may recall, negates government itself.

> Thus…I think, nobody will deny, that a hatred of the British Government and that of the United States go hand in hand. Nor is the reason

of this at all mysterious; it is not…as the Democrats have ingeniously observed, because "there is some dangerous connection between Great Britain and our public affairs"; *it is because they are both* pursuing the same line of conduct with respect to clubs and conspiracies; it is because they both possess the same radical defect, a power to suppress anarchy; it is, to say all in one word, because they are *governments….* It is not the form of a government, it is not the manner of its administration; it is the thing itself they are at war with, and that they must be eternally at war with.

Porcupine's Works, vol. 2, 34. Like Hamilton, what Porcupine refused to recognize was that Jefferson and his colleagues were not anarchists; they had in mind a definite system of government. The only difference was that it was based on opposite principles than those Hamilton and his quilled friend thought acceptable.

50. Thomas Jefferson to James Madison, May 15, 1793, *Writings of Jefferson,* vol. 9, 88–89.

51. James Thomson Callender wrote, "When the counsels of Mr. Hamilton shall…be completely unveiled, no suprize will remain at the resignation of Secretary Jefferson. The sole mystery seems to be, by what magic spell these two contending powers of light and darkness could act in unison, or even common civility, for a single day." *Sedgwick & Co. or A Key to the Six Per Cent Cabinet* (Philadelphia, 1798), 35.

52. John Adams complained of Hamilton's influence in later years and the problem Washington had of getting competent people to serve from 1794 on. "The truth is," Adams said, "Hamilton's influence over him was so well known, that no man fit for the Office of State or War would accept either. He was driven to the necessity of appointing such as would accept." John Adams to Thomas Jefferson, July 3, 1813, *Letters,* vol. 2, 349.

53. *The Anas, Writings of Jefferson,* vol. 1, 282–83.

54. Ibid., 317. Entry date October 1, 1792.

55. Thomas Jefferson to James Madison, April 3, 1794, *Writings of Jefferson,* vol. 9, 281.

56. Francis Wharton, *State Trials of the United States during the Administration of Washington and Adams* (Philadelphia: Carey and Hart, 1849), 102–97.

57. Ibid., 109.

58. Harry Marlin Tinkcom, *The Republicans and Federalists in Pennsylvania, 1790–1801: A Study in National Stimulus and Local Response* (Harrisburg, PA: Pennsylvania Historical and Museum Commission, 1950), 100.

59. Wharton, *State Trials*, 118. See also "Proclamation of George Washington," in *A Compilation of the Messages and Papers of the Presidents, 1789–1897*, ed. James Daniel Richardson (Washington, DC: Bureau of National Literature and Art, 1897), vol. 1, 150–54.

60. Wharton, *State Trials*, 159–61. See Hamilton's "detailed instructions to the Western Army," October 20, 1794.

61. James Madison to Thomas Jefferson, November 16, 1794, in *The Writings of James Madison*, ed. Gaillard Hunt (New York: G. P. Putnam's Sons, 1900), vol. 2, 18–19.

62. Alexander Hamilton to George Washington, November 11, 1794, *Works of Hamilton*, vol. 6, 65.

63. Thomas Jefferson to James Madison, December 28, 1794, *Works of Jefferson*, vol. 8, 156–59 (italics added).

64. Ibid. (italics added).

65. Ibid. (italics added).

66. Hamilton himself had described the basis for Madison's fear in *Federalist* No. 8, 67–68: "But standing armies, it may be replied, must inevitably... strengthen the executive arm of government, in doing which their constitutions would acquire a progressive direction toward monarchy." James Madison, Alexander Hamilton, and John Jay, *The Federalist Papers*, ed. Clinton Rossiter (New York: Penguin Putnam, 1961).

67. Thomas Jefferson to Benjamin Rush, January 16, 1811, *Writings of Jefferson*, vol. 11, 165–73 (italics added). See also *The Spur of Fame: Dialogues of John Adams and Benjamin Rush*, eds. John A. Schutz and Douglass Adair (San Marino, CA: Huntington Library, 1966), 2.

CHAPTER 4

The Principles of the American and French Revolutions

1. Thomas Jefferson to Thomas Mann Randolph, January 7, 1793, in *The Writings of Thomas Jefferson*, eds. Andrew A. Lipscomb and Albert Bergh, 20 vols. (Washington, DC: Thomas Jefferson Memorial Association, 1903) vol. 9, 13 [hereafter *Writings of Jefferson*]; see also Thomas Jefferson to Edmund Randolph, June 2, 1793, *Writings of Jefferson*, vol. 9, 107; and Thomas Jefferson to James Madison, June 29, 1793, *Writings of Jefferson*, vol. 9, 147.

2. *The Life and Writings of Thomas Paine*, ed. Daniel Edwin Wheeler, 10 vols. (New York: Parke, 1908), vol. 4, 220 [hereafter, *Paine*].

3. John Paul Jones to Marquis de La Fayette, June 15–26, 1788, in John Henry Sherburne, *Life and Character of the Chevalier John Paul Jones: A Captain in the Navy of the United States, During Their Revolutionary War* (New York: Wilder & Campbell, 1825, 301. An e-version is available at http://books .google.com/books?id=LeJ8NnY1AJUC&source=gbs_navlinks_s.

4. George Washington to Thomas Jefferson, January 2, 1788, in *The Papers of Thomas Jefferson*, ed. Julian P. Boyd (Princeton: Princeton University Press, 1950), vol. 12, 490 [hereafter, *Papers of Jefferson*].

5. Thomas Jefferson to George Washington, November 4, 1788, *Papers of Jefferson*, vol. 14, 330 (italics added).

6. William Cobbett, "A Summary View," in *Porcupine's Works*, 12 vols. (London: Cobbett and Morgan, 1801), vol. 7, 283 [hereafter, *Porcupine's Works*].

7. *Paine*, vol. 4, 196–97.

8. Ibid., 21.

9. Thomas Jefferson to Roger C. Weightman, June 24, 1826, in *The Life and Selected Writings of Thomas Jefferson*, eds. Adrienne Koch and William Peden (New York: Modern Library, 1944), 730–31.

10. See Paine's preface to the French edition (May 7, 1791) of *The Rights of Man*, *Paine*, vol. 4, xxv.

11. *Paine*, vol. 4, 2 (italics added).

12. In the essay *Novanglus*, written in 1774, John Adams referred to another author's attempts to dismiss the ideas "that all men by nature are equal; that kings are but the ministers of the people; that their authority is delegated to them by the people for their good, and they have a right to resume it, and place it in other hands, or keep it themselves, whenever it is made use of to oppress them." Adams then wrote, "*These are what are called revolution-principles. They are the principles of Aristotle and Plato, of Livy and Cicero, and Sidney, Harrington, and Locke. The principles of nature and eternal reason...It is therefore astonishing...that writers...should in this age and country...insinuate a doubt concerning them.*" *The Works of John Adams*, ed. Charles Francis Adams (Boston: Little, Brown, 1851), vol. 4, 15 [hereafter, *Works of Adams*]. The elder Adams was combating the sophistry of Daniel Leonard, a Massachusetts Tory. Needless to say, these were the basic principles underlying both the American and French Revolutions.

13. *Paine*, vol. 4, 22.

14. Ibid., 7–8.

15. Ibid., 27.

16. Ibid., 42–43.

17. Jacques Ellul, *Autopsy of Revolution* (New York: Knopf, 1971), 71.

18. Thomas Jefferson to James Madison, January 12, 1789, *Papers of Jefferson*, vol. 15, 232–33.

19. Anon., *An Impartial History of the Revolution in France*, 2 vols. (London, 1794), vol. 2, 357.

20. Thomas Jefferson to Richard Price, January 8, 1789, *Papers of Jefferson*, vol. 14, 420.

21. Thomas Jefferson to Diodati, August 3, 1789, *Papers of Jefferson*, vol. 15, 327.

22. Thomas Jefferson to Richard Price, January 8, 1789, *Papers of Jefferson*, vol. 14, 420.

23. Ellul, *Autopsy of Revolution*, 54.

24. *Paine*, vol. 4, 124–25. A New England clergyman, Jedidiah Morse, would see the same development taking place in America. He told his congregation that "the Jacobin Clubs, instituted by [Edmund] Genet, were a formidable engine for the accomplishment of the designs of France to subjugate this country. They started into existence by a kind of magic influence, in all parts of the United States, from Georgia to New Hampshire, and being linked together by correspondence, by constitutional ties, and…by oaths,…they acted upon one plan, in concert, and with an ultimate reference to the same grand objects….And," he added, "there is reason to believe their intention was…to produce a 'general explosion' or, in other words, a *revolution* in our country." Jedidiah Morse, *A Sermon, preached at Charlestown, November 29, 1798, on the Anniversary of Thanksgiving in Massachusetts* (Boston, 1798), 67.

25. Thomas Jefferson to John Jay, June 17, 1789, *Papers of Jefferson*, vol. 15, 190.

26. Thomas Jefferson to Francis dal Verme, August 15, 1787, *Papers of Jefferson*, vol. 12, 42.

27. William Short to John Jay, November 30, 1789, *Papers of Jefferson*, vol. 16, 3.

28. *Porcupine's Works*, vol. 7, 305.

29. "Fragment on the French Revolution," n.d., in *The Works of Alexander Hamilton*, ed. Henry Cabot Lodge, 10 vols. (New York: 1886), vol. 7, 377.

30. *Porcupine's Works*, vol. 2, 15.

31. Fisher Ames, "Equality II," in *Works of Fisher Ames* (Boston: T. B. Wait, 1809), 234–35 (italics added).

32. *Patrick Henry; Life, Correspondence and Speeches*, ed. William Wirt Henry, 3 vols. (New York: Charles Scribner's Sons, 1891), vol. 2, 576 (italics added).

33. Thomas Jefferson to Reverend Charles Clay, January 27, 1790, *Papers of Jefferson*, vol. 16, 129.

34. *Paine*, vol. 4, 103.

35. Thomas Paine to Thomas Jefferson, April 20, 1793, in *The Writings of Thomas Paine*, ed. Moncure D. Conway, 3 vols. (New York: G. P. Putnam's Sons, 1895), vol. 3, 132–33.

36. Thomas Jefferson to Destutt de Tracy, January 26, 1811, *Writings of Jefferson*, vol. 13, 20 (italics added).

37. Ibid., 19.

38. Thomas Jefferson to Judge William Johnson, June 12, 1823, *Writings of Jefferson*, vol. 15, 444. "I have been blamed for saying, that a prevalence of the doctrines of consolidation would one day call for reformation or *revolution*." See also Thomas Jefferson to Robert J. Garnett, February 14, 1824, *Writings of Jefferson*, vol. 16, 14.

39. Thomas Jefferson to Destutt de Tracy, January 26, 1811, *Writings of Jefferson*, vol. 13, 20–21.

CHAPTER 5

The Politics of Faction

1. For example, "Freedom of…political expression whether written or verbal was feared as a means of triggering conspiracies, internal disorders, wars, revolutions or some other disastrous train of events that might pull down… the State. In Leonard W. Levy, *Legacy of Suppression; Freedom of Speech and Press in Early American History* (Cambridge, MA: Harvard University Press, 1960), 7.

2. William Cobbett, "A Summary View," in *Porcupine's Works*, 12 vols. (London: Cobbett and Morgan, 1801), vol. 10, 18–19 [hereafter, *Porcupine's Works*]. Remember, it was not until 1826 that Sir John Hobhouse, then a member of Lords, derisively commented on "His Majesty's Opposition," indicating that he believed their presence an innocuous one. Richard Hofstadter believes that the idea did not gain acceptance in England until the 1840s, a full two generations after Jefferson's victory in 1800.

3. Bernard Bailyn, *The Ideological Origins of the American Revolution* (Cambridge, MA: Harvard University Press, 1967), 151

4. Richard Hofstadter, *The Idea of a Party System: The Rise of Legitimate Opposition in the United States, 1780–1840* (Berkeley: University of California Press, 1969), 9.

5. Thomas Jefferson to George Washington, September 9, 1792, in *The Works of Thomas Jefferson* (Federal edition), ed. Paul Leicester Ford, 12 vols. (New York: G. P. Putnam's Sons, 1904), vol. 7, 137–38 [hereafter *Works of Jefferson* (Federal ed.)].

6. Thomas Jefferson to George Mason, June 13, 1790, in *The Papers of Thomas Jefferson*, ed. Julian P. Boyd (Princeton: Princeton University Press, 1950), vol. 16, 493 [hereafter, *Papers of Jefferson*].

7. *Papers of Jefferson*, vol. 17, 172; see also *New York Daily Advertiser*, July 7, 8, and 9, 1790; and *Connecticut Courant*, July 15, 1790.

8. "A Citizen of America," *New York Journal*, July 27, 1790, in *Papers of Jefferson*, vol. 17, 181. See editorial note.

9. George Washington to the Acting Secretary of State, September 27, 1795, in *The Writings of George Washington from the Original Manuscript Sources 1745–1799*, ed. John C. Fitzpatrick, 39 vols. (1931–1944), vol. 34, 314–16 [hereafter, *Writings of Washington*].

10. Alexander Hamilton to John Jay, November 13, 1790, in *The Life of John Jay: with Selections from his Correspondence and Miscellaneous Papers*, ed. William Jay, 2 vols. (New York: J. & J. Harper, 1833), vol. 2, 202–3 [hereafter, *Life of John Jay*]. The Virginia Assembly had passed several resolutions, one of which stated: "An act making provisions for the debt of the United States as limits the right of the United States in their redemption of the public debt is dangerous to the rights and subversive of the interests of the people, and demands the marked disapprobation of the General Assembly." This was the spirit Hamilton wished killed.

11. In *The Idea of a Party System*, Hofstadter remarked, "In America…party opposition…had been carried on in the face of a firm conviction by each side…that the other was not legitimate, and in a healthy state of affairs would be put out of business" (page x). The reason for extinguishing the opposition, in the absence of any clearly defined loyal party system, could only have been the fear of potential revolution against the state.

12. Thomas Jefferson to Colonel John Harvie, July 25, 1790, *Works of Jefferson* (Federal ed.), vol. 6, 109.

13. Alexander Hamilton to Colonel Edward Carrington, May 26, 1792, in *The Papers of Alexander Hamilton*, eds. Harold C. Syrett and Jacob E. Cooke (New York: Columbia University Press, 1961), vol. 11, 429 [hereafter, *Papers of Hamilton*] (italics added).

14. Thomas Jefferson to James Madison, June 29, 1792, *Works of Jefferson* (Federal ed.), vol. 7, 130.

15. Alexander Hamilton to William Short, February 5, 1793, *Papers of Hamilton*, vol. 14, 7.

16. George Washington to John Jay, November 1, 1794, *Life of John Jay*, vol. 2, 233 (italics added).

17. Thomas Jefferson to James Monroe, May 5, 1793, in *The Writings of Thomas Jefferson*, eds. Andrew A. Lipscomb and Albert Bergh, 20 vols. (Washington, DC: Thomas Jefferson Memorial Association, 1903), vol. 9, 75 [hereafter, *Writings of Jefferson*].

18. James Madison to James Monroe, December 4, 1794, *The Writings of James Madison*, ed. Gaillard Hunt (New York: G. P. Putnam's Sons, 1900), vol. 6, 220–23 [hereafter *Writings of Madison*] (italics added).

19. James Madison to Thomas Jefferson, June 1, 1794, in *The Letters and Other Writings of James Madison* (published by order of Congress), 4 vols. (New York, 1884), vol. 2, 18 [hereafter, *Letters and Other Writings of Madison*]. An e-version is available at https://archive.org/details/letterswritings01madirich.

20. Thomas Jefferson to James Madison, December 28, 1794, *Writings of Jefferson*, vol. 9, 295.

21. James Madison to Thomas Jefferson, February 15, 1795, *Letters and Other Writings of Madison*, vol. 2, 35–36.

22. Oliver Wolcott to Oliver Wolcott Sr., May 3, 1794, in *Memoirs of the Administrations of Washington and Adams, Edited from the Papers of Oliver Wolcott, Secretary of the Treasury*, ed. George Gibbs, 2 vols. (New York: William Van Norden, 1846), vol. 1, 136.

23. Samuel Smith to Otho H. Williams, March 20, 1794, Papers of Otho Holland Williams, IX, no. 866, Maryland Historical Society, in Noble E. Cunningham Jr., *The Jeffersonian Republicans: The Formation of Party Organization, 1789–1801* (Chapel Hill: University of North Carolina Press, 1957), 69.

24. Henry William De Saussure to Richard Bland Lee, February 14, 1795, R. B. Lee Papers, Library of Congress.

25. William Wyche, *Party Spirit: An Oration, Delivered to the Horanian Literary Society, at Their First Anniversary Meeting, on the 10th of May, 1794, at Tammany Hall* (New York: T. and J. Swords, 1794), 15–16.

26. John Taylor of Caroline, *A Definition of Parties: Or the Political Effects of the Paper System Considered* (Philadelphia: Francis Bailey, 1794), 4–16.

27. James Madison to Thomas Jefferson, April 14, 1794, *Letters and Other Writings of Madison*, vol. 2, 10.

28. John Adams to Thomas Jefferson, May 11, 1794, in *The Adams-Jefferson Letters: The Complete Correspondence between Thomas Jefferson and Abigail and John Adams,* ed. Lester J. Cappon, 2 vols. (Chapel Hill: University of North Carolina Press, 1959), vol. 1, 255 [hereafter, *Letters*].

29. Fisher Ames to Thomas Dwight, March 9, 1796, in *Works of Fisher Ames* (Boston: T. B. Wait, 1809), 481.

30. George Washington to John Adams, August 20, 1795, *Writings of Washington,* vol. 34, 280 (italics added).

31. John Jay to George Washington, December 14, 1795, *Life of John Jay,* vol. 2, 260.

32. Thomas Jefferson to Philip Mazzei, April 24, 1796, *Writings of Jefferson,* vol. 9, 335–36.

33. Article II, Section 1, United States Constitution; superseded by the Twelfth Amendment.

34. David Hackett Fischer, *The Revolution of American Conservatism* (New York: Harper & Row, 1965), xi–xv, 10.

35. James Madison to Thomas Jefferson, December 19, 1796, *Writings of Jefferson,* vol. 6, 296–300.

36. Thomas Jefferson to James Madison, April 27, 1795, in *The Works of Thomas Jefferson,* ed. Henry A. Washington, 9 vols. (New York: Townsend MacCoun, 1884), vol. 4, 116–17 [hereafter, *Works of Jefferson* (Washington ed.)]. See also Thomas Jefferson to John Adams, December 28, 1796: "I have no ambition to govern men. It is a painful and thankless office," in *Works of Jefferson* (Washington ed.), vol. 9, 154. To Madison in January 1797, Jefferson noted, "For I think with the Romans that the general of today should be a common soldier tomorrow if necessary." *Works of Jefferson* (Washington ed.), vol. 9, 155.

37. James Madison to James Monroe, September 29, 1796, in Irving Brant, *James Madison, 1787–1800: The Father of the Constitution* (New York: Bobbs-Merrill, 1950), 444.

38. Alexander Hamilton to [unknown], 1796, *The Works of Alexander Hamilton,* ed. Henry Cabot Lodge, 10 vols. (New York: 1886), vol. 8, 419.

39. James Thomson Callender, *The American Annual Register, or, Historical Memoirs of the United States for the Year 1796* (Philadelphia: Bioren & Madan, 1797), 241.

40. George Cabot to Rufus King, August 14, 1795, in *Life and Letters of George Cabot,* ed. Henry Cabot Lodge (Boston: Little, Brown, 1877), 85. See also Charles Warren, *Jacobin and Junto* (Cambridge, MA: Harvard University Press, 1931), 173.

41. Christopher Gadsden, *A Few Observations on Some Late Public Transactions in and out of Congress, Particularly on the Dangerous and Seemingly Unconstitutional Manner the late Election for a Chief Magistrate was Conducted throughout the States of the Union* (Charleston, SC: Freneau and Paine, 1797), 9, 11–16 (italics added).

42. Thomas Jefferson to Aaron Burr, June 17, 1797, *Writings of Jefferson*, vol. 9, 402–4.

43. Aaron Burr to Thomas Jefferson, June 21, 1797, Jefferson Papers, CII, 17438, Library of Congress.

44. Thomas Jefferson to Aaron Burr, June 17, 1797, *Writings of Jefferson*, vol. 9, 402–4.

45. Thomas Jefferson to Colonel Thomas Bell, May 18, 1797, *Writings of Jefferson*, vol. 9, 387.

46. Thomas Jefferson to Peregrine Fitzhugh, June 4, 1797, Jefferson Papers, Duke University.

47. Thomas Jefferson to James Madison, August 3, 1797, *Writings of Jefferson*, vol. 9, 414.

48. Thomas Jefferson to Colonel Arthur Campbell, September 1, 1797, *Writings of Jefferson*, vol. 9, 419–20.

49. Thomas Jefferson to General Horatio Gates, May 30, 1797, *Writings of Jefferson*, vol. 9, 391.

50. Albert Gallatin to his wife, February 13, 1798, in *The Writings of Albert Gallatin*, ed. Henry Adams, 3 vols. (Philadelphia: J. B. Lippincott, 1879), 193–94. An e-version is available at http://oll.libertyfund.org/titles/gallatin-the-writings-of-albert-gallatin-3-vols.

51. Thomas Jefferson to James Madison, June 15, 1797, *Writings of Jefferson*, vol. 9, 399.

52. Thomas Jefferson to Aaron Burr, June 17, 1797, *Writings of Jefferson*, vol. 9, 403.

53. Thomas Jefferson to James Madison, March 29, 1798, *Writings of Jefferson*, vol. 10, 16.

54. Thomas Jefferson to James Madison, April 26, 1798, *Writings of Jefferson*, vol. 10, 31.

55. Thomas Jefferson to Edmund Pendleton, April 6, 1798, *Writings of Jefferson*, vol. 10, 26.

56. Thomas Jefferson to James Madison, April 12, 1798, *Writings of Jefferson*, vol. 10, 27–28 (italics added).

57. Thomas Jefferson to James Madison, April 26, 1798, *Writings of Jefferson,* vol. 10, 31.

58. John Adams to Jay McHenry, August 29, 1798, *The Works of John Adams,* ed. Charles Francis Adams (Boston: Little, Brown, 1851), vol. 8, 588.

59. *A Letter from George Nicholas of Kentucky, to his friend in Virginia, justifying the conduct of the citizens of Kentucky, as to some of the late measures of the General Government; and correcting certain false statements, which have been made in the different states, of the views and actions of the people of Kentucky* (Lexington, KY: John Bradford, 1798), 30–31. n.d.

60. John Adams to William Cunningham, Esq., March 20, 1809, in John Wood, *Suppressed History of the Administration of John Adams (from 1797 to 1801) as Printed and Suppressed in 1802* (Philadelphia: Walker & Gillis, 1846), 364. An e-version is available at https://archive.org/stream/suppressedhistoroowood/ suppressedhistoroowood_djvu.txt.

61. James Madison to Thomas Jefferson, May 20, 1798, *Writings of Madison,* vol. 6, 320–21.

62. James Madison to Thomas Jefferson, June 10, 1798, *Writings of Madison,* vol. 6, 324–25.

63. "Almanac Predictions," *Philadelphia Magazine and Review,* vol. 1, no. 1 (January 1799): 156.

64. Azel Backus, *Absalom's Conspiracy: A Sermon Preached at the General Election at Hartford in the State of Connecticut, May 10, 1798* (Hartford, CT: Hudson and Goodwin, 1798), 5–8.

65. Jedidiah Morse, *A Sermon, preached at Charlestown, November 29, 1798, on the Anniversary of Thanksgiving in Massachusetts* (Boston, 1798), 14 (italics added).

66. "A Friend to the Constitution." Author unknown, 3, 46. Huntington Library description estimates that it was "issued" c. 1799–1800.

67. Impartial Citizen, *A Dissertation upon the Constitutional Freedom of the Press* (Boston, 1801) 42, 44, 47 (italics added). An e-version is available at http://www.uark.edu/depts/comminfo/cambridge/impartial.html.

68. John Quincy Adams to Abigail Adams, June 27, 1798, *The Writings of John Quincy Adams,* ed. Worthington Chauncey Ford (New York: Macmillan, 1913), vol. 2, 323.

69. Thomas Jefferson to Anne W. Bingham, May 11, 1788, *Papers of Jefferson,* vol. 13, 151.

70. *Porcupine's Works,* vol. 8, 65.

71. John Adams to Thomas Jefferson, June 30, 1813, *Letters,* vol. 2, 346–47.

CHAPTER 6

The Kentucky and Virginia Resolutions and Threats to the First Amendment

1. For an excellent critique of taxation policies during the period, see Neil Charles Potash, "A Critique of Federalist Finances: The Direct Tax 1798–1800" (unpublished thesis, University of Maryland, 1964).

2. Alexander Graydon was not entirely wrong. Alexander Hamilton, whose influence during this period was near absolute, wrote to Theodore Sedgwick, Speaker of the House of Representatives, "I would add, as aid, the taxes... on stamps, collateral successions, new modifications of some articles of imports, and, let me add, saddle-horses." Alexander Hamilton to Theodore Sedgwick, no date other than 1798, in *The Works of Alexander Hamilton,* ed. Henry Cabot Lodge, 10 vols. (New York: 1886), vol. 8, 515–16. [hereafter, *Works of Hamilton*].

3. Potash, "A Critique of Federalist Finances," 50–51.

4. Francis Wharton, *State Trials of the United States during the Administration of Washington and Adams* (Philadelphia: Carey and Hart, 1849), 517–31.

5. Fisher Ames to Oliver Wolcott, January 12, 1800, in *Memoirs of the Administrations of Washington and Adams, Edited from the Papers of Oliver Wolcott, Secretary of the Treasury,* ed. George Gibbs, 2 vols. (New York: William Van Norden, 1846), vol. 2, 320.

6. John Adams to James Lloyd, February 11, 1815, in *The Works of John Adams,* ed. Charles Francis Adams (Boston: Little, Brown, 1851), vol. 10, 118.

7. Thomas Jefferson to James Madison, June 7, 1798, *The Works of Thomas Jefferson* (Federal edition), ed. Paul Leicester Ford, 12 vols. (New York: G. P. Putnam's Sons, 1904), vol. 8, 434 [hereafter, *Works of Jefferson* (Federal ed.)].

8. James Morton Smith, *Freedom's Fetters: The Alien and Sedition Laws and American Civil Liberties* (Ithaca, NY: Cornell University Press, 1956), 94.

9. Speech of July 10, 1798, quoted in Leonard W. Levy, *Legacy of Suppression; Freedom of Speech and Press in Early American History* (Cambridge, MA: Harvard University Press, 1960), 259. In a speech on July 5, 1798, Gallatin had referred to the bill as "a weapon used by a party now in power in order to perpetuate their authority and preserve their present places."

10. Thomas Jefferson to Stevens Thomson Mason, October 11, 1798, in *The Writings of Thomas Jefferson,* eds. Andrew A. Lipscomb and Albert Bergh,

20 vols. (Washington, DC: Thomas Jefferson Memorial Association, 1903), vol. 10, 61–62 [hereafter, *Writings of Jefferson*].

11. Alexander Hamilton to Oliver Wolcott, June 29, 1798, *Works of Hamilton,* vol. 8, 491.

12. Thomas Jefferson to John Taylor of Caroline, June 1, 1798, *Writings of Jefferson,* vol. 10, 44.

13. Adrienne Koch, *Jefferson and Madison: The Great Collaboration* (New York: Alfred A. Knopf, 1964), 187.

14. Thomas Jefferson to Stevens Thomson Mason, October 11, 1798, *Writings of Jefferson,* vol. 10, 62.

15. Kentucky Resolutions, Broadside, Huntington Library. For those readers who have not seen the Resolutions in their original form, they were printed on a single sheet approximately the size of one page of the *New York Times.* The text exhibited a short preamble followed by nine stated resolutions consisting of one or two paragraphs. All quotes in this section regarding the resolutions are from this source.

16. Thomas Jefferson to James Madison, November 17, 1798, *Writings of Jefferson,* vol. 10, 62–63 (italics added). While Jefferson did not wish to push matters to the extreme, his resolutions would nevertheless be interpreted in that light by those who wished to see the Alien and Sedition Laws enforced to the letter. Hence Robert Goodloe Harper claimed that the resolutions would produce "an armed opposition to these laws and consequently to this Government." *Annals of Congress,* V, 2430.

17. William Cobbett, *Porcupine's Works,* 12 vols. (London: Cobbett and Morgan, 1801), vol. 10, 16.

18. Jedidiah Morse, *A Sermon Exhibiting the Present Dangers, and Consequent Duties of the Citizens of the United States of America* (Charlestown, MA, April 25, 1799) 9, 15–16 (italics added). An e-version is available at https://archive.org/stream/sermonexhibitingoomorsrich/sermonexhibiting oomorsrich_djvu.txt. This had been a longstanding theme for Morse. In the previous year, he had charged that "FOREIGN INTRIGUE…has been operating in this country for more than twenty years past to diminish our national limits, importance and resources etc.," in A *Sermon, preached at Charlestown, November 29, 1798, on the Anniversary of Thanksgiving in Massachusetts* (Boston, 1798).

19. *Works of Hamilton,* vol. 8, 326.

20. *The Virginia Report of 1799–1800 Touching the Alien and Sedition Laws; together with the Virginia Resolutions of Dec. 21, 1798* (Richmond, 1850), 24–27 (italics added).

21. Ibid., 108.

22. "Extract of a letter from a gentleman of respectability in Richmond to his friends in this town, dated January 20, 1799," *Philadelphia Magazine and Review* (January 1799), Huntington Library, 54.

23. Ibid., 22–23.

24. Patrick Henry to Archibald Blair, January 8, 1799, in *Patrick Henry; Life, Correspondence and Speeches,* ed. William Wirt Henry, 3 vols. (New York: Charles Scribner's Sons, 1891), vol. 2, 609. Henry's alarm was echoed by Justice James Iredell, who wrote that Virginia was "pursuing steps which directly lead to civil war." Iredell to his wife, January 24, 1799, quoted in Griffith J. McRee, *Life and Correspondence of James Iredell,* 2 vols. (New York: Appleton, 1851), vol. 2, 543.

25. George Washington to Patrick Henry, January 15, 1799, in *The Writings of George Washington from the Original Manuscript Sources 1745-1799,* ed. John C. Fitzpatrick, 39 vols. (1931–1944), vol. 37, 87–88.

26. Thomas Jefferson to Elbridge Gerry, January 26, 1799, *Writings of Jefferson,* vol. 10, 76–79.

27. John Jay to Jedidiah Morse, January 30, 1799, in *The Life of John Jay: with Selections from his Correspondence and Miscellaneous Papers,* ed. William Jay, 2 vols. (New York: J. & J. Harper, 1833), vol. 2, 287–88.

28. Alexander Hamilton to Jonathan Dayton, 1799, *Works of Hamilton,* vol. 8, 517–22. The editor, Henry Cabot Lodge, placed the date in late January 1799 (italics added).

29. Alexander Hamilton to Theodore Sedgwick, February 2, 1799, *Works of Hamilton,* vol. 8, 525. The "two laws" referred to are the Alien and Sedition Laws (italics added).

30. James Madison to Thomas Jefferson, January 8, 1797, *The Letters and Other Writings of James Madison* (published by order of Congress), 4 vols. (New York, 1884), vol. 2, 110.

31. James Thomson Callender, *Sketches of the History of America* (Philadelphia: Snowden & McCorkle, 1798), 120.

32. Thomas Jefferson to James Madison, February 5, 1799, *Writings of Jefferson,* vol. 10, 96.

33. Thomas Jefferson to Colonel Nicholas Lewis, January 30, 1799, *Writings of Jefferson,* vol. 10, 89.

34. Thomas Jefferson to James Madison, February 5, 1799, *Writings of Jefferson,* vol. 10, 96.

35. Thomas Jefferson to Edmund Pendleton, February 14, 1799, *Writings of Jefferson,* vol. 10, 105.

36. Thomas Jefferson to Thomas Lomax, March 12, 1799, *Writings of Jefferson,* vol. 10, 123.

37. An example of this kind of effect Jefferson wished to create in Congress can be seen in his description of Bishop James Madison in late February 1799: "The tables of Congress are loaded with petitions…Thirteen of the twenty-two counties of this State [Pennsylvania] have already petitioned against the proceedings of the late Congress." Thus, if every state legislature, in addition to the national legislature, were so "loaded with petitions," the nation's representatives would hardly have time to discuss anything *but* the crisis that Jefferson saw coming. Thomas Jefferson to Bishop James Madison, February 27, 1799, *Writings of Jefferson,* vol. 10, 122.

38. Thomas Jefferson to James Madison, February 26, 1799, *Writings of Jefferson,* vol. 10, 121.

39. Thomas Jefferson to James Madison, February 26, 1799, in *The Papers of Thomas Jefferson,* ed. Barbara B. Oberg, 37 vols. (Princeton: Princeton University Press, 2004), vol. 31, 64. An e-version is available at http://rotunda.upress.virginia.edu/founders/TSJN.html.

40. Alexander Hamilton to Josiah O. Hoffman, 1799. No date is given, but the editor, Henry Cabot Lodge, has the letter listed in the period between July 10 and September or October 1799. *Works of Hamilton,* vol. 8, 354.

41. Thomas Jefferson to Edmund Randolph, August 18, 1799, *Writings of Jefferson,* vol. 10, 125–29.

42. Thomas Jefferson to James Madison, August 23, 1799. Quoted in Koch, *Jefferson and Madison,* 196–98. Despite the strategy and the tactics of "scission" and the reserved-rights clause, the author notes the following:

   > In the perspective of Jefferson's massive correspondence over the years, this is one of the most extreme statements that he ever made. The context of the fatal remark reveals how far he was willing to go in fighting "arbitrary" government. He was prepared to answer the dilemma: preserve civil liberties or cleave to the Union that proscribes them, by choosing the former. Thus, Jefferson placed no absolute value upon "Union." Compared to the extreme evil of the ruthless suppression of liberty, it appeared to him that the destruction of the compact that bound the states together was the lesser evil. This line of thought is in accord with his earlier judgment that only an Adam and Eve left upon earth, but left free, would be better than a host of men enslaved (page 199).

43. Thomas Jefferson to Wilson Cary Nicholas, September 5, 1799, *Writings of Jefferson*, vol. 10, 131. Jefferson wrote: "Mr. M[adison] who came, as had been proposed, does not concur in the *reservation* proposed above; and from this I recede readily, not only in deference to his judgment, but because, as we should never think of separation but for repeated and enormous violations, so these, when they occur, will be cause enough of themselves."

44. It is interesting to note Madison's objections in light of the fact that he had used the word "interpose" in the third Virginia Resolution of 1798. *Interpose* was not as blatant as *nullify* nor an expressed statement of the "reservation" of specific rights, but it did imply much the same meaning. The difference, however, was important: though vague, it made the point of determined resistance and also made it possible to be flexible on matters of principle.

45. Thomas Jefferson to Wilson Cary Nicholas, September 5, 1799, *Writings of Jefferson*, vol. 10, 132.

46. Text of the Kentucky Resolutions of November 14, 1799, in E. D. Warfield, *The Kentucky Resolutions of 1798: An Historical Study* (New York: G. P. Putnam's Sons, 1894), 123–26.

47. John Breckinridge to Thomas Jefferson, December 13, 1799, Warfield, *Kentucky Resolutions*, 123.

48. Thomas Jefferson to James Madison, November 26, 1799, W. C. Rives Papers, Library of Congress. Quoted in Koch, *Jefferson and Madison*, 203.

49. *Virginia Report*, 189-92.

50. *Communications of the Legislature of Virginia respecting the Alien and Sedition Laws and Instructions in reference to Resolutions of the General Assembly, 21st Day of December, 1798* (Richmond, 1800), Huntington Library, 48.

51. *Virginia Report*, 210 (italics added).

52. Ibid., 216, 212.

53. *Communications of the Legislature of Virginia*, 73; *Virginia Report*, 217.

54. *Virginia Report*, 222-30.

55. *Analysis of the Report of the Committee of the Virginia Assembly on the proceedings of sundry of the other States in Answer to their Resolutions* (Philadelphia, 1800), Huntington Library, 187.

56. We must keep in mind the fact that before 1800 there had never been a complete change of power in government without violence and bloodshed. A transfer of the reins of government from one faction to another thus meant that a violent revolution would occur.

57. *Analysis of the Report*, 187; *Virginia Report*, 225.

58. *Analysis of the Report,* 187, 226–27.

59. *Virginia Report,* 232.

60. *Virginia Report,* 230.

CHAPTER 7

The Politics of the Revolution of 1800: Prelude

1. Alexander Hamilton to Rufus King, January 5, 1800, *The Works of Alexander Hamilton,* ed. Henry Cabot Lodge, 10 vols. (New York, 1886), vol. 10, 358–59 [hereafter, *Works of Hamilton*].

2. *Newark* (NJ) *Centinel of Freedom,* April 1, 1800.

3. *Republican Meeting, at a meeting of Republican Citizens of the County of Burlington at the house of Joshua Rainear in Springfield, the 20th of September, 1800* (Mount Holly, NJ, 1800), 2. Quoted in Noble E. Cunningham Jr., *The Jeffersonian Republicans: The Formation of Party Organization, 1789–1801* (Chapel Hill: University of North Carolina Press, 1957), 155.

4. Theophilus Parsons to John Jay, May 5, 1800, in *The Correspondence and Public Papers of John Jay, 1794–1826,* ed. Henry P. Johnston, 4 vols. (New York: G. P. Putnam's Sons, 1890–93), vol. 4, 270. An e-version is available at http://oll.libertyfund.org/titles/2330.

5. Peter Van Schaak, quoted in David Hackett Fischer, *The Revolution of American Conservatism* (New York: Harper & Row, 1965), 52 (italics added).

6. Josiah Quincy to John Quincy Adams, November 23, 1804, in Adams Family papers, vol. 403. Quoted in Fischer, *Revolution of American Conservatism,* 59.

7. Colonel John Nicholas to George Washington, February 22, 1798, in Manning Dauer, "The Two John Nicholases," *American Historical Review* 45 (1940), 352.

8. "Reply of the Citizens of Hanover County, Virginia to the Circular Letters of the Democratic Society of Philadelphia," in *Gazette of the United States,* January 15, 1794. Quoted in Richard Buel Jr., *Securing the Revolution: Ideology in American Politics, 1789–1815* (Ithaca, NY: Cornell University Press, 1972), 128.

9. Cunningham, *The Jeffersonian Republicans,* 144–74. Cunningham has brilliantly described the structure of these committees and their organization state by state. A "General Standing Committee" of five members was established at Richmond, and Philip Norborne Nicholas was made its chair. This committee, entrusted with the overall direction of the campaign, was to act

as a central committee of correspondence; committees of correspondence, composed generally of five members, were appointed in eighty-nine counties and in Norfolk borough. In a few counties, where republican forces were weak, the committees did not have their full complement of members; and in three counties no committee was appointed, presumably because there were no trusted party members in those areas.

10. Philip Norborne Nicholas to Thomas Jefferson, February 2, 1800, Jefferson Papers, CVI, 1817, Library of Congress. Quoted in Cunningham, *The Jeffersonian Republicans*, 153.

11. *The Writings of Christopher Gadsden, 1746–1805,* ed. Richard Walsh (Columbia: University of South Carolina Press, 1966), 297–98. Printed in the *South Carolina State Gazette* and *Timothy's Daily Advertiser,* August 29, 1800.

12. Thomas Jefferson to James Madison, November 22, 1799, in *The Writings of Thomas Jefferson,* eds. Andrew A. Lipscomb and Albert Bergh, 20 vols. (Washington, DC: Thomas Jefferson Memorial Association, 1903), vol. 10, 133 [hereafter, *Writings of Jefferson*].

13. Thomas Jefferson to Uriah McGregory, August 13, 1800, *Writings of Jefferson,* vol. 10, 172.

14. Jefferson's recognition of this as a crucial matter was a carryover from his earliest days as a revolutionary. In the 1770s he had pointed out to John Adams the critical role that a reliable post office played: "I wish the regulation of the post office adopted by Congress last September could be put in practice.... The speedy and frequent communication of intelligence is really of great consequence.... Our people merely for want of intelligence which they may rely on are become lethargic and insensible of the state they are in." Thomas Jefferson to John Adams, May 16, 1777, in *The Adams-Jefferson Letters: The Complete Correspondence between Thomas Jefferson and Abigail and John Adams,* ed. Lester J. Cappon, 2 vols. (Chapel Hill: University of North Carolina Press, 1959), vol. 1, 4–5 [hereafter, *Letters*].

15. Fisher Ames to Timothy Dwight, March 19, 1801. Quoted in Charles Warren, *Jacobin and Junto* (Cambridge, MA: Harvard University Press, 1931), 160.

16. Uriah Tracy to Oliver Wolcott, August 7, 1800, in *Memoirs of the Administrations of Washington and Adams, Edited from the Papers of Oliver Wolcott, Secretary of the Treasury,* ed. George Gibbs, 2 vols. (New York: William Van Norden, 1846), vol. 2, 399–400 [hereafter *Administrations of Washington and Adams*].

17. Fisher Ames to James Bayard, August 6, 1800, *Works of Hamilton,* vol. 7, 562.

18. Alexander Hamilton to Rufus King, January 5, 1800, *Works of Hamilton*, vol. 10, 358.

19. Gouverneur Morris to Rufus King, June 4, 1800, in *The Life and Correspondence of Rufus King*, ed. Charles R. King, 6 vols. (New York: G. P. Putnam's Sons, 1895), vol. 3, 252 [hereafter, *Life and Correspondence of King*]. An e-version is available at https://archive.org/details/rufuskinglife03kingrich.

20. Warren, *Jacobin and Junto*, 150.

21. Theodore Sedgwick to Rufus King, November 15, 1799, *Life and Correspondence of King*, vol. 3, 146. See also George Cabot to Rufus King, January 20, 1800, *Life and Correspondence of King*, vol. 3, 183.

22. Fisher Ames to Timothy Pickering, October 19, 1799. Quoted in Warren, *Jacobin and Junto*, 149.

23. George Cabot to Rufus King, August 9, 1800, *Life and Correspondence of King*, vol. 3, 291–92.

24. Joseph Charles, *The Origins of the American Party System, Three Essays* (Williamsburg, VA: Institute of Early American History and Culture, 1956), 73. Adams and Jefferson, Charles asserts, may have, "joined forces against Hamilton at any time prior to the XYZ Affair." And the "support which both Adams and John Quincy Adams gave Jefferson after 1803–1804" indicates that "the ever present possibility of a coalition between the two was the High Federalist nightmare from 1797 on."

25. Thomas Jefferson to John Adams, December 28, 1796, *Writings of Jefferson*, vol. 9, 356–57.

26. Thomas Jefferson to John Adams, June 15, 1813, *Letters*, vol. 2, 332.

27. *Kentucky Gazette*, March 27, 1800 (extract of a letter from Philadelphia dated February 21, 1800), signed. "K. Herald."

28. William Cobbett, *Porcupine's Works*, 12 vols. (London: Cobbett and Morgan, 1801), vol. 12, 41–42 [hereafter, *Porcupine's Works*] (italics added). The editor, William Duane, left town until the legislative session ended and thus avoided punishment.

29. James Madison to Thomas Jefferson, March 15, 1800, in *The Papers of Thomas Jefferson*, ed. Barbara B. Oberg, 37 vols. (Princeton: Princeton University Press, 2004), vol. 31, 440.

30. Thomas Jefferson to Thomas Mann Randolph, February 2, 1800, *Writings of Jefferson*, vol. 10, 151.

31. Thomas Jefferson to Philip N. Nicholas, April 7, 1800, *Writings of Jefferson*, vol. 10, 163.

32. Matthew L. Davis to Albert Gallatin, March 29, 1800, Gallatin Papers, box 5, New York Historical Society. Quoted in Cunningham, *The Jeffersonian Republicans,* 177.

33. Mordecai Myers, *Reminiscences 1780–1814, Including Incidents in the War of 1812–14* (Washington, DC: Crane, 1900), 11. Quoted in Herbert S. Parmet and Marie B. Hecht, *Aaron Burr: Portrait of an Ambitious Man* (New York: Macmillan, 1967), 149.

34. Matthew L. Davis, *Memoirs of Aaron Burr: With Miscellaneous Selections from His Correspondence* (New York: Harper & Brothers, 1855), vol. 2, 55–64. An e-version is available at http://www.fullbooks.com/Memoirs-of-Aaron-Burr-Complete.html.

35. Davis, *Memoirs of Aaron Burr,* vol. 2, 61 (italics added).

36. Alexander Hamilton to John Jay, May 7, 1800, *Works of Hamilton,* vol. 10, 371–74. This directly contradicted Hamilton's logic during the Whiskey Rebellion. Then he noted, referring to those who merely refused to pay what they considered an unconstitutional tax on home brew, "You will observe an avowed object is to '*obstruct* the *operation* of the law.' This is attempted to be qualified by a pretence of doing it by 'every legal measure.' But 'legal measures to obstruct the operation of the law' is a contradiction in terms." Alexander Hamilton to John Jay, September 3, 1792, in *The Life of John Jay: with Selections from his Correspondence and Miscellaneous Papers,* ed. William Jay, 2 vols. (New York: J. & J. Harper, 1833), vol. 2, 211 [hereafter, *Life of John Jay*].

37. Alexander Hamilton to John Jay, May 7, 1800, *Works of Hamilton,* vol. 10, 371–74 (italics added). If Hamilton did not see it, his closest friend had predicted the disaster nearly a year earlier. "Burr has for two years past been a member of the Assembly, and by his arts and intrigues, he has done a great deal toward *revolutionizing* the state. It became an object of primary and essential importance to put him and his party to flight." Robert Troup to Rufus King, May 6, 1799, *Life and Correspondence of King,* vol. 3, 14.

38. *Porcupine's Works,* vol. 12, 139.

39. Editor's footnote, *Works of Hamilton,* vol. 10, 374. The fact was that Hamilton was wrong in any event and was guilty of those very things he had accused the Jeffersonians of promoting. At the formation of the government in 1788, Hamilton had foreseen this possibility. Convinced of his own ability to stay in power, he never dreamed that he was describing his own actions a decade later. For in a prophetic statement, which, had he read it in May 1800, might have turned the color of his cheeks, he wrote: "A spirit of faction, which is apt to mingle its poison in the deliberations of all bodies of men, will often

hurry the persons of whom they are composed into improprieties and excesses for which they would blush in a private capacity." *The Federalist Papers*, ed. Clinton Rossiter (New York: Penguin Putnam, 1961), No. 14.

40. Alexander Hamilton to Theodore Sedgwick, May 4, 1800, *Works of Hamilton*, vol. 10, 371. See also Alexander Hamilton to Theodore Sedgwick, May 8, 1800, *Works of Hamilton*, vol. 10, 374; and Timothy Pickering to William L. Smith, May 7, 1800, Pickering Papers, 13, Massachusetts Historical Society.

41. Alexander Hamilton to Theodore Sedgwick, May 10, 1800, *Works of Hamilton*, vol. 10, 375.

42. Alexander Hamilton to Timothy Pickering, May 14, 1800, *Works of Hamilton*, vol. 10, 376. Pickering was forced to resign on May 12, 1800. *Administrations of Washington and Adams*, vol. 2, 348. McHenry's actual resignation was May 6, 1800, but was made effective on June 1, 1800. James McHenry to John McHenry, May 20, 1800, *Administrations of Washington and Adams*, vol. 2, 346.

43. James Cheetham, *An Answer to Alexander Hamilton's Letter Concerning the Public Conduct and Character of John Adams, Esq., President of the United States* (New York: G. F. Hopkins, 1800). An e-version is available at https://tinyurl.com/p55axwf. Cheetham noted that Adams's sentiments "demonstrate[d] a prudent jealousy so essentially necessary in revolutionary times…A standing soldiery will become attached to their chief, and an ambitious chief, when a favourable opportunity occurs, will strike at the vitals of his country" (pages 5–6).

44. Hamilton actually implied that Adams fired Pickering because he "had been for some time particularly odious to the opposition party [the republicans], [and] it was determined to proceed to extremities." *Administrations of Washington and Adams*, vol. 2, 352 (italics added).

45. Alexander Hamilton to John Adams, August 1, 1800, *Works of Hamilton*, vol. 10, 382.

46. Fisher Ames to Rufus King, September 24, 1800, *Life and Correspondence of King*, vol. 3, 304.

47. George Cabot to Rufus King, July 19, 1800, *Life and Correspondence of King*, vol. 3, 278.

48. Theodore Sedgwick to Rufus King, September 26, 1800, *Life and Correspondence of King*, vol. 3, 308.

49. Robert Troup to Rufus King, October 1, 1800, *Life and Correspondence of King*, vol. 3, 315.

CHAPTER 8

The Politics of the Revolution of 1800: Revolution

1. George Cabot to Rufus King, August 9, 1800, in *The Life and Correspondence of Rufus King,* ed. Charles R. King, 6 vols. (New York: G. P. Putnam's Sons, 1895), vol. 3, 292 [hereafter, *Life and Correspondence of King*].

2. Alexander Hamilton to Oliver Wolcott, September 26, 1800, *The Works of Alexander Hamilton,* ed. Henry Cabot Lodge, 10 vols. (New York, 1886), vol. 10, 389 [hereafter, *Works of Hamilton*].

3. Alexander Hamilton to John Adams, October 1, 1800, *Works of Hamilton,* vol. 10, 390.

4. The pamphlet was published on October 22, 1800. A copy is printed in *Works of Hamilton,* vol. 6, 391–444.

5. Matthew L. Davis, *Memoirs of Aaron Burr: With Miscellaneous Selections from His Correspondence* (New York: Harper & Brothers, 1855), vol. 2, 65–66. In what was already an American political tradition, J. C. Hamilton, the general's son, wrote, "A *spy* had been placed in Hamilton's office." Hence the republicans were not above doing things for party purposes that were unbecoming.

6. Fisher Ames to Oliver Wolcott, June 12, 1800, in *Memoirs of the Administrations of Washington and Adams, Edited from the Papers of Oliver Wolcott, Secretary of the Treasury,* ed. George Gibbs, 2 vols. (New York: William Van Norden, 1846), vol. 2, 368 [hereafter *Administrations of Washington and Adams*].

7. Robert Troup to Rufus King, November 9, 1800, *Life and Correspondence of King,* vol. 3, 331–32. See also Robert Troup to Rufus King, December 4, 1800, *Life and Correspondence of King,* vol. 3, 340: "This letter (Hamilton's) continues to be disapproved here. I have not yet met with a dissenting voice here.…The letter has added much to his unpopularity here…likewise the case to the Eastward."

8. Alexander Hamilton to Timothy Pickering, November 13, 1800, *Works of Hamilton,* vol. 10, 391.

9. James Cheetham, *An Answer to Alexander Hamilton's Letter Concerning the Public Conduct and Character of John Adams, Esq., President of the United States* (New York: G. F. Hopkins, 1800), 11–15.

10. Richard Stockton to Oliver Wolcott, June 27, 1800, *Administrations of Washington and Adams,* vol. 2, 374.

11. George Cabot to Oliver Wolcott, June 14, 1800, *Administrations of Washington and Adams,* vol. 2, 370.

12. Theodore Sedgwick to Rufus King, September 26, 1800, *Life and Correspondence of King,* vol. 3, 308.

13. Cheetham, *An Answer to Alexander Hamilton,* 19–20. Unfortunately for Pinckney, his physical character lent itself to ridicule. Cheetham, a Jeffersonian supporter, accused Hamilton of insulting the nation by offering him for the presidency and told an anecdote to make the point: "If Heliogabilus could insult the Roman Senate by introducing a horse to its councils, may not designing politicians have their views in advancing and promoting the election of an animal more particularly distinguished by the length of his ears, than the energy of his mind."

14. Tunis Wortman, *A Solemn Address to Christians and Patriots* (New York: David Denniston, 1800), 31–32. An e-version is available at http://oll.liberty fund.org/titles/sandoz-political-sermons-of-the-american-founding-era -vol-2-1789-1805.

15. *Salem Gazette,* March 29, 1799. Quoted in Charles Warren, *Jacobin and Junto* (Cambridge, MA: Harvard University Press, 1931), 110.

16. William Bingham to Rufus King, August 6, 1800, *Life and Correspondence of King,* vol. 3, 285 (italics added).

17. Alexander Hamilton to James A. Bayard, August 6, 1800, *Works of Hamilton,* vol. 10, 387.

18. Quoted in Charles O. Lerche Jr., "Jefferson and the Election of 1800: A Case Study of the Political Smear," *William and Mary Quarterly,* third series, vol. 5 (1948), 480.

19. Gideon Granger to Thomas Jefferson, June 4, 1800, Jefferson Papers, CVII, 182, 198–99, Library of Congress. Quoted in Noble E. Cunningham Jr., *The Jeffersonian Republicans: The Formation of Party Organization, 1789–1801* (Chapel Hill: University of North Carolina Press, 1957), 204.

20. Fisher Ames to Oliver Wolcott, January 12, 1800, *Administrations of Washington and Adams,* vol. 2, 320.

21. John Ward Fenno, *Desultory Reflections on the New Political Aspects of Public Affairs in the United States of America since the Commencement of the Year 1799* (New York, 1800), 52 (italics added).

22. John Adams, "4th Annual Address," November 22, 1800, *A Compilation of the Messages and Papers of the Presidents, 1789–1897,* ed. James Daniel Richardson (Washington, DC: Bureau of National Literature and Art, 1897), vol. 1, 297–98 [hereafter, *Messages and Papers*].

23. "To the People of New Jersey" (Princeton, NJ, September 1800), in *History of American Presidential Elections 1798–1968,* ed. Arthur Schlesinger Jr., 4 vols. (New York: Chelsea House, 1971), vol. 1, 136.

24. Thomas Jefferson to Robert R. Livingston, December 14, 1800, in *The Writings of Thomas Jefferson*, eds. Andrew A. Lipscomb and Albert Bergh, 20 vols. (Washington, DC: Thomas Jefferson Memorial Association, 1903), vol. 10, 177–78 [hereafter, *Writings of Jefferson*]. See also Thomas Jefferson to Samuel Adams, February 26, 1800, *Writings of Jefferson*, vol. 10, 153; and Thomas Jefferson to Gideon Granger, August 13, 1800, *Writings of Jefferson*, vol. 10, 167.

25. Marcus Brutus (pseud.), *Serious Facts, Opposed to "Serious Considerations": or, The Voice of Warning to Religious Republicans* (New York, October 1800), 2.

26. Ibid., 4.

27. Abraham Bishop, *Connecticut Republicanism: An Oration on the Extent and Power of Political Delusion Delivered in New-Haven, on the Evening preceding the Public Commencement, September, 1800* (New Haven: September 1800), i (italics added).

28. Alexander Hamilton to James A. Bayard, August 6, 1800, *Works of Hamilton*, vol. 10, 387.

29. Peter Freneau to Seth Paine, December 2, 1800. Quoted in Cunningham, *The Jeffersonian Republicans*, 236.

30. Within two weeks Jefferson would write to Madison: "Though as yet we do not know the actual votes of Tennessee, Kentucky, and Vermont, yet we believe the votes to be on the whole, J[efferson] seventy-three, B[urr] seventy-three, A[dams] sixty-five, P[inckney] sixty-four. Rhode Island withdrew one from P[inckney] [given to John Jay]. There is a possibility that Tennessee may withdraw one from B[urr], and Burr writes that there may be one vote in Vermont for J[efferson]. But I hold the latter impossible, and the former not probable; and that there will be an absolute parity between the two republican candidates." Thomas Jefferson to James Madison, December 19, 1800, *Writings of Jefferson*, vol. 10, 184. Jefferson's information was accurate and reflected the final arrangement of electoral votes.

31. Thomas Jefferson to Colonel Aaron Burr, December 15, 1800, *Writings of Jefferson*, vol. 10, 181.

32. Thomas Jefferson to Tench Coxe, Esq., December 31, 1800, *Writings of Jefferson*, vol. 10, 188.

33. Thomas Jefferson to James Madison, December 19, 1800, *Writings of Jefferson*, vol. 10, 184.

34. James Madison to Governor James Monroe, December 1800, in *The Letters and Other Writings of James Madison* (published by order of Congress),

4 vols. (New York, 1884), vol. 2, 165 [hereafter, *Letters and Other Writings of Madison*].

35. James Madison to Thomas Jefferson, December 20, 1800, *Letters and Other Writings of Madison*, vol. 2, 166.

36. Henry Adams, *The Life of Albert Gallatin* (New York: Peter Smith, 1943), 241. Noting a conversation she had had with Burr, Maria Gallatin wrote, "Burr says he has no confidence in the Virginians, they once deceived him, and they are not to be trusted."

37. Thomas Jefferson to Tench Coxe, Esq., December 31, 1800, *Writings of Jefferson*, vol. 10, 188.

38. George Cabot to Rufus King, December 28, 1800, *Life and Correspondence of King*, vol. 3, 354.

39. Joseph Hale to Rufus King, December 29, 1800, *Life and Correspondence of King*, vol. 3, 357.

40. Oliver Wolcott to his wife, December 31, 1800, *Administrations of Washington and Adams*, vol. 2, 462.

41. Uriah Tracy to James McHenry, December 30, 1800, McHenry MS, Library of Congress. Quoted in Morton Borden, *The Federalism of James A. Bayard* (New York: Columbia University Press, 1955), 81.

42. Stevens T. Mason to John Breckinridge, January 15, 1801, Papers of Breckinridge Family, 18, 3156, Library of Congress. Quoted in Cunningham, *The Jeffersonian Republicans*, 242.

43. Quoted in Herbert S. Parmet and Marie B. Hecht, *Aaron Burr: Portrait of an Ambitious Man* (New York: Macmillan, 1967), 164.

44. Alexander Hamilton to Oliver Wolcott, December 16, 1800, *Works of Hamilton*, vol. 10, 392–93 (italics added).

45. In the historical literature of the "Election of 1800," little has been made of Hamilton's role in the intrigue among the various factions that were to decide whether Jefferson or Burr would acquire the presidency. Matthew Davis, in his attempt to exonerate Burr totally from any complicity whatever in the election intrigue, barely mentions Hamilton's name. In *The Jeffersonian Republicans*, Cunningham positively denies that Hamilton had much influence in the election (page 245). In a more recent study by Parmet and Hecht, *Aaron Burr: Portrait of an Ambitious Man*, Hamilton is still considered to have not been "particularly influential" (page 167). Morton Borden's account in *The Federalism of James A. Bayard*, by far the most scholarly and reasonable explanation of the intricate negotiations among the factions, makes note of Hamilton at several points and recognizes that he may have

at least influenced Bayard (see Borden's footnote 92, page 221). None of the secondary accounts I have seen, however, mentions Hamilton's conscious willingness to follow a policy of dividing the "two chiefs," thereby promoting unnecessary intrigue among already dangerously divided factions and running the risk of plunging the country into civil war.

46. Alexander Hamilton to Oliver Wolcott, December 17, 1800, *Works of Hamilton,* vol. 10, 393–97; see also Alexander Hamilton to Theodore Sedgwick, December 22, 1800, *Works of Hamilton,* vol. 10, 397–98.

47. See Robert Troup to Rufus King, December 31, 1800, on the declining status of Hamilton as the unqualified leader of the Federalists. *Life and Correspondence of Rufus King,* vol. 3, 358–59.

48. Wolcott, for example, responded to Hamilton's letters of December 16 by saying, "that of the 16th I communicated to Mr. Marshall and Mr. Sedgwick." Oliver Wolcott to Alexander Hamilton, December 25, 1800, *Administrations of Washington and Adams,* vol. 2, 460.

49. Alexander Hamilton to Gouverneur Morris, December 26, 1800, *Works of Hamilton,* vol. 10, 401.

50. Alexander Hamilton to James A. Bayard, December 27, 1800, *Works of Hamilton,* vol. 10, 402–3.

51. John Quincy Adams to Thomas Boylston Adams, December 30, 1800, *The Writings of John Quincy Adams,* ed. Worthington Chauncey Ford (New York: Macmillan, 1913), vol. 2, 491 (italics added).

52. *The Diary and Letters of Gouverneur Morris,* ed. Anne Cary Morris, 2 vols. (New York: Charles Scribner's Sons, 1888), vol. 2, 396–97. An e-version is available at http://oll.libertyfund.org/titles/1857.

53. Gabriel Christie to Samuel Smith, December 19, 1802, Samuel Smith MS, Library of Congress. Quoted in Borden, *Federalism of James A. Bayard,* 82.

54. *The Anas, Writings of Jefferson,* vol. 1, entry of January 2, 1804, 442–43.

55. *The Anas, Writings of Jefferson,* vol. 1, entry of December 31, 1803, 442. An incident surrounding one David A. Ogden, who solicited support for Burr, was another example. See Nathan Schachner, *Thomas Jefferson,* 2 vols. (New York: Appleton, 1951), 653.

56. James Madison to Thomas Jefferson, January 10, 1801, *Letters and Other Writings of Madison,* vol. 2, 166–67.

57. Gouverneur Morris to Nicholas Low, February 8, 1801. Quoted in Jared Sparks, *The Life of Gouverneur Morris: With Selections from His Correspondence and Miscellaneous Papers; Detailing Events in the American Revolution,*

the French Revolution, and in the Political History of the United States, 3 vols. (Boston: Gray & Bowen, 1832), vol. 3, 152.

58. See Alexander Hamilton to Gouverneur Morris, January 9, 1801, and Alexander Hamilton to James A. Bayard, January 16, 1801, *Works of Hamilton,* vol. 10, 407–8, 412–17. The latter is a masterful example of Hamilton's rhetorical ability and is the most skillful analysis of Burr and his philosophy that I have seen.

59. *Philadelphia Aurora,* February 6, 1801. Quoted in Borden, *Federalism of James A. Bayard,* 219.

60. Joseph H. Nicholson to a Constituent, January 15, 1801, MS, Pennsylvania Historical Society. Quoted in Schachner, *Thomas Jefferson,* 654.

61. George Erving to James Monroe, January 25, 1801, Monroe MS, Library of Congress. Quoted in Borden, *Federalism of James A. Bayard,* 87.

62. "Plan at time of Balloting for Jefferson and Burr. Communicated to Nicholas and Mr. Jefferson," *The Writings of Albert Gallatin,* ed. Henry Adams, 3 vols. (Philadelphia: J. B. Lippincott, 1879), vol. 1, 18–23.

63. Fisher Ames, "Laocoon No. 2," in *Works of Fisher Ames* (Boston: T. B. Wait, 1809), 112.

64. John Vaughan to Thomas Jefferson, January 10, 1801, Jefferson MS, Library of Congress. Quoted in Borden, *Federalism of James A. Bayard,* 88.

65. William Cobbett, *Porcupine's Works,* 12 vols. (London: Cobbett and Morgan, 1801), vol. 12, 175 [hereafter, *Porcupine's Works*]. The rumor was probably fact if Jefferson's response to Governor McKean on February 2, 1801, can be taken as an answer. In the letter Jefferson addressed himself to the electoral corruption that had occurred in Pennsylvania, New York, and elsewhere. He mentioned that it was "too soon" to make a decision in "atrocious cases…of Federal officers obstructing the operation of State governments. One thing I will say, that, as to the future, interference with elections, whether of the State or general government, by officers of the latter, should be deemed cause of removal, because the constitutional remedy by the elective principle becomes nothing, if it may be smothered by the enormous patronage of the general government." *Writings of Jefferson,* vol. 10, 195.

66. *Porcupine's Works,* vol. 12, 178.

67. Samuel Tyler to Governor James Monroe, February 9, 1801. Quoted in *William and Mary Quarterly,* first series, vols. 1–3 (1892–1895), 102–3. Tyler was a former member of the Virginia House of Delegates in 1798–1799, who had been sent by Monroe to the New York elections as an observer. He was then a member of the Governor's Council.

68. An anonymous observer wrote a description of the election proceedings, which was discovered by Professor Peter P. Hill of George Washington University in the Paris archives and translated from French in October 1968. The long letter was forwarded by the French consul, Joseph Philippe Le Tombe. The letter was published in the *Los Angeles Times*, October 27, 1968, sec. G2 [hereafter, Eyewitness].

69. Samuel Tyler to James Monroe, February 11, 1801. Quoted in *William and Mary Quarterly,* first series, vols. 1–3 (1892–1895), 104.

70. Thomas Jefferson to James Monroe, February 15, 1801, *Writings of Jefferson,* vol. 10, 201.

71. Samuel Tyler to James Monroe, February 11, 1801. Quoted in *William and Mary Quarterly,* first series, vols. 1–3 (1892–1895), 104.

72. *Porcupine's Works,* vol. 12, 182.

73. Ibid.

74. Eyewitness (italics added).

75. *Porcupine's Works,* vol. 12, 186–87.

76. Eyewitness.

77. *Baltimore American and Daily Advertiser,* February 14, 1801. John Adams in later years would express his feelings on the violent expectations of the time. Writing of the turbulent events leading up to Jefferson's election, he stated, "Let me repeat to you once more, sir, the faction was dizzy. Their brains turned round. They know not, they saw not the precipice upon which they stood....To dispatch all in a few words, a *civil war* was expected." John Adams to James Lloyd, February 6, 1815, *The Works of John Adams,* ed. Charles Francis Adams (Boston: Little, Brown, 1851), vol. 10, 115.

78. *Porcupine's Works,* vol. 12, 190.

79. Thomas Jefferson to James Monroe, February 15, 1801, *Writings of Jefferson,* vol. 10, 201 (italics added).

80. *The Anas, Writings of Jefferson,* vol. 1, 452. At the same time, Jefferson wrote, Adams and Hamilton wished "the will of the people" respected. Thomas Jefferson to Thomas Mann Randolph, February 23, 1801, *Writings of Jefferson,* vol. 18, 233.

81. Alexander Hamilton to James A. Bayard, January 16, 1801, *Works of Hamilton,* vol. 10, 412–19.

82. Caesar Rodney to Thomas Jefferson, December 28, 1800, Jefferson MS, Library of Congress. See Borden, *Federalism of James A. Bayard,* 87.

83. Davis, *Memoirs of Aaron Burr,* vol. 2, 130–31.

84. Ibid., 133.

85. Ibid., 135-37. This led to a controversy in which Jefferson later categorically denied any conversation between himself and Smith on the subject. See *The Anas, Writings of Jefferson,* vol. 1, 450.

86. Davis, *Memoirs of Aaron Burr,* vol. 2, 133–37. General Smith's testimony was given in a deposition to the Supreme Court of the State of New York, *James Gillespie v. Abraham Smith,* April 15, 1806.

87. For an explanation of Bayard's maneuvering, I am indebted to Morton Borden and his account in *Federalism of James A. Bayard,* 87–96.

88. Eyewitness. The eyewitness's testimony was later corroborated by Alexander Hamilton. "It is believed to be an alarming fact that, while the question of presidential election was pending in the House of Representatives, parties were organizing in several of the cities in the event of there being no election, to cut off the leading Federalists and seize the government." Alexander Hamilton to James A. Bayard, April 6, 1802, *Works of Hamilton,* vol. 10, 436. Another writer, Ezra Witter, spoke of "the threatened invasion of New England from the middle States, particularly Pennsylvania, unless they [the Federalists] withdrew their support from Mr. Burr....Much was said of the number, and valor, and determination of Governor McKean's militia." Ezra Witter, *Two Sermons on the Party Spirit and Divided State of the Country, Civil and Religious* (Springfield, MA, April 9, 1801), 11.

89. *Porcupine's Works,* vol. 12, 190.

90. Eyewitness. Ezra Witter noted "the threats and menaces, lately addressed to several members of Congress, because they voted for Mr. Burr instead of Mr. Jefferson, as President of the United States." *Two Sermons on the Party Spirit,* 11.

91. *The Correspondence and Miscellanies of the Hon. John Cotton Smith,* ed. William W. Andrews (New York: Harper & Brothers, 1847), 219–20. The description of the caucus was made by Smith.

92. James A. Bayard to Samuel Bayard, February 22, 1801, in "Papers of James A. Bayard, 1796–1815," ed. Elizabeth Donnan, *Annual Report of the American Historical Association for the Year 1913,* vol. 2, 131–32.

93. James A. Bayard to Alexander Hamilton, March 8, 1801, in *The Works of Alexander Hamilton, Comprising His Correspondence,* ed. John C. Hamilton, 7 vols. (New York: C. S. Francis, 1851), vol. 6, 523.

94. Eyewitness.

95. "Inaugural Address," March 4, 1801, *Messages and Papers,* vol. 1, 312.

96. Thomas Jefferson to Spencer Roane, September 6, 1819, *Writings of Jefferson*, vol. 15, 212.

Afterword

1. Thomas Jefferson to Samuel Kercheval, July 12, 1816. An e-version is available at http://www.constitution.org/tj/ltr/1816/ltr_18160712_kercheval.html.

2. Thomas Jefferson to David Humphreys, March 18, 1789, *Papers of Jefferson*, vol. 14, 676–77.

Acknowledgments

*I*T'S BEEN FORTY YEARS SINCE THIS BOOK WAS FIRST PUBLISHED, AND after looking over the acknowledgments section of that first edition, I find that almost everyone is gone. I've also realized how little has changed. At that time I was a graduate student and dependent on professors and fellow students for survival and inspiration. Forty years later I am still learning and dependent for my survival on a small group of creative people I wish to acknowledge.

Keith Quincy and Jim Headley have contributed to an ongoing conversation about revolution, terrorism, and American institutions. Together they have raised more questions than I will ever be able to answer. Kathleen Huttenmaier, Dick Donley, and Marty Seedorf have been exceptional in their friendship and at least tolerant of my ideas.

My economic survival has depended on the generosity of six especially creative men who allowed me to invent and teach courses that were outside the usual curriculum and, as a result, enabled me to remain vitally interested in my teaching: Larry Kizer, Mick Brodska, John Neace, Don Richter, Claudio Talarico, Esteban Rodriguez-Marek, and Mark Baldwin have never wavered in their commitment to excellence.

Two other men have been my friends for more than forty years, and one in particular was instrumental in the writing of *The American Revolution of 1800*. Don Utter, a friend since college days, talked with me about the book for years. Richard E. Kipling, then a Research Fellow at The Center for the Study of Democratic Institutions, was a constant intellectual gadfly. He not only asked questions but critiqued each and every chapter (sometimes over and over again) for the four long years it took to complete.

Dick literally kept me writing whenever I became discouraged or bogged down after making arguments about faction and party that opposed every established historian and political scientist in America. Without his encouragement and his insights, derived from a brilliant background in political theory, I might have stopped writing altogether.

Finally, I wish to acknowledge Thom Hartmann for making the Fortieth Anniversary Edition possible. Thom rescued the thesis from an intellectual graveyard and brought it back to life. He somehow became immersed in the book's ideas and has illustrated in his contributions both the importance and the relevance of those ideas for our time. For his efforts I will be forever grateful and not the least for his connecting me with Neal Maillet of Berrett-Koehler. Thom threw me sight unseen into a pack of wild Jeffersonians, and for over a year—a long year, I might add—it has been a delightful experience.

And lastly, I would be remiss (sacrificed at high noon is more like it) if I did not acknowledge my wife, Karen, who during this past year has not only done *all* the cooking, cleaning, entertaining, and taking care of Sally, our dog, but has demonstrated unequivocally that women are not just equal to men but superior. This Chicago-born, totally urban orchestral violinist and gifted pianist transformed herself into a strong and resolute "pioneer" woman. She not only trundled six cords of wood and built fires at all hours of the day and night to keep our house warm, but in her spare time typed the entire manuscript and endnotes and learned every new computer program required by the editors. In sum, Karen transcended the eighteenth century to function expertly in the twenty-first and then chose to return to sanity and fill our rotunda with music in the Jeffersonian tradition.

Index

About the Authors

DAN SISSON was born in Washington, DC, and educated at St. John's College Prep in the city. Following his military service, he received his BA from California State University at Long Beach and his MA and PhD from the Claremont Graduate School and The Center for the Study of Democratic Institutions in Santa Barbara, where he was in residence for six years. He has taught at colleges and universities from California to Alaska, been a politician—running for Congress in 1976, a journalist in Alaska, a writer for *Field & Stream* magazine, where for 13 years he described the many outdoor adventures he had with his son, Alan, in Oregon and Alaska. He currently teaches at Eastern Washington University as an adjunct in the Engineering Department and lives in the mountains of eastern Washington with his wife, Karen, in a near-full-sized replica (90 percent) of Thomas Jefferson's Monticello that he built himself. His forthcoming book, a work in history and political theory, is to be titled *The First American Coup d'Etat*.

THOM HARTMANN is an internationally syndicated talk-show host heard by more than 2.75 million listeners each week and simulcast on television in more than 40 million homes. He is also a *New York Times* best-selling author of twenty-four books, including *The Last Hours of Ancient Sunlight. Talkers* magazine named Thom ninth on its "2013 Heavy Hundred" list. His newest book is *The Crash of 2016*.

Berrett–Koehler
BK Publishers

Berrett-Koehler is an independent publisher dedicated to an ambitious mission: *Creating a World That Works for All*.

We believe that to truly create a better world, action is needed at all levels—individual, organizational, and societal. At the individual level, our publications help people align their lives with their values and with their aspirations for a better world. At the organizational level, our publications promote progressive leadership and management practices, socially responsible approaches to business, and humane and effective organizations. At the societal level, our publications advance social and economic justice, shared prosperity, sustainability, and new solutions to national and global issues.

A major theme of our publications is "Opening Up New Space." Berrett-Koehler titles challenge conventional thinking, introduce new ideas, and foster positive change. Their common quest is changing the underlying beliefs, mindsets, institutions, and structures that keep generating the same cycles of problems, no matter who our leaders are or what improvement programs we adopt.

We strive to practice what we preach—to operate our publishing company in line with the ideas in our books. At the core of our approach is stewardship, which we define as a deep sense of responsibility to administer the company for the benefit of all of our "stakeholder" groups: authors, customers, employees, investors, service providers, and the communities and environment around us.

We are grateful to the thousands of readers, authors, and other friends of the company who consider themselves to be part of the "BK Community." We hope that you, too, will join us in our mission.

A BK Currents Book

This book is part of our BK Currents series. BK Currents books advance social and economic justice by exploring the critical intersections between business and society. Offering a unique combination of thoughtful analysis and progressive alternatives, BK Currents books promote positive change at the national and global levels. To find out more, visit **www.bkconnection.com**.

Berrett–Koehler
Publishers

A community dedicated to creating
a world that works for all

Dear Reader,

Thank you for picking up this book and joining our worldwide community of Berrett-Koehler readers. We share ideas that bring positive change into people's lives, organizations, and society.

To welcome you, we'd like to offer you a free e-book. You can pick from among twelve of our bestselling books by entering the promotional code **BKP92E** here: http://www.bkconnection.com/welcome.

When you claim your free e-book, we'll also send you a copy of our e-newsletter, the *BK Communiqué*. Although you're free to unsubscribe, there are many benefits to sticking around. In every issue of our newsletter you'll find

- A free e-book
- Tips from famous authors
- Discounts on spotlight titles
- Hilarious insider publishing news
- A chance to win a prize for answering a riddle

Best of all, our readers tell us, "Your newsletter is the only one I actually read." So claim your gift today, and please stay in touch!

Sincerely,

Charlotte Ashlock
Steward of the BK Website

Questions? Comments? Contact me at bkcommunity@bkpub.com.

Certified

Corporation
bcorporation.net